INNS, ALES
AND DRINKING CUSTOMS OF
OLD ENGLAND

Frederick William Hackwood was born in 1851. He wrote many books on social history and folklore, among the list of which are such fascinating titles as *Dragons and Dragon Slayers, The Romance of Food and Feasting, The Story of the Shire, Old English Sports,* and *Legends, Traditions, Myths and Symbols.* Most of his work was profusely and carefully illustrated with line drawings, etchings, photographs, woodcuts – whatever would illuminate his subject most appropriately – and was always carefully researched and detailed.

Paul Jennings (the humorous writer) has spent his life in or with brackets, since childhood in Coventry (he was its Boy Soprano), education at its King Henry VIII School (and subsequently at Douai) till now when he still sings as an obscure tenor (in the far from obscure Philharmonia Chorus, with the jollier members of which he often drinks if there is time after the rehearsal before his train to some point about thirty miles from his home at Orford [practically in the North Sea; look, *more* brackets]). The pubs there are the King's Head and the Jolly Sailor, but he has been in many others during his career as scriptwriter for the COI (about British dentistry, British carpets, British schools, British *everything),* copywriter (he once initiated a letter in Latin to all 22,000 Catholic clergy telling them to fly BEA, as it then was), The Observer's first regular humorist (with his column Oddly Enough, 1949-66), his freelance work for Punch, Telegraph Magazine, Sunday Times, Financial Times, Radio Times, Guardian, you name it (unless it's called Reader's Digest), his publication of 15 books of his own pieces, 1 novel, 3 children's books, 4 anthologies, you name it (no, don't, they're mostly out of print, except Golden Oddlies in the Methuen Library of Classic Humour [advt. More brackets. Very grand company, e.g. Thurber, to whom he once gave dinner (well of course his wife did all the work) Noel Coward, Saki etc., but they are all dead except Tom Lehrer and him]). He is not dead, at the time of writing, or even drunk. He has never been drunk in his life. But he liked this book about drink so much he would have written the Foreword for nothing (but fortunately they did offer him some money. Not a little, not a lot. Like always).

THE ELECTION—CANVASSING FOR VOTES. BY HOGARTH.

Reproduced from the picture in Sir John Soane's Museum, Lincoln's Inn Fields, by kind permission of the Curator.

INNS, ALES
AND DRINKING CUSTOMS OF
OLD ENGLAND

Frederick W. Hackwood

with a Foreword by
PAUL JENNINGS

Bracken Books
LONDON

This edition published 1985 by Bracken Books,
a division of Bestseller Publications Ltd,
Brent House, 24 Friern Park, North Finchley, London N12.

ISBN 0 946495 25 4

Printed and bound by Grafoimpex, Yugoslavia.

Foreword

PAUL JENNINGS

In a mad sort of way it is simultaneously pleasant and impossible to imagine the author of this divinely wide-ranging, endlessly curious compendium for compotators (*what* a useful word, see page 344; here have I been drinking for years with all kinds of men – commentators, commuters, competitors, computators and computer-men among others – and never thought so to latinise my fellow-drinkers) going in for *Mastermind* on television.

"Our second competitor is Mr Frederick W. Hackwood, author, who has chosen for his subject Inns, Ales and Drinking Customs. Your first question is: how many doors were there in Valhalla?"

"Five hundred and forty."

"Correct. What is a fuddling cup?"

"A group of cups or beakers cemented together, but with a hole drilled through each partition and connecting all the cups, so that the drinker could not empty one without emptying all."

"Correct. Where is the highest inn in England?"

"The Tan Hill Inn, at Stainmoor, in the North Riding" (don't forget this would have been in 1909, in the good old days before they messed up the old counties and when Mr Hackwood could write that *"until a generation ago* a large snuff-box for the free use of customers was to be found in most well appointed public houses", my italics). It still *is* the highest, according to the Guinness Book of Records.

"Correct. What is the derivation of the drink called punch?"

"The Hindustani *panch*, or five, from the same Aryan root as the Greek *penta;* it was so called because it contained five ingredients."

"Correct. Can you name these ingredients?"

"Originally they were arrack, sugar, lime juice, spice and water. In 1694 –"

"Correct. What was called by Dr Johnson 'a hateful tax levied upon commodities'?"

"Excise Duty, imposed by Parliament in 1643, early in the Civil War. But in 1694 –"

It would be no good, you see. Mr Hackwood clearly knew or could find out everything, and no doubt manfully restrained himself from pointing out that *punch* shares its root with Punjab ("five rivers"), but he would have been far too leisurely, too discursive, too enquiring – in short too good a man to have as compotator – to fit into the quick yes-or-no, get-on-to-the-next-fact rhythm of the modern quiz. He belongs to a time when there was all the time in the world, he would certainly have wanted to stop at the punch question to go on with the marvellous tale of what actually happened in 1694, one of my favourite stories in the book, about Admiral Russell's party in "Alicant" where there was so much punch in a marble fountain that a small boy rowed round it in a boat to serve the *six thousand* guests who – but you can read it for yourself on page 350.

Like all really good compendia, this one manages to achieve, by its very inclusiveness and range, a sense of open-endedness, of that infinite and delightful feeling of potentiality which comes to some only after a drink or two but which a man like R. L. Stevenson (for instance) had all the time;

> The world is so full of a number of things
> I'm sure we should all be as happy as kings

Thus, although it contains a great deal more about definitions and derivations of *beer* than most of us are likely to have known before (it's the same root as *barley*, there is ½% of alcohol in bread, and that word itself comes from the Saxon *bréowan*, "brew"), it does not attempt the impossible task of differentiating between the terms "ale" and "beer". The Oxford English Dictionary says ale is "a beverage made from an infusion of malt by fermentation, flavoured with hops or other bitters." It gives more or less the same definition for beer, but then adds "formerly distinguished from *ale* by being hopped, but now generic, including ale and porter. See ALE." Well, we've seen ALE. But my encyclopaedia, very rightly, says the word "ale" is "never used to denote the black beers, stout and porter."

His historical perspective alone would prevent Mr Hackwood from leaving this question anything but open-ended. He knows (page 44) that

> Hops and turkeys, carp and beer
> Came into England all in one year

the year "assigned" he says with the wariness of the true historian, being 1520; and he tells us that once "beer" was the term for the first, stronger liquor from the first mashing of the malt, never mind about hops. It was a Saxon term, and although he is kind

enough about the Roman *tabernae* at fixed intervals on their great
roads, no doubt offering more wine and less beer the nearer they got
to Rome, it is clear where his heart lies. Indeed the chapter nobly
headed "The Universality of Ale" begins with one splendid, unargu-
able sentence which would be taken as the core of the book. "Beer
ranks with bread – the respective products of the two principal
indigenous cereals – as the traditional sustenance of Englishmen."

Whilst I should have liked to confront him with a splendid observation of Thackeray's – "Fancy a hundred thousand Englishmen,
after a meal of stalwart beef ribs, encountering a hundred thousand
Frenchmen, who had partaken of a trifling collation of soup, turnips,
carrots, onions and Gruyère cheese. Would it be manly to engage at
such odds? I say no!" – and say "what about roast beef?", the key
word in that sentence is *indigenous*. Whilst Mr Hackwood is not given
to mere chauvinistic boasting (though there is plenty of good old
nostalgia, a very different thing), even in that playful Thackeray vein,
it is clear that not very deep down he thinks there is nothing much
worth drinking south of Dover.

This is very much a book about the English, as well as their (and
the Germans', see Valhalla and those doors, page 33) national drink;
you may see why even the Scots and Irish, let alone the wine-
drinking countries (last paragraph on page 38) have had to be
excluded not from any kind of nationalistic ill-will but simply
because there were so many areas – social, legal, historic, poetic,
musical (oh, those lovely drinking songs, how I should like to know
the music for the one by Huffy White on page 337!), you name them,
to be covered that there wasn't room for anything else.

No doubt anyone who has given any thought at all to drinking and
English pubs and the rest of it will be able to find some point not
covered. I myself, for instance, have always wanted to get to the truth
(or otherwise) of the explanation sometimes offered for those little
swivelling glass partitions, at eye level, which you still find in the
more ornate, luxurious and wonderfully, Englishly *subdivided* pub:
that apprentices were not supposed to drink, and their masters did
not particularly like to be *seen* drinking by the apprentices; so the
masters in the Saloon Bar, and the apprentices in the Public (or the
Snug, or perhaps even the Private), could each turn these things
round when they required invisibility from the others.

Mr Hackwood has nothing on this. But he has plenty on the inns
of fiction, on inn signs, on drinking vessels, on certain bogus
ceremonies and rites at a Highgate coaching inn, on (who would have
thought it?) a marvellously uncomfortable official way of testing ale

by making a puddle of it on the bench, sitting in this for half an hour during which time the ale tester would "converse, he would smoke, he would drink with all who asked him to, but he would be careful not to change his position any way." If his leather breeches then stuck to the bench, there was too much sugar (and therefore not enough alcohol) in the beer (page 107).

Some readers will have heard some versions given here of pub names, their origins and transmogrifications; most people know "The Goat and Compasses" is alleged to be a corruption of "God Encompasseth Us". I had heard of both "Catherina Fidelis" and Caton Fidèle (the faithful governor of Calais) for "The Cat and the Fiddle". But "Peg and Wassail" (see pegged drinking cups) for "Pig and Whistle" was new to me, as was "The Beehive" at Grantham, the only pub with a *live* sign, a real beehive outside (still there, as I have just telephoned to check). And hands up who knew about the Chemical Inn at Oldbury, or even the story about "The Same Yet" (page 301).

Knowing Ipswich (as who doesn't?) I was surprised to see the famous old song with the refrain *But* (or *And*) *bryng us in good ale* (my favourite verse being *Bryng us in no podynges, for therein is al Godes good, nor bryng us in no veneson, for that is not for owr blod, But* etc.) was from a collection called "The Ipswich Minstrel"; and I'd like to be sure that the verb "to tip" (*orig. obsc.,* says the OED cautiously) came from the initials of a box in inns labelled To Insure Promptitude . . .

But what an infinite number of items are finds which will stay with the reader for ever, from knowing where Cardinal Wolsey, as a mere vicar, got drunk at a village feast, to the delightful information that in the 18th century coffee was called such things as "ninny-broth" and "Turkish gruel". And how good to learn that – but you need only look at the copious chapter-headings, themselves little masterpieces of invitatory précis, to see that Mr Hackwood, as a compotator, has no competitor.

Analytical Table of Contents

CONTENTS

CONTENTS

CONTENTS

CONTENTS

CONTENTS

CONTENTS

CONTENTS

CONTENTS

CONTENTS

CONTENTS

CONTENTS

CONTENTS

CONTENTS

CONTENTS

CONTENTS

CONTENTS

CONTENTS

CONTENTS

List of Illustrations

LIST OF ILLUSTRATIONS

Inns, Ales, and Drinking Customs of Old England

I

GENESIS OF ALES AND INNS

The taste for strong drink—Biblical references—Ale-brewing an
Egyptian industry five thousand years ago—An innless England
inconceivable—The taverns of Roman-Britain (*Tabernæ*)—How
Roman public-houses were conducted—The German peoples
dubbed "the sons of malt"—Ale the beverage of the Teuton
gods—A stream of ale from the udders of Heidrun, the goat of
Valhalla—Served round by Valkyries—The mighty drouth of
the gods—The mythological search for the many-fathomed
brewing caldron—Drunkenness honourable among the Anglo-
Saxons—Mead or Meathe, Metheglin, and Hydromel, varieties
of the Saxon drink made from fermented honey and water—
Old recipes for making it—Excessive drinking among the Danes
—The origin of the word "ale"—Rise of the English ale-house
—The restrictive laws of Ina to regulate ale-booths—Public
establishments of three kinds among the Saxons, namely, the
ale-house, the wine-house, and the inn—And three kinds of ale
—Ancient Britons charged with drunkenness—Swinish excesses
of the English mentioned in "Ivanhoe"—England a beer-
drinking country for climatic reasons.

WHEN did primitive man develop a taste for palatable,
stimulating drinks in preference to pure and refreshing
water? Who was the first to give way to the transient
delights of intoxication? Drunkenness resulting from

the juice of the grape is certainly as old as the days of Noah (Genesis ix. 21) ; and wine was recognised as the beverage of festivity by that first miracle at Cana of Galilee (John ii.)—to say nothing of its adoption as an element in the chief of the Christian sacraments.

The brewing of ale, as the frescoes on its ancient temples have revealed, was a skilled industry in Egypt five thousand years ago, and the ancient city of Pelusium was as noted for its breweries as for its university.   A thousand years later the Egyptian reformer was demanding a reduction in the number of ale-houses then existing in the land.   The outcry could have had little practical effect, as yet another thousand years later the university students of Pelusium were found neglecting their studies for the seductions of the beer-houses.

Thus it will be seen the ancient Egyptians were habitual beer-drinkers for ages, the art of brewing having no doubt been introduced into the Nile Valley by the primitive settlers.   It certainly required settled habits to develop the art of brewing from corn, and prehistoric man, being generally of nomadic habits, had doubtless contented himself with the fermentation of drinks made from wild honey or wild fruits.   Or it may have been that ale became the national beverage because the land of Egypt was ill-suited to the cultivation of the vine.

Herodotus ascribes the first discovery of the art of brewing " barley-wine " to Isis, the wife of Osiris ; and a beverage of this nature, perhaps made from wheat, barley, and honey, is mentioned by Xenophon, 401 B.C.

On the decline of the Egyptians and the rise of the Greeks and the Romans, the wine of the grape became the beverage of civilisation.   With the Romans the story of ales and inns moves in due course in this country.

Some one has said that an "innless" England is inconceivable.   Certain it is that inns made their appearance

AN ENGLISH INN OF THE FOURTEENTH CENTURY.
(From the Louterell Psalter.)

[*Page* 64.

A ROADSIDE ALE-HOUSE.
(From a Fourteenth Century MS.)

[*Page* 64.

CHAUCER'S PILGRIMS SEATED ROUND THE TABLE OF THE
"TABARD," AT SOUTHWARK.

(A reproduction of Caxton's engraving in his second edition of
the "Canterbury Tales." 1484.)

[*Page* 261.

MOTHER LOUSE, THE ALE-WIFE.

[Page 66.

in this country with the very earliest dawn of civilisation.

When the Romans constructed roads in any part of their empire, as they did in Britain, not only was the initial outlay upon them exceedingly heavy, but they had to be maintained and regulated at enormous expense. The office of Curator Viarum was one of considerable honour and equivalent emolument. At fixed intervals along the road stood "mansiones," the keepers of which, called "mancipes," stopped all passengers to examine their "diplomata," or passports.

Nearer the centre of the empire, if not in every one of the distant provinces, there were stationed along the roads at convenient distances apart "mutationes," or places where post-horses could be taken or changed, which were termed "agminales," and which were conducted by "veredarii," otherwise postilions. The keepers of these posting-houses were called "statores."

It was by means of these posts that Constantine, the son of Constantius Chlorus, made his rapid and celebrated journey from the East to join his father in Britain; and as it is known that these "mutationes" continued to the coast of Gaul it may fairly be inferred that they were not discontinued to York, which was not only the capital of Britain, but an imperial residence.

But, what is more to our present purpose, there were also to be found along these Roman roads—though not perhaps at any regular or fixed distances apart, but wherever the traffic warranted the expenditure of so much private enterprise—houses of entertainment for man and horse, which were the Roman equivalent for, and prototype of, the good old English wayside hostelry. The classical name for these roadside refreshment taverns were "diversoria," "cauponæ," or "tabernæ diversoriæ"; and for those who kept them, "diver-

sores" or "caupones." At these Tabernæ (or Tavernæ),
the earliest of our roadside inns, food and a night's
lodging were always procurable.

These Romano-British taverns were places of rest and
refreshment, and in no sense mere calling-places for the
set purpose of consuming strong drink. Doubtless wine
was supplied in them as part of the refreshment, but
quite as a subsidiary feature of the entertainment. The
English inn, as equivalent to a drinking-shop, was not till
the advent of the English; but how soon after the Anglo-
Saxon invasion the "ale-house" appeared it would be
impossible to say.

In Romanised Britain there were doubtless inns and
public-houses as in Italy at that time. Herculaneum
had no less than nine hundred public-houses; and from
a placard discovered on the wall of a house in that ruined
city, offering the lease of one, it is gleaned that such
houses of entertainment had galleries at the top and
balconies or green arbours, and also baths. The dining-
room was in the upper storey; and although it was the
custom of the Romans to recline at their meals, yet when
they refreshed themselves at these places they invariably
sat. The landlord had a particular dress, and the landladies wore a *succinct* or tucked-up dress, and brought
the wine to their customers in vases. They had common
drinking vessels, not unlike those in use in more modern
times, and sometimes the flagons were chained to posts.
The imagination easily pictures, as a replica of this, an
inn of the Romano-British period in this country. Chess
was regularly played; and it is thought that the painting
of the fronts of inns, or of posts at inn doors, in chequer
patterns like a chessboard—a practice which came down
to almost recent times—was derived from this custom of
the ancient classical inn. To this day the "Chequers"
is a common inn sign to be found in all parts of England;

and in some instances it may, of course, be derived from the heraldic shield of the neighbouring landowner.

With the decline of Rome and the spread of Teutonic influence, malt liquor again came to the front, at least so far as England and Northern Europe are concerned. Indeed, so addicted were the German conquerors to the inordinate use of this kind of strong drink, the Emperor Julian had not inaptly dubbed them "sons of malt"; and Tacitus, two centuries or more before him, had made similar allusions to the German love of malt beer.

The religious beliefs in which the English race was cradled made "ale" the beverage of the gods. The Norse mythology of our Teuton forefathers taught that the gods were like unto themselves in that they were big and burly, with huge appetites, delighting in feasts of fat meat, which were always washed down with tankards of strong ale. The spirits of the dead who had fallen in battle feasted every day in Valhalla, a mighty banqueting-hall with 540 doors, in which Woden entertained those warrior souls for ever, never insulting their worthiness by setting water before them, but satisfying their prodigious thirsts with a copious supply of strong ale that never failed. For in the centre of this hall was kept the goat Heidrun, who nibbled at the branches of the mighty ash whose roots went down to the very ends of the world; and from her udders flowed a stream of ale that every day filled a jar so large that all the warriors could drink from it and yet not empty it. This heavenly drink—in this chapter of Anglo-Saxon mythology we surely arrive at the prototype of the modern barmaid—was poured out by the Valkyries, tall and beautiful maidens, who helped the heroes in battle and carried their spirits after death to Valhalla, where they tended them afterwards, and where in particular they ministered most assiduously to their ever-glorious thirsts.

In the episode of the feast given to Thor by Ægar, the
sea-god, although the table was laden with meat of every
kind set upon dishes of gold and silver, yet because
there was no beer when the mighty Thunderer called for
it, the adventurous search was undertaken for a many-
fathomed brewing caldron, of a capacity suited to the
drouth of a god. And so throughout the whole mythology of our English progenitors it is ale, always ale,
which the gods cry out for, and which is deemed the
only beverage worthy of divine drouthiness.

Our Saxon forefathers were notoriously addicted to
the use of ale and mead, and regarded drunkenness
as rather honourable than otherwise ; for the man who
could withstand the intoxicating effects of strong drink
longest was the most admired and the one most
respected among them.

The Saxon Mead was not a malt liquor. Mead, or
Meathe, was made with the washings of the honeycomb,
after the honey had been taken out, which was boiled
with spices, and fermented. The process of preparing
Mead, or Metheglin, or as another and later variety
was called, Hydromel, varied slightly in different parts
of the country. It was usually made after the pure
honey had been extracted, of the last crushing of the
comb, boiled with water and fermented. In the earlier
centuries it was made by boiling both comb and honey
and mixing the liquor with sweetwort. In the process of
boiling the wax of the comb rises to the surface of
the liquid and is skimmed off for beeswax. The liquid
is then strained, and boiled again with spices added
to suit taste. In the remoter country districts this
beverage, called Methegle, or Metheglum, is still prepared
and drunk by the cottagers.

The best time to make Metheglin is a little before
Michaelmas, and the drink then made will be excellent

towards the beginning of spring. The process, according to an old recipe two hundred years old, is to—

"Take live honey which naturally runs from the combs (that from swarms of the same year is best), and put so much of it into clear spring water that when the honey is dissolved thoroughly an egg will not sink to the bottom, but easily swim up and down therein ; then let the liquor boil in a brass or rather copper vessel, for about an hour's time or more, and by that time the egg swims above the liquor about the breadth of a groat. Next morning it may be barrelled up, adding to the proportion of fifteen gallons, an ounce of ginger, half an ounce of cinnamon, cloves and mace of each an ounce, all grosly pounded, for if beat fine it will always float in the Metheglin and make it foul, and if they be put in while it is hot the spice will lose their spirits. A small spoonful of yest may be also added at the bung-hole to increase the working, but it must not be left to stand too cold at first that being a principal impediment to its fermentation. As soon as it has done working stop it up, close and let it stand for a month, then draw it off into bottles, which if set in a refrigeratory will become a most pleasant vinous liquor, and the longer it is kept the better it will be. By the floating of the egg you may judge of its strength, and it may be made more or less strong at pleasure by the addition of more honey or more water, and by long boiling it is rendered most pleasant and durable. When Metheglin is boiling it is not necessary to scum it, for the scum being left behind will be of use and help to the fermentation. There are divers ways of making Metheglin, and several green plants are prescribed to be used, such as sweet-briar leaves, thyme, rosemary, &c., which yet are not to be taken green by them that intend to make a lively, quick and brisk liquor ; green and raw herbs dulling and flatting the spirits of the liquor to which they are added ; neither will any green herb yield its virtue so easily as when dry; but spice and aromatic herbs are very necessary to add a flavour to Metheglin and abate its too luscious taste.

For making a "White" variety of Metheglin, a number of other herbs were boiled together for the flavouring, including sweet marjoram, violets, strawberry leaves, borage, agrimony, fennel, and some of those before mentioned together with coriander and caraway seeds.

A seventeenth-century recipe for making "Mead of the best sort," is to—

"Take twelve gallons of water and slip in the whites of six eggs; mix them well with the water and twenty pounds of good honey; let the liquor boil an hour, and when boiled add cinnamon, ginger, cloves, mace and a little rosemary; as soon as it is cold put a spoonful of yest to it, and tun it up, keeping the vessel filled as it works; when it has done working, stop up close, and when fine bottle it for use."

These recipes give us a very fair notion of the real nature of this ancient English beverage.

If we are to accept the evidence of Lord Coke we are indebted to the Danish invasion for our propensity to make ale the national beverage. This eminent authority, in fact, puts the case stronger than that. He says that King Edgar, in permitting the Danes to inhabit England, first brought excessive drinking among us. The word "ale" came into the English language through the Danish *öl*. At any rate, after the advent of the Norsemen, the English left off drinking water and began to drink ale as the regular everyday beverage of the people. In the succeeding reign a law was made that if any man quarrelled and beat another in an ale-house, he should pay a fine to the value of sixteen shillings of the money then current. This, however, is by no means the first mention of an English ale-house, nor yet of the first restrictive measure in connection therewith; earlier mention occurs in the laws of Ina, King of Wessex, and the regulating laws were called for by the numerous "ale-booths" and "ale-stonds" which had been set up in England by the year 728.

Although among the Anglo-Saxons there were three kinds of establishment open to the public, the Ale-house (*eala-hus*), the Wine-house (*win-hus*) and the Inn (*cumen-hus*), accommodation for travellers was always difficult to find on a journey. Travellers were accustomed to inquire for hospitable persons in the neighbourhood; and the religious houses would always entertain visitors for three days together, if requested. Till the time of Edward I., Lord Berkeley's farmhouses were used by wayfarers as houses of call.

Allusions to the ale-house range widely and frequently over the centuries of English history, from the regulation of the "eala-hus," by the laws of Ethelbert (616), to the phraseology of present-day licensing law.

It will be thus seen that from the earliest times the law sought to exercise some restrictive influences over the consumption, if not over the sale, of strong drink. There can be little doubt that ale-houses soon came to have a definite status in the country, and that the ale-houses became inns. By common law a man might erect and keep an inn or ale-house to receive travellers ; at first no licence was necessary, or even the giving of recognisances for keeping good order.

Sharon Turner in his "History of the Anglo-Saxons," speaks of mead and wine being used, but says the chief drink among this people was ale, of which he names three kinds : "clear ale," "mild ale," and "Welsh ale."

Let our national propensity to beer-swilling be traceable to Norse or to Saxon ancestry, whichever it may, it must not be thought the early Celtic inhabitants of this country were guiltless of the weakness of inebriety. The British historian St. Gildas, recently identified as the Welsh warrior-poet, Aneurin, who wrote a poem on the battle of Cattraeth, in Lothian, has latterly had some authority attached to his Latin treatise in which he accuses the British chieftains of going into battle drunk, and so bringing about the ruin of Britain. What saith the modern Welsh Puritan to this ?

In Saxon England the monks and clergy undoubtedly

drank more than was good for them, notwithstanding that priests were forbidden to eat or drink where ale was sold. At Abingdon Monastery there was a great bowl presented by the noble founders which was used to fill each brother's drinking-horn twice a day with mead, and on festival days, of which the calendar was nearly full, twice a day also with wine.

The modern Englishman may still regard ale as his national beverage, but he has long ago overcome the swinish indulgence in it which characterised his Anglo-Saxon forbears. It was the custom, for instance, at the funeral of a great Saxon noble (as we may read in Sir Walter Scott's " Ivanhoe," chapter xli.), for open house to be kept, and great " hogsheads of ale set abroach to be drained at the freedom of all comers." On such occasions, we read, "the naked Saxon serf drowned the sense of his half-year's hunger and thirst in one day of gluttony and drunkenness."

It may fairly be claimed that for a thousand years beer held its sway in this country.

Climatic causes have stood in the way of England becoming a wine-drinking country ; a similar reason perhaps has prevented the adoption of ardent spirits as the national beverage—beer-drinking England is less damp and chilly than whisky-drinking Ireland, less cold and rigorous than whisky-drinking Scotland.

II

MEDIÆVAL BREWING

English ale supreme as a food adjunct—Historical and literary references to old English ale—Monastic brewing—Burton Abbey brewery—The foundation of the Burton-on-Trent staple —The secret of Burton's pre-eminence in the production of the national beverage—Herbs formerly used as flavourings— Malt always the foundation of ale—Dr. Plot's account of the Burton method of brewing in 1686—The Burton "knack of fincing" Ling used in lieu of hops at Shenstone near Lichfield—"Maulted oats"—Oxford University authorities find difficulties in enforcing their bylaws for the brewing of "wholesome ale"—Introduction of the hop-vine—Early prejudice against it—Called the "wicked weed" and regarded as an adulterant—Ale, and hopped ale or beer—The terms "beer," "barley," and "barm" considered—Derivation of the term "double X" and "treble X"—How the monk used the magic broomstick to bring him beer (a humorous quotation from "Ingoldsby").

FROM the earliest days of civilisation, and in nearly every quarter of the globe, man's indulgence in stimulants has been almost universal. His use of narcotics, the best known of which are tobocco, opium, and bhang, although widespread, has not been nearly so pronounced.

The Japanese have their saké, a beer made from rice; the Tartars their koumiss, a fermented drink made of mare's milk; the Mexicans, their pulque, prepared from the juice of the agave; the South Sea Islanders, a fermented liquor made from the shrub called kava;

while many of the different tribes and races of Africa drink a native kind of beer.   But of all the intoxicating drinks used as a food adjunct, English ale, if not supreme, has certainly the most interesting history.

When we go back to mediæval times, be it remembered that tea and coffee were unknown and undreamt of ; that brandy, gin, and rum were as yet undiscovered ; and that wine then, as it is now, was the rich man's beverage. Some ardent spirits, known as cordials, were to be found in the mansions of the great, and were generally kept by the lady of the house among her simples, and only dealt out to favoured friends on special occasions by the thimbleful.   The beverages of the common people were almost exclusively water, cider, and beer.

Among the Anglo-Saxons, as we have seen, the chief drink was ale ; the Norman Conquest wrought little or no change in the national beverage, which practically retained its early English character till the introduction of hops.

It is a matter of history that King John died of a surfeit of peaches and new cider ; and in Magna Charta there was a clause providing a standard measurement by which ale and wine should be sold.

The popularity of ale in those times is to be gathered from the allusion of the poets.   Chaucer, in his " Canterbury Pilgrims," says of the Cook: " Wel coude he knowe a draught of London ale."   Shakespeare in *Henry V.* (Act III., Scene 2) makes the Boy Camp-follower say :—

"Would I were in an ale-house in London."

And in *Henry VI.*, Part 2 (Act IV., Scene 2), the demagogue Jack Cade declares he would " make it felony to drink small beer."

Brewing was an accomplishment cultivated in most

old English monasteries, just as at the present day the extraction of essential oils for the concoction of liqueurs and cordials is largely carried on in a number of the Continental monasteries. In Saxon and mediæval times the office of Cellarer was one of the most important in English religious houses ; and according to Scott's " Ivanhoe" Burton-on-Trent Abbey in the time of Cœur-de-Lion had already acquired a reputation for its conventual ale.

The whole of Burton's present-day commercial prosperity is the outcome of that ancient monastic practice. In pre-Reformation days the abbot was lord of the manor, and the abbey with its dependencies was then practically the town. In those times, according to the local legend—

> "The Abbot of Burton brewed good ale,
> On Fridays when they fasted—"

and being an artful abbot, who preferred that his ale should have time to mellow, the legend proceeds—

> "But the Abbot of Burton never tasted his own
> As long as his neighbour's lasted."

The earliest historical reference to this particular conventual beer is one of the year 1295, when, sometimes called " cicer," it would appear to be a common article of consumption among the dependents of the abbey. It is also an historical fact that when Mary, Queen of Scots, was a prisoner in Tutbury Castle (1584) she was supplied with beer from " Burton three myles off."

It must by no means be thought that the pre-eminence of Burton ales has been derived by brewing it from the inexhaustible waters of the Trent; the secret of its success lay in the peculiar suitability of the water supplied by its numerous wells, the chemical or natural properties of which confer those potable qualities so much approved by the connoisseur. The water passes through some gypsum beds in the neighbourhood.

A side-light has recently been thrown on the manner in which native enterprise availed itself of this undoubted natural advantage. It appears that the great carrying business, so widely known as Pickfords, was established in 1640, when road traffic had to be performed mainly by the use of pack-horses, and has only grown to its present enormous dimensions by the overcoming of trade rivalry from time to time. In 1723 there was a small carrier near Burton. His name was Bass. Upon his round he sold a home-brewed beer prepared in his spare time. The demand for the beverage grew to such an extent that he sold his carrying business to Pickfords and devoted himself exclusively to brewing. Such was the commencement of the great Burton house of Bass.

Since the liquor called Ale was first made by fermenting an infusion of malt, countless experiments have been tried for its improvement in every direction. Before hops were used for flavouring ale the ground-ivy was sometimes employed, from which circumstance it acquired the name of Ale-hoof. To give the liquor an aromatic flavour, the costmary was also tried, in which use this plant was commonly called Ale-cost.

As to the ingredients of ale, and the early methods of brewing it in this country, an old monkish chronicler has left on record this interesting piece of information :—

" Some abstemious souls have their home decoctions of broom, of bay berries, of ivy berries ; their sloe wine and their currant wine ; but men, in good sooth are believers in amber ale of malt, or of unmalted oats."

Staffordshire having risen to pre-eminence in the production of the commodity, it is from a history of this county—Dr. Plot's, written in 1686—we are best able to gain an insight into the earlier developments of the process.

Plot calls it "the *art* of making good ale," which, he says, is "nothing else but boyled water impregnated with mault."

"In the management of which," he continues, alluding to the brewers of Burton, "they have a knack of fineing it in three days to that degree that it shall not only be potable, but as clear and palatable as one would desire any drinke of the kind to be ; which, though they are unwilling to own it I guess they doe by putting alum or vinegar into it whilst it is working ; which will both stop the fermentation and precipitate the lee, so as to render it potable as when it has stood a competent time to ripen."

The learned historian makes us furthermore acquainted with the nature of some of the other ingredients. He says : "About Shenstone"—which is a village contiguous to the city of Lichfield—"they frequently used *Erica vulgaris* heath, or Ling, instead of Hopps, to preserve their beer, which gave it no ill taste."

But what is more interesting, he also alludes to the use of oats for brewing purposes. "They sometimes here make mault of oats ; which, mixed with that of barley, is called dredg mault ; of which they make an excellent fresh, quick sort of drink." He also mentions the use of "French barley, that is, a plant between wheat and barley, which runs to mault as well as other barley, and makes a good sort of drink."

One more extract from the old gossip must be added, for it discloses a rather curious practice. "At some places they still thrash their corn after the ancient manner, *sub dio*, as I saw them upon the pavement in the open streets at Burton-on-Trent."

What was true of Burton Abbey was equally true of many other conventual establishments throughout the land.

In 1434 it was placed on record "how great evils arise both to the clerks and to the townsmen of the city of Oxford owing to the negligence and dishonesty of the brewers of ale"; whereupon the brewers were all brought together by the Commissary in the Church of the Blessed Virgin Mary, where each was made to swear most solemnly on the holy evangelists that he would thereafter "brew ale that was good and wholesome so far as his ability and human frailty" permitted him.   That there might be no possible doubt as to what constituted good ale, the University authorities proceeded to lay down minute directions concerning the methods of brewing to be employed in that city.   Notwithstanding these precautions and the strictness of the surveillance exercised, it was found impossible to enforce these bylaws long together; in 1449 the stewards and manciples of Canterbury College lodged a complaint against nine brewers who had brewed "an ale of little or no strength, to the grave and no mean damage of the University and Town."   Again in 1464 the Commissary ordered that a brewer named John Janyn should refund the sum of eightpence to Anisia Barbour, to whom he had sold a cask of ale for 20d., whereas, said the judgment, "in our opinion and that of others who have tasted it, it is not worth more than 12d."

It was the hop-vine which made ale, as we know it now, "the wine" of our country, recognised by Englishmen as a better drink than ypocras, mead, or methlin. According to an old rhyme—

> "Hops and turkeys, carp and beer,
>   Came into England all in one year."

The date assigned is 1520; and, says that picturesque writer, Mr. Ford Madox Hueffer, putting the words in the mouth of a Kentish squire of those Tudor times—

"The Almains call the plant 'hopfen,' but 'hop' is a good enough word for me. From Bohemia cometh this goodly vine that I am minded to plant in the county of Kent. With its aid is made that good drink that we call Brunswick Mum. But the Almains call it 'bier,' for it is made from the bere or barley plant. It is like our ale, but not so sweet."

It would appear, however, that the hop had been known in this country almost a century previous to the date mentioned, inasmuch as Henry VI. had prohibited the brewers from using hops, and the prohibition was repeated by Henry VIII., who, by the way, was a great lover of spiced ale—that is, the old English unhopped ale.

Whether the hop was introduced into this country by a Kentish merchant or, as is sometimes stated, by Flemish immigrants, there can be no gainsaying the fact that the innovation was regarded with strong disapproval. For a long time the hop was considered an adulterant, and the use of the "wicked weed" was checked by legislation for a century or more. The prejudice was put into a formal petition presented to Parliament by the Common Council of the City of London, asking that the employment of hops might be prohibited, because they not only spoilt the taste of the drink, but endangered the lives of the people. However, the improvement made in the liquor by the new constituent came at last to be generally recognised, although for many years the beer brewers kept themselves distinct from the ale brewers, who alone originally constituted the Brewers' Company of London.

As to the interchangeable terms "ale" and "beer," it may be observed that in olden times beer was considered the superior variety of ale, and usually sold at twice its price ; whereas nowadays at Burton-on-Trent and many other places the classification is reversed. In former times beer was the stronger liquor, because it was the brew from the first mashing of the malt. The term "beer" was used by the Anglo-Saxons, but seems to have fallen into disuetude until the name was revived to distinguish *ale* from *hopped ale*. At the present day, while the term ale does not apply to porter or stout, beer embraces all kinds of malt liquors.

That there is some connection between the words *beer* and *barley* is highly probable.

Richard Verstegans, the accomplished Anglo-Saxon scholar of the sixteenth century, says our Saxon ancestors called August the "gerst month" because it yielded the barley, the ancient name for which was gerst, "the name of barley being given to it by reason of the drinke therewith made, called beere." He also derives the word *barm*, through the form *berham*, from the same source. "This excellent and healthsome liquor, beere," he proceeds, "antiently also called *ael*, as of the Danes it is yet (beere and ale being in effect all one), was first of the Germans invented and brought into use."

Be it observed, this variety of ale, the characteristics of which were the agreeable bitter flavour and the improved keeping qualities, both imparted by the hops, was also of Teutonic origin.

To the association of ale-brewing with monastic life we owe the familiar marking of beer barrels with X, or XX, or XXX. These marks came to be interpreted as signifying the relative alcoholic strength of the drink, and people came to speak of "double X" or "treble X," as we now speak of Pale, Mild, or Strong ales. But the custom of marking barrels in this way arose in former times when monasteries were recognised brewing centres, the original idea being that of a sort of trade-mark guarantee ; for in shape the crosses were at first more akin to the crucifix, and served to indicate that by the oath of the monks, "sworn on the cross," the beer was of sound quality, fit to drink.

We are reminded of the same association by the genial Ingoldsby's " Lay of St. Dunstan," an imaginary monastic

ELINOVR RVMMIN,

The famous Ale-wife of *England*.

Written by Mr. *Skelton*, Poet Laureat to King

Henry the egiht.

When Skelton *wore the Lawrell Crowne,*
My Ale put all the Ale-wiues' downe.

LONDON

Printed for *Samuel Rand* 1624.

[Page 69.

INNS AT THE SOUTHWARK ENTRANCE TO LONDON IN SHAKESPEARE'S TIME.

(A part reproduction from Visscher's map.)

[*Pages* 70, 212.

episode of the "yere of our Lorde IX hundred & XXV, that tyme reynynge in this londe, Kinge Athelston." The gist of this humorous piece of rhyming is the plan of Peter the Lay-Brother to obtain the control of St. Dunstan's magic broomstick in order that he may make it bring him beer; so that if we are to believe the reverend and witty Mr. Barham, monastic ale even in Saxon times was a beverage highly to be desired. Poor Lay-Brother Peter, however, got too much of it; for the magic broomstick, at first bringing him the coveted ale by the flagon, presently brought it by the barrel; and not content with this bounty, next "started the hoops" and deluged all the cell with ale, faster than the discomfited Lay-Brother could drink it. And when in desperation he seized the officious broomstick and broke it in two, his plight was made worse, for each part set to work harder than ever to bring him supplies. To quote the droll "Ingoldsby":—

> "For both now came loaded with Meux's entire;
> Combe's, Delafield's, Hanbury's Truman's—no stopping—
> Goding's, Charrington's, Whitbread's continued to drop in
> With Hodson's pale ale, from the Sun Brewhouse, Wapping.
> (The firms differed then, but I can't put a tax on
> My memory to say what their names were in Saxon).
>   To be sure the best beer
>   Of all did not appear,
> For I've said 'twas June, and so late in the year
> The 'Trinity Audit Ale' is not come-at-able,
> As I've found to my great grief when dining at that table."

And so, when his brethren opened the door of the cell—

> "The Lay-Brothers nearest were up to their necks
> In an instant, and swimming in strong double X;
> While Peter, who, spite of himself now had drank hard,
> After floating awhile, like a toast in a tankard,
>   To the bottom had sunk,
>   And was spied by a monk,
> Stone-dead, like poor Clarence, half-drown'd and half drunk."

There are other authorities who trace these old-time barrel marks to other sources. One, for instance, refers them to the ancient practice of the Guild of Coopers. Every cask to contain beer was to have a capacity of XXXVI. gallons, and a cask to hold ale only XXXII. gallons ; and the wardens of the craft who went round to examine the work for illegal sizes are said to have passed the good vessels of standard size by marking on each one, two, or three crosses, according to the quality of liquor it was intended for.

Dr. Brewer, in " Phrase and Fable," says the X on beer casks indicates beer which had to pay ten shillings duty, and hence it came to mean beer of a given quality. Two or three crosses, he says, are mere trade marks, intended to convey the notion that the contents were twice or thrice as strong as that which paid a ten shillings duty. If the learned doctor is correct, this marking cannot possibly date back any farther than the year 1643, when a duty was first imposed on ale, cider, and perry—in fact, when the whole system of excise or inland impositions was originated—and the tax on strong beer was only 2s. 6d. (which, of course, may be put as XXX pence) per barrel at the outset.

III

THE INFLUENCE OF THE CHURCH

The "Merrie England" of ancient times an ale-drenched England
—The Church's recognition of alcoholic merriment—"Church
Ale" a parochial duty—Managed by the churchwardens—The
Whitsun Ale—Described by Carew—by Aubrey—by Douce—
The Easter Ale or Clerk Ale—Jolly Absolon, Chaucer's
frivolous Parish Clerk—The Help Ale or Bid Ale on behalf of
the poor—Christening Ales—"Give Ales" from bequests—And
Bride Ales—Parish Wakes, their origin and degradation—Sale
of Wake Ale illustrated by a Derbyshire example—Puritan disapproval—Wolsey drunk at a village feast—Bishop Grindal's
injunction (1572)—Beadle and churchwardens—In search of
tipplers during church-time—Latest survival of Church drinkings in Rogation processions.

THE close connection between the ancient monasteries
of the land and the evolution of the national beverage
suggests the consideration of the influence exercised by
the Church at large upon the English habit of beer-
drinking. A review of old Church customs cannot fail
to disclose the prevalence of ale as the beverage of the
people. In these chapters "Merrie England" stands
revealed as an ale-drenched England.

Many ancient inns in this country possessed a religious,
or quasi-religious character, when attached to monastic
houses for the accommodation of pilgrims. The offerings of pilgrims at shrines and altars were a prolific
source of income to many mediæval religious founda-

tions. One such hostelry in old Southwark bore the sign of the " Three Brushes," painted like the holy-water brushes which are used at the *asperges* in the commencement of the Mass in the Catholic Church. Further reference to these ancient inns of monastic origin or association, will be made in a later chapter.

In pre-Reformation times there were plenty of opportunities for deep drinking. First of all tobacco was unknown, so that when a man once sat himself down with his pot of beer he had nothing to do but drink— there was no pipe to take his attention from his liquor.

Mother Church did not, perhaps, purposely invent excuses for guzzling, with her " idle-wakes, church-ales, helpe-ales, and heathenish riots at bride-ales " ; but the priests and parsons were consistently lenient to those who got drunk on ecclesiastical malt. And in the old Roman Calendar there were no less than ninety-five Saints' Days to be kept as holidays—days, that is, almost ear-marked for indulgence in alcoholic merriment.

Ale was so prevalent as a drink in olden times it gave its name to quite a number of festivals, some of them parochial meetings, some social gatherings, but all held with ecclesiastical sanction, if not directly under Church auspices. There were Church Ales, Whitsun Ales, Clerk Ales, Bride Ales, and what not. It was no doubt the influence of the Church which, in the earlier period, kept them pure by preserving a proper and reverent spirit at their observance.

The parochial gatherings were usually held in some large barn, and were often honoured by the presence of the squire and his lady, who came with their piper and taborer, and perhaps sipped a little ale themselves as they looked on at what were supposed to be, and, let us hope were, the sober joys of our simple ancestors.

At the Church Ales it was the practice for the churchwardens to buy or receive presents of malt with which to brew a quantity of beer. In some parishes there was a church house for the accommodation of this recognised parochial duty. Here were stored spits and cooking utensils as well as vessels for ιbrewing, so that a feast might be provided to add to the enjoyment, if not to induce a greater thirst for the consumption of the Church ale. The edibles, too, were generally the gift of the parishioners, so that the amount of clear profit which the churchwardens reaped by the sale of their ale might be all the larger ; and the proceeds were duly devoted to the relief of the poor, or some other worthy parochial object. These Church Ales were recognised assemblages of pleasure-seekers, where the young folk danced and revelled, while their elders looked on approvingly.

The great point, so far as our present purpose is concerned, is that whatever the occasion for these parish festivals—and in the course of the year several might be held in each village—they were commonly known as Ale Feasts, and sometimes briefly called Ales ; being so named because ale was the predominant liquor. Undoubtedly the most popular, and the most universal, was the one held at the best part of the English summer—Whitsuntide.

The customs prevailing at Whitsun Ales varied in different localities, but probably to a slight degree only. Carew gives the following description of the Cornish form of merriment on these occasions :—

"For the church-ale, two young men of the parish are yerely chosen by their last foregoers to be wardens, who, dividing the task make collection among the parishioners, of whatsoever provision it pleaseth them voluntarily to bestow. This they employ in brewing, baking, and other acates [purchased provisions], against Whitsuntide, upon which holidays the neighbours met at the church house, and there merily feed on their owne victuals, each contributing some petty portion to the stock, which, by many smalls, groweth to a meetly greatness ; for there is entertayned a kind of emulation between these wardens, who, by his graciousness in gathering, and good husbandry in expending, can best advance the churche's profit. Besides, the neighbour parishes at those times lovingly visit one another, and frankly spend their money together. The afternoons are consumed in such exercises as olde and yonge folk (having leysure) doe accustomably weare out the time withall. When the feast is ended, the wardens yeeld in their accounts to the parishioners ; and such money as exceedeth the disbursement is layd up in store, to defray any extraordinary charges arising in the parish, or imposed on them for the good of the countrey or the prince's service ; neither of which commonly gripe so much, but that somewhat stil remayneth to cover the purse's bottom."

From Aubrey's "Wiltshire" we extract the following seventeenth-century account:—

"There were no rates for the poor in my grandfather's days ; but for Kingston St. Michael (no small parish) the church ale of Whitsuntide did the business.   In every parish is (or was) a church-house to which belonged spits, crocks, &c., utensils for dressing provisions. Here the housekeepers met, and were merry, and gave their charity. The young people were there too, and had dancing, bowling, shooting at butts, &c., the ancients sitting gravely by and looking on. All things were civil, and without scandal."

A later authority, the antiquary Douce, writes :—

"At present the Whitsun ales are conducted in the following manner.   Two persons are chosen, previously to the meeting, to be lord and lady of the ale, who dress as suitably as they can, to the characters they assume. A large empty barn, or some such building is provided for the lord's hall, and fitted up with seats to accommodate the company.   Here they assemble to dance and regale in the best manner their circumstances and the place will afford ; and each young fellow treats his girl with a riband or favour. The lord and lady honour the hall with their presence, attended by a steward, sword-bearer, purse-bearer, and mace-bearer with their several badges or ensigns of office.   They have likewise a train-bearer or page, and a fool or jester, drest in a party-coloured jacket, whose ribaldry and gesticulation contribute not a little to the entertainment of some part of the company.   The lord's music, consisting of a pipe and tabor is employed to conduct the dance. Some people think this custom is a commemoration of the ancient Drink-lean, a day of festivity, formerly observed by the tenants and vassals of the lord of the fee, within his manor ; the memory of which, on account of the jollity of those meetings, the people have thus preserved ever since. The glossaries inform us that this drink-lean was a contribution of tenants, towards a potation of ale, provided to entertain the lord or his steward."

A minor celebration was held in some places at Easter ; and as the ale officially brewed and sold in the church-yards at this season was for the benefit of the Parish Clerk, the Easter festivities were called Clerk Ales—they were, in fact, the parochial gatherings at which the parish officers were enabled to collect their dues.

Evidence that in mediæval times there was no antagonism between the public-house and the house of God, is afforded by the character of Jolly Absolon in "The Miller's Tale." Chaucer describes this gay and frivolous Parish Clerk (in those times an ecclesiastic of inferior rank, but a "cleric") as one who was not above tuning his guitar wherewith to solace the hearts of tavern-wenches :—

> ". . . well could he play on the gitern.
> In all the town was brewhouse nor tavern
> That he not visited with his solas
> There as that any gaillard tapstere was."

The Help Ale was a festive gathering at which the contributions were made specially to help some poor person in distress, the object in view being not dissimilar to that of the present-day theatrical benefit ; sometimes it was known as a Bid Ale, inasmuch as a general bidding or invitation was given out in order that the patronage might be larger, and the benefit accruing from the entertainment all the greater.

Of the other celebrations mentioned some were of the nature of family rejoicings rather than parochial institutions, and marked such epochs of human life as births, deaths, and marriages.

Christening Ales were held when happy parents entertained their relations at a family gathering for the observance of the baptismal rite, and Bride Ales in celebration of a wedding ; Give Ales were the outcome of bequests designed to keep the deceased donor's memory green ; at all of which assemblages for festivity there was a ready flow of ale, and as four quarts could be had for a penny no one needed to wait long for a drink.

A Bride Ale, or as it was more shortly called in the Anglo-Saxon tongue, a " Bredale," was an ancient form of marriage feast celebrated by the consumption of specially provided ale.   For family gatherings they were attended by unusually large numbers—

> " No man may telle yn tale
> The people that was at that bredale,"

says an ancient allusion to one of these old English marriage celebrations.   Another form of festival, also intimately connected with Church life, was the parish Wake.

As every town, parish, and village practically held its Wake at a different time, according to the position of the Saints' Days in the Calendar, and as it was customary on such occasions for every parishioner to invite kinsfolk and friends from far and near, these patronal festivals offered even greater opportunities for drunkenness. Originally held in the churchyards, they had, owing to the licentious practices they encouraged, to be removed from the sacred precincts, and they came to be held in the public thoroughfares long before the Reformation ; and when morris-dancing, and the "hobby horse had been forgot," the "sealed quarts" at the ale-house door remained their only attraction.

Wakes, for their origin, have been traced back to the Agapæ, or love feasts of the Early Christians, which in turn had a basis upon ancient pagan rites. The people, on the birthday of the saint whose relics were deposited in their parish church, came together and made booths of the trees adjoining the church, and in them celebrated the feast with thanksgiving and prayer. Says an old author, they came " to churche with candellys burnyng, and would wake and come toward night to the church in their devocion." But as early as the reign of King Edgar there was issued a canon that the people should not betake themselves to drunkenness and debauchery on these occasions.

Certain it is that as these Wakes or Watch-night festivals fell away from the original purpose of their institution, they became more popular in the sense that they afforded unbridled opportunities for the drinking of enormous quantities of ale—opportunities of which each parish in turn availed itself to invite its neighbours to patronise its special brew, then and there to take a willing tribute of them in the sale of Wake ale.

In some instances the inhabitants of one or more parishes were mulcted in a certain sum according to mutual agreement. Thus we find an ancient stipulation of this kind, couched in these terms :—

"The parishioners of Evertoon and those of Okebrook in Derbyshire agree jointly to brew four ales, and every ale of one quarter of malt, between this and the feast of St. John the Baptist next coming, and every inhabitant of the said town of Okebrook shall be at the several ales ; and every husband and his wife shall pay twopence, and every cottager one penny. And the inhabitants of Elverton shall have and receive all the profits comming of the said ales, to the use and behoof of the church of Elverton ; and the inhabitants of Elverton shall brew eight ales betwixt this and the feast of St. John, at which ales the inhabitants of Okebrook shall come and pay as before rehearsed ; and if any be away one ale, he is to pay at t'oder ale for both."

In some parishes "wardens" were specifically appointed to look after the commercial side of this parochial victualling and drinking, which was looked upon as legitimate Church business.

The Church Ales have long since passed out of date ; but Wakes and Fairs, as purely secular institutions and entirely divorced from the Church, have in many places survived to modern times.

All these Church-organised festivities fell out of favour after the Reformation, when Puritanism lifted up its voice against such profanation. For under the newer conditions, involving the withdrawal of the countenance of the Church, the old reverent spirit had been completely lost, and much debauchery had crept in. Shakespeare gives some idea of this when he adverts to the song in *Pericles :—*

> " It hath been sung at festivals
> On ember days, and holy ales."

Truth, however, compels the confession that in the later Tudor times, excesses did frequently creep in at these celebrations. It is to be feared that many church-wardens salved their consciences with the comforting reflection that the harder their patrons drank the more their parish would benefit. Consequently they encouraged many fillings and allowed repeated refillings of the capacious black-jacks ; so that these meetings for social intercourse, affording as they did useful opportunities for the free intermingling of all ranks and classes of society, ultimately degenerated into mere drunken carnivals, though their origin had grown out of loving pity and a godly charity.

At a village feast held at Lymington, near Yeovil, about the year 1500, a very notable incident occurred. The vicar of the parish at that time was no less than

Thomas Wolsey ; and he, becoming inebriated in the course of the day's festivities, came in that condition under the notice of the austere Sir Amias Poulett, a local magistrate of great authority, who, without more ado, clapped the future cardinal into the stocks, to the scandal of his parishioners, though apparently not greatly to the detriment of the culprit's future career.

It would be wrong to think that no clerical mind of bygone times ever felt the impropriety of the Church's lending its countenance to the vicious practice of openly indulging in strong drink. Bishop Grindal, in his Injunctions to the Clergy issued at York in 1572, directly deals with the evil in the following order :—

"Ye shall not keep, or suffer to be kept in your parsonage or vicarage houses, tippling houses or taverns, nor shall ye sell ale, beer, or wine."

The practice in the later centuries was for the churchwardens and the beadle, or some other of the Church officials, to sally forth on Sunday morning at the commencement of the reading of the second lesson, and to visit all the public-houses in the neighbourhood of the church. Any one found tippling during Church service was instantly apprehended and placed in the stocks, which not unfrequently stood near the churchyard gates. The wardens apparently administered the law in these cases without the aid or intervention of the magistrates.

One other old custom in which copious drinking often occurred under the cognisance of, if not with the approval of the Church, cannot be omitted, because it lingered till comparatively recent times.

There is no need to go into the history of that interesting old custom, so highly necessary in an unlettered age, which was known as Beating the

Bounds. Every one who has read of these perambulations knows how largely the drinking of ale entered into their observance, and this under the eye and with the tacit consent of the Church. The clergy and choristers and other Church officials always headed the procession, which not only included the principal parishioners, but tailed off into the boys and youths and all the riffraff of the neighbourhood, the main attraction being the bountiful supplies of ale which were freely distributed at certain inns and stopping-places along the line of the parish boundaries. The drinking at the inns was not considered an unfit concomitant with the reading of the gospel at the various gospel trecs along the route, a custom which in its origin was purely a religious ceremony, held in Rogation Week.

> "Now comes the day wherein they gad abrode,
>   With crosse in hand,
> To boundes of every field and round about
>   Their neighbour's lande."

IV

THE MEDIÆVAL INN

The monastic inn or guest-house—The terms "Inn," "Hostel," and "Hotel"—The "Inns of Court"—Family mansions used as occasional inns—The plot of *She Stoops to Conquer*—Public inns of the Middle Ages—An "Inn" signifying a stage on a journey —Internal arrangements of a mediæval inn—The common alehouse—A bush, or Ale Stake, as a sign—Evil reputation of alehouses—The "Ale-wife" and the "Ale-draper"—Christopher Sly and the "fat Ale-wife of Wincot"—The tricks of dishonest "Ale-wives"—Restrictions of the Edwardian period—The functions of an inn—Victuallers and vintners—And ale-house keepers—Their obligations—Restrictive legislation at the Reformation (1552)—The number of taverns strictly limited—Licences first become necessary for ale-houses—And for inn-keepers who retailed ale—Disorderly houses indictable as nuisances—Inns for travellers needing no licence—Ale-houses the resort of disorderly characters (1496)—Skelton's description of the Ale-wife—Stow's account of the disreputable and dangerous ale-house at Billingsgate—An improvement in English inns by the close of the sixteenth century.

IF, as it has been asserted, the Roman inns or official posting-houses which had been established along all the main roads at about twenty miles or so apart, had been all rudely swept away by the Anglo-Saxon invaders, then we may accept it that for two or three centuries at least this country afforded no accommodation, no places of rest and refreshment, for travellers and wayfarers; and that this deficiency existed till such times as monasteries had been planted up and down the length and breadth of the land.

As the centuries went by, and travel became more general, the monasteries found their guest-chambers insufficient for the growing demands upon them, and hence arose the necessity of subsidising the lodging-houses, which in due time became inns. Some of these religiously-founded inns had chapels attached to them, in which the traveller on arrival returned thanks for the safe accomplishment of his journey so far, and where again on his departure he besought the protection of the saints during the remainder of his journeying. The Pilgrims' Inn at Glastonbury and the New Inn at Gloucester are among these monastic legacies.

As previously mentioned, some of the monasteries had a direct interest in attracting such visitors as came to make offerings at a shrine. The offerings and oblations of pilgrims often formed a considerable source of income to the religious foundation which was fortunate enough to possess a popular shrine.

A direct succession from monastic guest-houses to public inns might possibly be traced in some of the more venerable of our ancient hostelries by the local historian who would devote himself to the task with the necessary ability and enthusiasm.

The " Bell " at Tewkesbury, a fine half-timbered house considerably more than three hundred years old, seems to have stood within the precincts of the abbey ; its velvet-turfed bowling-green near the confluence of the Avon and the Severn, and bounded by a fine old yew hedge, has every appearance of having been anciently within the pleasaunce of the monks. This inn, it may be noted, is the scene of the once famous and still widely read novel, " John Halifax, Gentleman."

Besides those of our oldest inns which had their

foundations as monastic lodging-houses, others were originally family mansions of the nobility.

The word "Inn" is of good Saxon origin, and at first signified a chamber, although it came to be applied generally to a mansion, like the French word "hôtel." Hence, Clifford's Inn was once the mansion of De Clifford ; Lincoln's Inn the family residence of the Earls of Lincoln ; Gray's Inn the town house of the Lords Gray ; and so on.

Both terms "Inn" and "Hostel" were formerly employed as synonymous with a house used as a lodging-place, and were not confined to drinking taverns, as at the present day. For example, the "inns" or halls which were so numerous in Oxford and Cambridge before the erection of colleges, were merely lodging-houses for the scholars, though kept under strict regulation by the college authorities. Similarly the Inns of Court in London were originally provided for the lodging of the law-students there.

It was nothing unusual in olden times for the country houses of the nobility, during the absence of the owners, to be used as inns for the accommodation of travellers. At inns or guest-houses of this description it was customary to hang out as signs the arms of the owner ; and hence the origin of so many heraldic signs given to public-houses—a subject which will be treated later with a fulness its interest deserves.

As a matter of fact, the town house of the Earls of Warwick in ancient times was known as Warwick Inn. It was situated in Warwick Lane, and when the puissant "Kingmaker," as Richard Neville, Earl of Warwick, was called, came to London in 1458, he lodged a retinue of six hundred men in this house, all in red jackets, embroidered with the famous family badge of the Bear and Ragged Staff.

Existing inns converted from old family mansions belong to a later date, and generally they have been permanently used as houses of public entertainment ever since their conversion. It would, perhaps, be impossible to find an example of an inn which in the far-away centuries (when the scarcity of accommodation for travellers demanded the expedient) was used as a public inn during the temporary absence of its owners, and reverted to its original status on the family's return into residence.

That the private mansion of a great family would readily lend itself to the various requirements and specific uses of a public inn is quite conceivable. The idea of such conversion has been often utilised for fiction, and can be proven in fact. Taking the latter first, it will be found that the "Golden Lion" at Barnstaple—worth seeing for a richly moulded ceiling depicting a number of Biblical subjects, and having enormous pendants of the period of James I.—was formerly the mansion of the Earls of Bath.

And then, playgoers may recall, a number of leading incidents in Goldsmith's comedy, *She Stoops to Conquer*, hinge on the mistaking Squire Hardcastle's country residence for a public inn. Young Marlow, on his way to pay a first visit to his affianced but unknown ladylove, Miss Hardcastle, is purposely and mischievously sent to the house, by her clownish half-brother, Tony Lumpkin, under the impression it is an inn, dubbed for the nonce "The Buck's Head." Now, as young Marlow is exceedingly bashful in the presence of ladies, but by no means so with chambermaids, the fun of the play arises when Miss Hardcastle, made aware of her lover's mistake as to the identity of the house, pretends to be a chambermaid, and thus "stoops to conquer." Goldsmith admirably works out all the possibilities of resemblance

COURT ROOM, VINTNERS' HALL.

[Page 76.

BEER STREET.

By Hogarth.

(From a copy of Hogarth's Works, kindly lent by Messrs. Myers & Co., of Holborn.)

[Page 133.

between an old English family mansion, with its ample resources and lavish hospitality, and a large wayside hostelry on a well-frequented road.

In the fourteenth century the monasteries were the resort of the very poor and of the very rich, the good monks receiving the former of their charity, while the latter (from whom their patrons and founders were drawn) were received of right or of courtesy, the common inns of the Middle Ages being often too dear for the one and too miserable for the other.

The inns at that period generally found their regular customers among the merchants, small landowners, packmen, and other travelling members of the middle class. How the various social ranks freely fraternised in these fourteenth-century inns we may gather from Chaucer's "Tales," in which we see the knightly pilgrim did not disdain to dine with a miller, a cook, and a ploughman.

In some old English towns, as Rochester, Salisbury, Glastonbury, Sherborne, Malmesbury, Fotheringay, Ludlow, Grantham, and York, may still be found the remnants of ancient buildings originally erected as public inns ; some of them are still used for that purpose, while some have been diverted to other uses. That an inn was understood to signify a stage on a journey, may be gathered from Spenser's *Faery Queen* (vi. 3) :—

> "Now, when as Phœbus with his fiery waine,
> Unto his inne began to draw apace——"

As to the internal arrangements of a mediæval inn, there was little comfort and less privacy. A number of beds were placed in one room, and each customer purchased of the host what he required, chiefly meat, a little bread, and some beer. Frugal as these arrangements appear, such extortionate prices were charged for simple victuals

of this description that Parliament was petitioned to
intervene, and in 23 Edward III. a statute was pro-
mulgated to constrain hostellers to sell food at a
reasonable tariff.

The beds, however, could not be considered dear
at a penny a head in London, and something less in the
country, servants being generally charged at half these
rates. The modern traveller might think them dear at
any price when it is stated that they were invariably
overrun with fleas, bugs, and other vermin.

In addition to the inns where wayfarers slept at nights
there were lesser establishments along the highway, and
nearly always at the road crossings—mere calling-places
known as ale-houses. These could always be seen a
long way off if the weary traveller but raised his eyes
to look ahead for the one common sign which distinguished them all.   From above the front door of
every ale-house projected a long, horizontal pole, on
the top of which was a thick bush. In the towns it
became necessary to regulate the length and height of
these signs, as not infrequently they were affixed so low
as to endanger the heads of horsemen riding along the
narrow thoroughfares of a crowded city. An Act of
1375 restricted them to a maximum of 7 feet above
the public road.

Chaucer makes allusion to the Ale Stake thus, in
his Prologue, written in the year 1386 :—

> "A garland had he set upon his head
> As great as it were for an ale-stake."

Also this sign was sometimes called an Ale Pole ; as
thus, Holinshed, writing in 1587, says :—

> " Booths and Ale-poles are pitched at St. James his gate."

The Ale Stakes set up in front of ale-houses, by way of

signs, and sometimes known as Ale Poles, have by some writers been confused with Maypoles. Skelton, however, uses the second name—

> "Another brought her bedes
> Of jet or of cole
> To offer to the Ale-pole."

While another old writer (Bansley) employs the other—

> "For lyke as thee jolye ale-house
> Is always knowen by the good ale-stake," &c.

The reputation of many of these houses, flaunting their sign of a thick bush, or a bundle of green branches, was notoriously so shady that some of their frequenters did not always care to be seen entering them.

> "Some, lothe to be espyde
> Start in at the backe syde
> Over the hedge and pale
> And all for the good ale."

The incorrigible toper manifested as strong an objection to being thrust from the front door; as Shakespeare amusingly illustrates in the case of the bibulous Christopher Sly, in his Induction to *The Taming of the Shrew*. In this play we get a thumb-nail sketch of the old-time ale-house; and "Marian Hacket, the fat Ale-wife of Wincot," is no doubt a type of her class.

The question has been asked, Does a hostess attract custom more than a host? There is certainly something comfortable in the sound of the word "Ale-wife"; infinitely more so than in the term "Ale-draper," which was sometimes applied to the ale-house keeper of the opposite sex.

The old-time prototype of the Rev. Stiggins failed not, in his pursuit of good liquor and cheap, to make love to the comely Ale-wife; and in some cases perhaps found the lady not unwilling to receive his attentions, if the whispered invitation contained in the old rhyme is to be relied upon—

> " Kiss me, and tell me true ; and when they fail
> Thou shalt have bigger potts and stronger ale."

But the Ale-wife was not always comely, if always willing ; she was not even cleanly, as is exemplified in the traditional " Mother Louse."

The ancient practice, both in England and in Scotland, was to put Ale-wives who brewed and sold bad beer into the cucking-stool and punish them with a sound ducking. It was quite characteristic of Scots' laws that such dishonest brewsters should forfeit the ale, which was ordered to be "distributed to the pure folke." But why poor folk should have to drink the ale which was too evil for others is one of those things which only thrifty Scotsmen can explain.

By a statute of Edward I. (1285), none but freemen were allowed to keep ale-houses in London ; and from the chronicles of the old historian Spelman it may be gathered that the attempt to limit the number of public-houses in a given area is no new thing. He says :—

" In the raigne of King Edward the Third only three taverns were allowed in London : one in Chepe, one in Walbrook, and the other in Lombard Street."

The houses at which this restrictive legislation of the Edwardian period was levelled were clearly not the inns or hostels, which were then too few, but the common ale-houses and wine taverns used as mere drinking-shops.

Clearly the earliest function of an inn was to refresh and lodge travellers ; this was afterwards extended to supplying the wants of those who were not otherwise able to provide themselves with large quantities of drink and provisions. The victuallers, as these sellers of food and drink were called, were an ancient trade corporation when the Vintners' Company of London was founded in 1437. In course of time, however, common ale-house keepers came to be called victuallers. The vintners, as their name implies, kept wine-shops, which were generally known as taverns. Inns for the lodgment of travellers remained comparatively few till the period of the Reformation.

If any ale-house keeper or innkeeper refused to lodge a traveller, a Justice of the Peace might compel him to it ; or the Constable might present it as an offence at the next sessions ; or the party refused might have an action on the case. But he could not be compelled to sell victuals unless (it is naïvely added) the traveller tendered the money upon being required to do so.

In the reign of Edward VI. (1552) the number of taverns in London was restricted to 40 ; in York to 8 ; in Bristol to 6 ; in Norwich, Hull, Exeter, Canterbury, Gloucester, Chester, Cambridge, and Newcastle-upon-Tyne to 4 each ; and in Westminster, Lincoln, Shrewsbury, Salisbury, Hereford, Worcester, Southampton, Ipswich, Winchester, Oxford, and Colchester to 3 each.

Up to the period of the statute of Edward VI., it had been lawful for any one to keep an ale-house without a licence, for it was recognised as a means of livelihood not prohibited by law, although if kept in a disorderly manner it became indictable as a nuisance.

But mark the distinction again made between the two classes of public-house. This statute did not extend to inns, " for these are for lodging travellers " ; but if the inn degenerated into a mere drinking-shop, " and the master or innkeeper suffer men to sit tippling there in a disorderly manner, it shall be taken to be an ale-house," said the Act of 1552.

And so the Sessions Court, or alternatively the two justices, were empowered to put down ale-houses at their discretion, and further to take recognisances of ale-house keepers not to " use any unlawful games, or keep disorders in their houses."

It now, however, became necessary for any person keeping an ale-house to be licensed in sessions, or by two justices (one of the " quorum ") on pain of three days' imprisonment and a fine to be imposed by the quarter sessions. The Act, it may be mentioned, placed no restraint on the old practice of selling malt liquors at fairs.

Though at common law it had been lawful at one time for any person to build an inn for the reception of travellers without any licence from the justices, if the innkeeper sold ale by retail to persons other than travellers, without a licence to do so, he was punishable.

It would appear that as the common ale-houses had increased in number they had suffered in reputation, having become in many places the resort of disorderly characters of all kinds ; so much so that in 1496 (11 Henry VII.) an Act had been passed by which power was given to two justices to refuse permission to sell ale. Then had come this Act, half a century later, positively requiring that every ale-house should be licensed, either in sessions or by at least two justices. The punishment for infringement of this law was commitment for three days without bail, and the offender not to be set at large till he had entered into recognisances with two sureties not to keep an ale-house ; which recognisance being certified to the next quarter sessions, was to be sufficient conviction to mulct him in a fine of twenty shillings.

In early Tudor times some of the ale-houses in towns

and cities were often the resort of bad characters of all
sorts—cut-purses, harlots, and others who drank and
diced all day, and left their haunts only under cover of
the night. The poet Skelton, tutor to Henry VIII., in
one of his ballads describes a typical Ale-wife as a
detestable old creature with a crooked nose, humped back,
grey hair, and wrinkled face.

> "She breweth noppy ale,
> And maketh thereof poorte sale
> To travellers, to tynkers,
> To sweters, to swynkers,
> And all good ale drinkers."

The Ale-wife thus immortalised was Elinour Rummin,
of the " Running Horse," Leatherhead, Surrey, who is
always depicted with two cups in her hands, the symbol
of her calling.

Stow, in his account of London between the years
1560 and 1590, thus depicts a disreputable and dangerous
inn kept by a sort of Elizabethan Fagin :—

"One Wotton, a Gentleman born, and sometime a Merchant of
good Credit, but falling by Time into Decay . . . kept an Alehouse
at Smart's—very near Billingsgate. . . . And in the same house he
procured all the Cutpurses about the City to repair to his House.
There was a School-house set up, to learn young Boys to cut Purses :
two Devices were hung up, the one was a Pocket, the other was a
Purse. The Pocket had in it certain Counters, and was hung about
with Hawk's bells, and over the top did hang a little Sacring Bell.
The Purse had silver in it. And he that could take out a Counter
without any Noise was allowed to be a public Foyster. And he that
could take a piece of silver out of the Purse without Noise of any of
the Bells was adjudged a judicial Nypper, according to their Terms
of Art. A Foyster was a Pickpocket, a Nypper was a Pickpurse or
Cutpurse."

By the close of the sixteenth century the character of
English inns had greatly improved. The constant resort

to the markets and fairs caused inns to flourish along all the great high-roads. How numerous they were, and the kind of accommodation they provided, may be seen by a glance at the illustration showing the Southwark approach to London Bridge in Shakespeare's time.

These English inns were under better regulation than those on the Continent at this period. The English host was not, as those on the Continent were, a despot among his guests. Each guest, who could pay for it, was lodged in a well-furnished chamber, amply supplied with clean linen, and of which he could hold the key. If the traveller lost anything, the landlord was responsible; but although the host of Tudor times had the reputation of being honest, it is to be feared the tapsters and chamberlains were sometimes in collusion with the thieves and robbers who infested the highways, to the terror of solitary travellers.

V

VINTNERS AND TAVERNS

Old English vineyards and native wine—Introduction of Bordeaux
wines (1154)—Vintners established in London—The Vintry or
wine docks—A Vintner Lord Mayor in 1314—Another in 1356
entertains royalty—Vintners' Hall, 1357—Vintners incorporated,
1437—Their charters—Their arms—Guienne wines—Varieties
—Malmsey and other Rhenish wines—Gascony, Spanish, and
Canary wines—Sack, and Shakespearean references thereto—
Ruling prices and lucrative business—Adulterat. 1 wine con-
fiscated, 1428—The Gascony wine trade regulated—The
"Three Cranes" in the Vintry—Literary allusions—Pepys'
experience there in 1661—Vintners' Hall—Vintners' Company's
right to keep swans on the Thames—Retail wine-shops called
" Taverns"—Where a man may get drunk with more credit
and apology than in a common ale-house—Charles I. and the
Vintners' Company—Patents of monopoly condemned by Parliament—Unscrupulous patentees punished—Vintners' archives
suffered in the Fire of London, 1666—A Vintners' Song of the
City pageant in Anne's reign—Privileges of a " free Vintner "—
Failed in Birmingham because it is not a " thoroughfare town."

LET it not be vainly imagined that ale and mead were
the only English-made beverages of ancient times. The
Saxons cultivated vineyards, and made an inferior kind
of wine from the juice of the grape. In Norman times
there was a vineyard within the precincts of the Tower of
London, and many old towns in England still have
street-names and place-names, like Vineyard and Vinegar,
indicative of the sites once occupied for the household

71

industry of wine-growing and wine-making. Some antiquaries, however, contend that the Saxons used the
English word "vineyard" for "orchard," and that
Saxon wine was nothing more than cider or perry. It
may be safely assumed that the juice of the grape grown
under the dull grey skies [of this country would not be a
very generous liquor ; and certain it is that whatever the
nature of the native wine may have been, it was entirely
discarded at an early date in favour of that imported
from the sunny land of France.

The traffic in Bordeaux wines is said to have commenced about 1154, when Henry II. married Eleanor of
Aquitaine. The wine merchants became known as Vintners, and the place on the Thames bank where, till the
year 1300, they landed their wares—which they were
obliged to sell within forty days—was called the Vintry.

A Vintner literally signifies a man who sells wine, and
both the term and the occupation were at one time prac-
cally unknown outside London. Wine merchants nowadays generally sell spirits, and sometimes ale as well as
wines, so that the restricted meaning of the term Vintner
has long since been lost.

Of the high standing of the Vintners we get some idea
from Stow, who tells us that in the neighbourhood of the
"Three Cranes," near Cheapside, was the great house
called the "Vintrie," where, in 1314, Sir John Gisors,
Lord Mayor and Constable of the Tower, resided, as did
Sir Henry Picard, Vintner, who was Lord Mayor in 1356,
and who "in one day did sumptuously feast Edward,
king of England, John, king of France, the king of
Cypress, then lately arrived in England, Edward, Prince
of Wales, with many noblemen and others."

In 1357 Sir John Stodie, a wealthy Vintner, gave the
land on which the Vintners built themselves a trade or
guild hall, as well as a number of almshouses. It is

probable the Vintners acted as a fraternity long before they were incorporated as a City Company by Henry VI. in 1437, because we read of the Gascon wine merchants being powerful enough to hold serious contentions with the citizens of London in the time of Edward I.

From the reign of Edward III. to that of James I. the Vintners obtained six royal charters, and the Company's arms, granted by Henry VI., included a crest which very appropriately comprised a Bacchus and loving-cup.

Guienne was one of the chief places from which wine was imported for English consumption in those times ; but a list of the period enumerates the following varieties as being largely dealt in : Muscadell, a rich wine ; Malmsey, Rhenish ; Dale wine, a sort of Rhenish ; Stum, a strong new wine ; Gascony wine ; Alicant, a Spanish wine made of mulberries ; Canary wine, or sweet sack (the grape of which was brought from the Canaries) ; Sherry, the original sack, not sweet ; Rumney, a sort of Spanish wine. Sack, of which the convivial Sir John Falstaff was such a lenient connoisseur, was a term somewhat loosely applied at first to all white wines.

The sack mentioned by Shakespeare as the favourite beverage of Falstaff—the "sherris sack," as Sir John calls it—was evidently the wine of Xeres, in Spain. That Falstaff drank sugar with it is also proof that it was not a sweet wine. An old ballad in " Pasquil's Palinodia " has this chorus—

> " Give me sacke, old sacke, boys,
>   To make the muses merry,
> The life of mirth and the joy of the earth
>   Is a cup of good old sherry."

Also as to this sack, of which Shakespeare makes so much capital, it is extremely doubtful if it were known in England so early as the time of Henry IV. ; it was an

imported wine, and is said to have derived its name
either from being *vin sec*, or a peculiarly dry wine—did
it not need the addition of much sugar?—or from being
carried in sacks of Spanish goat-skins.

With regard to the prices of foreign wine which prevailed in olden times, it is significant that although it
was not allowed that "Gascoyne wine should sell for
more than fourpence, nor Rhenish wine above sixpence
the gallon," there were four Vintners who attained to the
office of Lord Mayor within the reign of Edward III.
The City records throw some light on the way this
business was conducted.

In the last-mentioned reign John Peche, a wealthy
citizen, was fined and imprisoned for having obtained
a monopoly for the sale of sweet wines. John Raine-
well, Lord Mayor in 6 Henry VI., having discovered that
the Lombard wine merchants adulterated their sweet
wines, ordered, in his great wrath, 150 vessels to be staved
in, "so that the liquor running forth, passed through the
cittie like a stream of rainwater in the sight of all the
people, from whence there issued a most loathsome
savour."

In the same reign grievous complaints were made of
the adulteration of Gascon and Guienne wines, and a
petition was made to Parliament, praying that all wine
casks from Gascony, "tonnes, pipes, and hogsheads,"
should be of the full and true measure.

It was in this reign, as previously mentioned, that the
Vintners' Company was established; and a charter from
the same monarch forbade that any but such as were
enfranchised by the craft should trade in wines from
Gascony; and Gascoigners were forbidden to sell wine
except in the tun or pipe. All wines coming to London
were to be unloaded above London Bridge, at the
Vintry; and the right was given to the Company, to be

exercised by four members, elected annually, to search
all taverns to see that the prices and all the various trade
regulations were strictly adhered to.

As showing how trade begets trade, it may be mentioned that merchant Vintners might buy cloth, while, on
the other hand, the Gascoigne merchant might purchase
dried fish in Cornwall and Devon, also herrings and
cloth in what other parts of the kingdom they pleased.

In London a favourite inn sign was the "Three
Cranes," generally represented pictorially by three birds
of this name. But this sign really originated from the
three lifting cranes in the Vintry by which the heavy
casks of wine were unloaded from boats and lighters in
the river.

The "Three Cranes" in the Vintry was a famous
tavern in the time of James I., and was much frequented
by the wits of Ben Jonson's time. In his play *Bartholomew Fair* this dramatist says :—

"A pox o' these pretenders to wit ! your 'Three Cranes,' 'Mitre,'
and 'Mermaid' men ! not a corn of true salt, not a grain of right
mustard amongst them all !"

There is a similar allusion in his play, *The Devil is an
Ass*—

"Nay, boy, I will bring thee to the sluts and the roysters,
At Billingsgate, feasting with claret-wine and oysters ;
From thence shoot the bridge, child, to the 'Cranes' in the
Vintry,
And see there the gimblets how they make their entry."

It was at the same house of entertainment that Pepys,
as recorded in his famous Diary, under date January 23,
1661–2, suffered bitter mortification in having to dine
there with some poor relations ; not only was the com-

pany distasteful to the snobbish Secretary, but the accommodation seems to have been very deficient, for he describes the best room in the tavern as a "narrow dogg-hole," and the meal served in it as "a sorry poor dinner."

Not far away, in Upper Thames Street, stood Vintners' Hall—a most interesting building.   As mentioned in another place, the public-house sign, "The Swan with Two Necks," is derived from the practice of the Vintners' Company marking their swans, kept on the open Thames, with two nicks cut in the beak, at every swan-hopping season when account is taken of the young birds hatched since the previous marking.   This stocktaking usually occurs in August, and at one time the Vintners' Company had five hundred birds on the river.

The mark of the Company is two straight lines made in the shape of a V, which perhaps may stand as the initial of the word Vintner, or it may be a chevron, which is a portion of the Company's coat-of-arms—"a chevron between three tuns, argent."

In olden times the retail establishments of Vintners were commonly known as taverns.   "A tavern," says Bishop Earle, writing in 1628, "is a degree above an ale-house, where men are drunk with more credit or apology.   If the vintner's nose be at the door, it is a sign sufficient ; but the absence of this is supplied by the ivy bush."

The term "Vintner," again, is not nowadays restricted to one who keeps a wine-shop, to one who merely "sells wine to be consumed on the premises."   It generally has the wider signification of "licensed victualler."

King Charles I. extorted forty shillings a tun from the Vintners, and in return prohibited the wine coopers from exporting wines.   Licences for retailing wine were at the same time granted by the Vintners' Company for the

King's benefit. He also forbade the sale of wines in bottle instead of measures. Soon afterwards, in 1641, royal patents received their death-blow from Parliament, when two patentees, Alderman Abell and Richard Kilvert, were heavily fined for having obtained an exclusive patent for wines.

These men, it appeared, were found to have "in their hands, which they deceived the King of, £57,000 upon the wine licence ; the Vintners of London, £66,000 ; the wine merchants of Bristol, £1,051 ; all of which moneys were ordered to be immediately raised on their lands and estates, and to be employed to the public use." The heavy exactions of these unscrupulous patentees were thus rightly recovered for the benefit of the state, and the whole business of patent-hunting fully exposed and condemned.

Many valuable and interesting documents of the Company kept at the first hall were unfortunately lost in the Fire of London, 1666. A song which was sung in hall by the Vintners at the last City pageant in the time of Queen Anne, and one which is no mean example of a city poet's verse, ran in this wise :—

"Come, come, let us drink the Vintners' good health ;
'Tis the cask, not the coffer, that holds the true wealth ;
If to founders of blessings we pyramids raise,
The bowl, not the sceptre, deserves the best praise.
Then next to the Queen, let the Vintners' fame shine ;
She gives us good laws, and they fill us good wine.

Columbus and Cortez their sails they unfurled
To discover the mines of an Indian world,
To find beds of gold so far they could roam ;
Fools ! fools ! when the wealth of the world lay at home.
The grape, the true treasure, much nearer it grew ;
One Isle of Canary's worth all the Peru.

Let misers in garrets lay up their gay store
And keep their rich bags to live wretchedly poor ;
'Tis the cellar alone with true fame is renowned,
Her treasure's diffusive, and cheers all around.
The gold and the gem's but the eye's gaudy toy,
But the Vintner's red juice gives health, life, and joy."

Membership with an old City Company like the Vintners' anciently carried with it many privileges, as came out in the evidence given in a case tried some quarter of a century ago at Birmingham. A "free Vintner" of the City of London, named Pruday, opened a wine-shop in the High Street of the Midland Metropolis, without taking out any licence therefor in the ordinary way. Naturally enough an Excise prosecution followed, when Pruday pleaded that as a "free Vintner" he was entitled to trade in wine, untrammelled by any licensing authority, not only within the limits of the City of London, but "anywhere along the king's highway from Dover to Berwick, where the king's courier ran." [1] Doubtless there was some

[1] A charter was granted to the Vintners' Company on February 2, 1611, for the benefit of the freemen of the Company and "also for the better maintenance of our subjects being sailors of this our kingdom of England," enabling the freemen to sell wine in the city of London and "within three miles from the walls or ports of the city," and "also in all and singular other cities and seaports called port-towns within our kingdom of England and in all other cities and towns known by the name of thoroughfare towns where our couriers, commonly called posts, were set up and limited to, in the common road usually frequented and used by foreigners or natives between Dover and London and between London and Berwick, wheresoever any freeman or freemen of the mistery aforesaid now dwell or dwelleth or hereafter shall happen to dwell."

On June 7, 1889, the Vintners' Company issued to their members an order defining the area over which the privilege could be exercised as follows : 1. In the City of London and within three miles from the walls or gates of the City ; 2. In the following cities and seaports in England described in the charter as "porte-towns," namely : Sandwich, Faversham, Rochester, Dover, Chichester, Rye, Southampton,

GIN LANE.

By Hogarth.

(From a copy of Hogarth's Works, kindly lent by Messrs. Myers & Co., of High Holborn.)

[*Page* 134.

"Neglected by their parents, educated only in the streets, and falling into the hands of wretches who live upon the vices of others, they are led to the gin-shop, to drink at that fountain which

ancient prerogative of this kind, making the Vintners free not only of the City of London, but of all high-roads from "Dan to Beersheba," from one end of the kingdom to the other; but in this case Pruday failed to substantiate his claim apparently on the ground that the "high street" of Birmingham, at any rate, was not one of the privileged roads. It was felt that such chartered privileges ought to be, if they were not, obsolete.

Poole, Weymouth, Lyme Regis, Exeter, Dartmouth, Barnstaple, Bridgwater, Plymouth, Minehead, Bristol, Gloucester, Chester, Liverpool, Pressal, Carlisle, Berwick, Newcastle, Kingston-upon-Hull, Boston, Lynn, Great Yarmouth, Ipswich, and Colchester; 3. In the following cities and towns on the post-roads between London and Dover and London and Berwick, described in the charter as "throughfare towns," namely : Dartford, Gravesend, Rochester, Sittingbourne, Canterbury, Margate, Sandwich and Dover on the first-named road, and Waltham, Ware, Royston, Babraham, Caxton, Huntingdon, Stilton, Stamford, South Witham (Lincolnshire), Grantham, Newark, Tuxford, Scrooby, Doncaster, Tenybridge, Tadcaster, York, Wetherby, Boroughbridge, Catterick, Bowes, Burghe, Penrith, Carlisle, Northallerton, Darlington, Durham, Newcastle-on-Tyne, Hexham, Thirlwall, Morpeth, Alnwick, Belford, and Berwick, on the last-named road.   By the Inland Revenue Act, 1862 (25 & 26 Vict. c. 22), no freeman of the Vintners' Company shall be entitl d to sell wine in more than one separate and distinct house or premises at the same time without taking out the proper Excise licence in that behalf ; nor shall any freeman be entitled to exercise the said privilege unless he shall have previously made an entry of the house or premises in which he intends to sell wine with the proper officer of Excise, in the manner directed in s. 5 of the Excise Management Act, 1834.

The privilege of selling wine as a freeman of the Vintners' Company extends only to persons whose freedom has been obtained by patrimony or servitude and their widows (Board's Order, February 26, 1830, Order of Vintners' Company, March 12, 1839).

The Houses of Vintners are expressly excluded from the provisions of the Ale-house Act, 1828 ; Beer-house Acts, 1830–1840 ; Wine and Beer-house Act, 1869 ; and Licensing Act, 1872.

VI

BREWERS AND BREWERIES

From a domestic industry to an organised trade—St. Adrian chosen patron saint of brewers—Ale regarded as a necessary food—No reduction of its output allowed—"A withdrawer of such victual from a city" regarded as a traitor—Regulations for a standard quality and fixed price—The Brewers' Company—Convicted of selling "dear ale" (1422)—Location of the London breweries—Exportation of English ale in Tudor times—A harassed trade (1591)—Arbitrary legislators ignore fluctuations in price of materials—A lucrative trade—Cromwell a brewer—A severe censure on brewers by a writer of 1621—Literary and biographical associations—Mrs. Thrale—"Miss Haversham"—"Angela Marsden Messenger"—William Hucks, M.P.—George III.'s visit to Whitbread's London Brewery.

IN early English times, when brewing was a domestic industry, the trade was entirely in the hands of women ; hence the origin of the terms Ale-wife and Brewster, already commented upon.

In " The Vision of Piers Plowman " (1377) we read of—

" The best and brounest ale that brewsters sellen,"

and in another part of the poem that—

" Beton the brewstere bad him good morwe [morrow]."

We have seen brewing carried on as an important part of the old English household economy, and we have seen the same thing glorified and conducted on a larger scale in the monastic life of the period. But exactly when brewing developed into an organised industry no man can say with certitude, although references to it as such are to be found almost as early as Robert Langland.

Stow, for instance, informs us that in 1414 "one William Murle, a rich maltman and bruer of Dunstable, had two horses all trapped with gold." Brewing would appear always to have been a lucrative calling.

The brewing trade, having become a recognised industry for men, selected and appropriated, after the manner of all mediæval guilds of workmen, a patron saint. St. Bacchus, whose day is so appropriately held on the seventh of the best brewing month, October, was not selected; it was St. Adrian, whose day appears in the Calendar on September 8th, who, for some reason not apparent, has been chosen patron saint of the brewing fraternity.

Friction often arose between the authorities and the brewers respecting the quality of the liquor brewed, and the prices at which it was sold. Also it was incumbent upon the brewers in old time to keep up an adequate supply of good ale, just as we nowadays insist upon a proper supply of pure water; the former, however, was regarded more as a question of food supply, while the latter is mainly a hygienic precaution. The brewers were not allowed to cause any inconvenience by a sudden reduction of their output, on the plea, perhaps, that the State-regulated prices were unremunerative to them, or on any other excuse whatever. In 1533 the authorities of the City of London ordered that if it came to the knowledge of the Mayor and Aldermen that "any of the saide brewers, of their frowarde and perverse myndes, shall

at any time hereafter sodenly forbeare and absteyne
from bruyinge, whereby the king's subjects should bee
destitute or onprovided of drynke," no less a penalty
would be imposed upon the recalcitrant brewers than
the confiscation of their breweries—their establishments, it was ordained, would be taken possession of
by the City Council, who would put others into the
brew-houses, and, if need be, supply them with materials
to produce the ale, which in the days of bluff King
Hal was regarded as one of the necessaries of life.

Any one who refused to brew, or produced a less
quantity than he or she had been accustomed to brew,
was regarded as "a withdrawer of victual from the
city," which, in the old fighting days, was tantamount
to being a traitor ; and the ordinances then in force
for keeping up the quality and fixing the price, awarded
to brewers so offending, the penalties of imprisonment
and disqualification to follow the trade of a brewer
within the liberties of the City of London for ever.
From the severity of these trading regulations, particularly those relating to a standard quality always
accompanying a fixed price, it may be guessed that
disputes between the Common Council of the City
and the Brewers' Company were of frequent occurrence.

There is evidence for believing that the brewers, who
succeeded the Ale-wives of earlier times, had been
formed into a trade guild long before they received
their first royal charter of incorporation. This formal
recognition was granted in 1445 by Henry VI., to
"The Master and Keepers or Wardens & Commonalty
of the Mystery or Art of Brewers of the City of
London." The craft had possessed their own Hall as
early as 1422.

The brewers of London, after their incorporation,
for a long time regulated the brewing trade in the

City and eight miles around. The present Brewers'
Hall in Addle Street, Cheapside, is a modern building.

In 1422 the famous Richard Whittington laid an
information before his successor in the lord mayoralty,
Robert Childe, against the Brewers' Company, for
selling "dear ale," when they were convicted in the
penalty of £20, and the masters were ordered to be
kept in prison until they paid it.

The breweries of London in Tudor times were
located on the river-side below St. Katherine's, near
the Tower, and are marked on a map of the period,
"Bere houses." These breweries were subject to the
usual vexatious, though useful surveillance, of the
times.

Henry VII., in 1492, licensed one John Merchant,
a Fleming, to export 50 tuns of ale "called berre";
and by Elizabeth's reign the demand for English strong
ale had evidently increased, as we find 500 tuns being
exported at one time to Amsterdam—probably, Pennant
the antiquary surmises, for the use of our thirsty army
in the Low Countries. The exportation of ale, though
formerly requiring royal licence, seems to have been
free at this period, except in scarce times when it was
checked by proclamation.

The introduction of French wines in the twelfth
century did not oust home-brewed ale as the beverage
of the people. Not only did the supremacy of the
native beverage remain unchallenged, but English ales
began to acquire a reputation abroad. So long as the
rule-of-thumb methods of the old Ale-wives prevailed,
so long as brewing was little more than a domestic
industry, restrictions and interferences on the part of
the authorities were practically uncalled for.

But when brewing passed into the hands of masculine
brewers, who employed improved processes and used

better appliances, when it attained to the importance of a commercial undertaking—one indeed which involved nothing less than the manufacture of what was regarded as a necessary of life, as one of the chief sources of nourishment for the bodies of the English people—then arose a condition of harassed trading for the brewers, from which they did not escape for centuries.

The reason for this chronic state of friction between the brewers and the authorities is not far to seek. Ale being a necessary of life and a source of national strength, an adequate supply of it, of a standard quality of wholesomeness, and at a prescribed price easily accessible to the average pocket, was demanded by the Legislature. But even supposing the price fixed by law for a commodity of standard quality and legal measurement is a fair one at the time it is made, it does not follow that the price will always remain a fair and remunerative one to the producer. It was this ignorance of the first principles of political economy which was at the root of all the trouble in which the brewers found themselves time after time. Variations in the price of material, particularly the higher prices which, with increased consumption, ruled for barley, were utterly disregarded by arbitrary legislators. In 1591 the Brewers' Company protested against being compelled to sell their ale at a price which had been fixed upon sixty years previously ; they went so far as to advance the price in defiance of the existing ordinances ; but such high-handed procedure was promptly checked, and the brewers were again reduced to a becomingly submissive attitude by her imperious Majesty, Queen Elizabeth.

As brewing has generally been lucrative, the opportunities of life have not been denied to its followers, and one of the most caustic things said of our present-day politicians is that the "step from beerage to the peerage" is an easy one under a system of party politics. It is a noteworthy fact that the chiefest Puritan of Puritan England was, amongst other things, a brewer—no less a personage than the Lord Protector of England, the great Oliver Cromwell. That the calling was not then without its critics may be gathered from an author of the year 1621, quoted by Hone :—

"Of all the trades in the world, a brewer is the loadstone which draws the customes of all functions to it. It is the mark or upshot of every man's ayme, and the bottomless whirlepoole that swallowes up the profits of rich and poore. The brewer's art (like a wilde kestrell) flies at all games ; or like a butler's boxe at Christmasse, it is sure to winne, whosoever loses. Your innes and alehouses are brookes and rivers and their clients are small rills and springs, who all (very dutifully) doe pay their tributes to the boundless ocean of the brewhouse. For, all the world knowes, that if men and women did drinke no more than sufficed nature ; if drinking were used in any reason, or any reason used in drinking, I pray ye what would become of the brewer then ? Surely we doe live in an age wherein the seven deadly sins are every man's trade and calling. Every stiffe potvaliant drunkard is a post-beam which holds up the brewhouse ; for as the barke is to the tree, so is a good drinker to the brewer."

Brewers and breweries occur in biography and literature as well as in politics. Mrs. Thrale, the intimate friend of Dr. Johnson, was married against her will to Henry Thrale, a brewer whose brewery on his death was sold to the Barclays for £135,000. In fiction we meet in Charles Dickens' "Great Expectations" the eccentric Miss Havisham, who lived the life of a recluse at the deserted brewery of her dead-and-gone family, from which all the scents of brewing had long since evaporated, its yard being but a wilderness of empty casks and sour lumber.

A similarly interesting character in fiction is the philanthropic Angela Marsden Messenger of Sir Walter

Besant's famous novel, "All Sorts and Conditions of Men." The wealth she distributes so generously and so wisely has all been derived from a great brewery, of which she is the sole surviving owner. As she says of herself :—

"I am the brewery. I am Messenger, Marsden, & Company myself, the sole partner in what my lawyer sweetly calls the concern. . . . Why my very name—I reek of beer, I am all beer, my blood is beer. . . . I only wonder they did not call me Marsden-and-Company Messenger."

Also there have been loyal and patriotic brewers—real personages. The first called to mind was at one time M.P. for Abingdon, Mr. William Hucks, who is called to mind by what has not unjustly been said to be " at once the most pretentious and the ugliest ecclesiastical edifice in London," St. George's Church, Bloomsbury. It was built about 1731 by one of Wren's pupils, who chose for his model the original Mausoleum, or tomb of Mausolus, which was one of the " seven wonders of the world," and must have been an architectural monstrosity. The church has a tower and spire—rather incongruous features in a " classical " edifice—and the summit of the steeple is crowned by a statue of George I., attired as a Roman Senator. This statue was the gift of the aforesaid loyal brewer, Mr. William Hucks, M.P., and inspired the contemporary epigram :—

" The King of Great Britain was reckoned before
  The ' Head of the Church' by all good Christian people ;
  But his brewer has added still one title more
  To the rest, and has made him the ' Head of the Steeple ! ' "

Hogarth has immortalised St. George's, Bloomsbury, by choosing this respectable church as the background for his " Gin Lane."

Then just as good King Edward recently paid a friendly visit to the great Staffordshire breweries of Lord Burton, so once upon a time did the eccentric but well-meaning George III. pay a visit to Whitbread's London brewery. The episode was satirised by the lively " Peter Pindar," otherwise Dr. John Wolcot :—

> " Red-hot with novelty's delightful rage,
> To Mister Whitbread forth he sent a page,
> To say that majesty proposed to view,
> With thirst of wondrous knowledge deep inflamed,
> His vats, and tubs, and hops, and hogsheads famed,
> And learn the noble secret how to brew."

VII

THE UNIVERSALITY OF ALE

Bread and beer, the traditional sustenance of Englishmen—Even from before the Conquest—Bread and ale associated in ancient benefactions—As at St. Paul's, London—And St. Cross, Winchester—Cakes and ale for every festive occasion—Referred to in "Poor Robin's Almanack"—Ale, the chete loaf, and the manchet at the royal breakfast-table—Queen Bess's estimate of strong ale—Excessive ale-drinking in the Elizabethan period —Ale the foundation of all old English merrymakings— Herrick's allusion to "nut-brown mirth"—Scott's reference to festive ale-drinking—Ale regarded as the national beverage—Varieties and qualities of ales—Strong beer and lithe beer—Single and "doble-doble"—"Dagger-ale," "huff-cap," "dragon's milk," and "merry-go-down"—Humming ale—Small beer—Anecdote of Pulteney, Earl of Bath, being "cured" by small beer—Epitaph on one killed by small beer—Pit beer— Broken beer—Ale brewed to celebrate an heir's outcome— Yorkshire "stingo"—The fame of various local brews—As London, Burton, Nottingham, and Newcastle— Brasenose and Trinity Colleges—Manchester and Warrington—Banbury and Derby ales—"Old Burton"—How Nottingham ale was made—Birmingham "stingo" (1763)—An imported ale called Mum—The Brunswick recipe for brewing it—An English adaptation of it—A petition of 1673 against Brunswick Mum as detrimental to health—Porter introduced 1760—The terms "Porter," "Entire," and "Stout"—Tennyson's reference— George Borrow's defamation of Chester ale—Sion Tudor, the fourteenth-century ale expert—William IV. and cheap ale— Old customary drinkings—Leet ale—Tithe ale—Foot ale— Marriage ale—Child ale—Walking-stick ale, Journey ales, &c.

BEER ranks with bread—the respective products of the two principal indigenous cereals—as the traditional sustenance of Englishmen. Philologists tell us the word Bread is derived from the Saxon *bréowan*, "brew." Beer is capable of the widest definition, as made from farinaceous grain; wheat and other grains than barley having been at various periods malted for its production. The earliest use of beer as the beverage of the country has been traced back by tradition to the faraway Bronze Age. Bread was the burnt-offering of old, and beer was the libation. We are also assured by the old rhyme that—

> "King Hardicanute 'midst Danes and Saxons stout
> Caroused in nut-brown ale and dined in grout,"

—grout being a heady kind of ale prepared from malt that had been slightly burnt in an iron pot.

Indeed, says an authority :—

> "Ale for antiquity may plead and stand
> Before the Conquest conquering the land."

The Anglo-Saxons maintained the credit of their Teutonic origin in being mighty drinkers; yet, mighty topers as the English were, it may be doubted if they have ever outdone the Germans in beer-swilling, notwithstanding the assertion of Iago that "your Dane, your German, and your swag-bellied Hollander, are nothing to your English" in powers of drinking.

Bread and beer is typical English fare ; and whatever changes of diet have been brought about in recent times by modern modes of living, there can be no gainsaying the truth that once upon a time the English liked it, and believed in it. It was deemed a rational, as it was accepted as a national regimen.

There were for centuries, and are to this day, clerical officials in St. Paul's Cathedral, London, known as Cardinals, who are responsible for the good conduct and regular attendance of the choir; and their recompense for the performance of these duties was always set down as "a large allowance of bread and beer."

The association of beer with bread occurs in numbers of old-time benefactions. The well-known Winchester Dole is a gift of ale and bread to any wayfarers who ask for it. It was originated about the year 1140 by Bishop Henry de Blois, founder of the hospital of St. Cross in that city; and in the porch of that ancient building it has been dispensed for hundreds of years. In recent times the distribution of the benefaction has been restricted to thirty persons a day.

In olden times corn, malt, ale, and beer were favoured commodities which could only be exported from this country by royal licence. In old England no festive occasion from New Year to Christmastide, from a christening to a funeral, could be properly celebrated without the consumption of cakes and ale. Church doles even, in some parishes, provided cakes and ale for specified festivities; Dr. Plot, in his "History of Staffordshire," makes allusion to this custom; and Shakespeare betrays the fact that the consumption of these viands on these occasions was seldom marked by moderation, when he wrote—

"Dost thou think, because thou art virtuous, there shall be no more cakes and ale?"

As late as 1676, in "Poor Robin's Almanack," we have the traditional association of "cakes and ale"—

"At Islington
A fair they hold,
Where cakes and ale
Are to be sold.

> At Highgate, and
> At Holloway
> The like is kept
> Here every day.
> At Totnam Court
> And Kentish Town,
> And all those places
> Up and down."

About the same period the much-quoted diarist, Pepys, writes in April, 1664 : "Home to the only Lenten supper I have had of wiggs (buns) and ale."

In old England ale and bread long continued to be the chief items even of the royal breakfast. The quantity of ale consumed by ladies at breakfast was considerable, for in the reign of Henry VIII. the maids-of-honour were allowed for breakfast "one chete loafe, one manchet, two gallons of ale, and a pitcher of wine."

A chete loaf was one for cutting up, while a manchet was a loaf of the finest wheaten flour. We may read of a certain Lady Lucy who made a mighty tonic of the national brew. Her breakfast was "a chine of beef, a loaf, and a gallon of ale ; and for her pillow-meal a posset porridge, a generous cut of mutton, a loaf, and a gallon of ale."

There is an amusing letter written by the Earl of Leicester to Lord Burleigh as to the lack of sufficiently strong ale for Queen Elizabeth at Hatfield. "There is not one drop of good drink for her there. We were fain to send to London and Kenilworth and divers other places where ale was ; her own bere was so strong as there was no man able to drink it."

It was Queen Bess's matured opinion that beer was "an excellent wash." Right well did this typical English queen enjoy a quart of ale for breakfast, though her more fastidious sister, Queen Mary, preferred a flask of Canary. But then Mary was not "all English."

In the reign of Elizabeth Englishmen reverted to the characteristic vices of their rude Anglo-Saxon progenitors, gluttony and drunkenness becoming rife. "What a coil have we," says a writer of the period, " this course and that course, removing this dish higher, setting another lower, and taking away a third. A general might in less space remove his camp, than they stand disposing of their gluttony. From Gluttony in meats let me descend to superfluity in drink "—and so on.

It was beneath contempt to drink anything less than ale. There was no compromise with temperance drinks. For, says a quaint old writer of the period, "Some abstemious souls have their home decoctions of broom, of bay berries, of ivy berries, their sloe wine, and currant wine ; but men, in good sooth, are believers in amber ale of malt, or of unmalted oats."

Ale, says that acknowledged authority, Mr Edwin A. Pratt, formed the very foundation of the merrymakings, feasts, festivals, and functions in hall, in cottage, or on village green, which were characteristic of our country at the period it had won for itself the name " Merrie England." Had the use of good old English ale been abolished in those bygone centuries, he contends, mediæval England might have been more sober, but it certainly would have been duller ; he argues, in fact, the disappearance of these old-time merrymakings has made village life so unutterably dull, that we are able to see in it at least one reason why our population is steadily deserting the village for the attractions of the town.

That no old English festivity was possible without the accompaniment of ale, we are fully reminded by the outpouring of Herrick :—

"Thy Wakes, thy quintals, here thou hast,
Thy maypoles, too, with garlands graced,
Thy morris-dance, thy Whitsun-ale,
Thy shearing feasts which never fail,
Thy harvest-home, thy wassail-bowl
That tossed up after fox-i'-th'-hole,
Thy mummeries, thy Twelfth-night Kings
And Queens, thy X-mas revellings ;
Thy nut-brown mirth, thy russet wit,
And no man pays too dear for it."

A " quintal," it may be explained, was a wedding sport in which young men ran a tilt on horseback to win a garland from a high pole ; and the strange phrase " fox-in-the-hole " is but a poetical way of describing the tongue which laps up the strong drink of the festive bowl with relish.

Sir Walter Scott similarly alludes in " Marmion," to the prevalence of ale-drinking on these occasions :—

"England was merry England when
Old Christmas brought his sports again ;
'Twas Christmas broached the mightiest ale,
'Twas Christmas told the merriest tale ;
A Christmas gambol oft would cheer
A poor man's heart through half the year."

A learned disquisition of the year 1620 presents us with the views of an erudite French physician on this subject :—

" The English have a drink which they call Ale and which is thought the wholesomest liquor that could be drank ; for whereas the body of man is supported by natural heat and radical moisture, there is no drink conduceth more to the preservation of the one, and the increase of the other, than Ale ; for while the Englishman drank Ale they were strong, brawny, and able men and could draw an arrow an ell long ; but when they fell to wine and beer they were found to be impaired in their strength and age."

This at least shows how the wine-drinking Frenchman looked upon the Englishman and his beer-drinking proclivities.

Beer has come to be acknowledged as the national beverage of England. At a recent Conference of Brewers, Lord Burton claimed that this country owed its high and proud position among the nations of the earth simply on account of its characteristic dietary, "Beef and Beer." Whereupon some one made the waggish comment, "Why drag in the Beef?"

That simplest of all English meals, good bread and cheese moistened by a draught of sound beer, is by no means the least nutritive. Quite recently (says *The Hospital*) beer has been authoritatively claimed, not only as possessing a real dietetic value, but as being *par excellence* the most nutritive of alcoholic beverages, though admittedly an unsuitable food for the obese. When a man drinks good beer he eats and drinks at the same time, just as when he eats a bowl of soup—the terms "eat" and "drink" are curiously but inconsistently used as connoting the difference between what is merely quenching our thirst, and what is actually consuming nourishment. It is thus a recent Special Commission on Beer seeks to remove, as being thoroughly unjust, the long-standing prejudices against malt liquor as a food adjunct. Then there is the medicinal aspect of ale and stout, in their hypnotic action. Stout is one of the most harmless of hypnotics, the hypnotic principle being derived from the hops.

There were always several varieties or qualities of ale. There was beer and there was strong beer ; clear ale or lithe beer ; there was single and double-brewed beer, the latter being the famous "doble-doble" of Queen Elizabeth's time.

The prices and the strength of vendible ales were

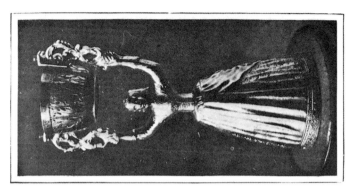

MILKMAID CUP, VINTNERS' HALL.

[Page 347.

PEPYS' LOVING CUP.

[Page 142.

[Photo]

[Pictorial Agency.

The Coffee-house Politicians.

Page 362.

THE TOPERS' SENTENCE ON A SNEAKER.

[Page 148.

regulated and fixed by law for several centuries, and varied but slightly, till the time of Henry VIII., when the brewers bestirred themselves to get the prices raised. Their agitation was directed chiefly towards escaping liability to brew " single " beer, for which the legal price was two shillings a kilderkin, whereas " double " beer sold at twice that price.

Beer (as we have seen in Chapter II.) was a designation at one time more honourable than Ale ; the name, however, seems to have disappeared from common use between the time when honey-sweetened Mead was popular, till its revival, when the introduction of the flavouring hop called forth the term Beer again, to differentiate bitter hopped-ale from the older and sweeter variety.

When the earliest Licensing Act was passed in 1552, the Assize of Ale fixed the price at one penny per quart ; among the qualities of strong ale then drunk were those known by a variety of slang names, such as " dagger ale," " huff cap," " dragon's milk," and " merry-go-down."

Although Burns writes of " ill-brewn drink," it was an old Black Country toper's saying that there was " no such thing as bad ale—there was some better than others." Notwithstanding this dictum, it is well known that the varying strength and condition of ales have given rise to a nomenclature indicative of standard. Single and Double are terms of obvious meaning. A Humming ale was perhaps so called because it was strong enough to make the drinker's head hum. Small beer was the weaker after-brew, and generally considered so refreshing that it was regularly used to cool the head and quench the parching thirst after an overnight bout of drunkenness ; and reference to such use will be found in the older poets, from Shakespeare downwards. " For

God's sake, a pot of small ale," was the first cry of Christopher Sly, when he woke up from his drunken slumbers.

John Timbs, the antiquarian miscellanist, relates the following anecdote of a "cure" by small beer :—

"About 1730 Pulteney, afterwards the Earl of Bath, lay for a long time at Lord Chetwynd's house of Ingestre, in Staffordshire, sick, very dangerously, of a pleuritic fever. This illness cost him an expense of 750 guineas for physicians; and, after all, his cure was accomplished merely by a draught of small beer. Dr. Hope, Dr. Swynsen, and other physicians, from Stafford, Lichfield, and Derby, were called in, and carried off about 250 guineas of the patient's money, leaving the malady just where they found it. . . . When two physicians who were Pulteney's friends arrived they found his case to be quite desperate, and gave him over, saying that everything had been done that could be done. They prescribed some few medicines, but without the least effect. He was still alive, and was heard to mutter, in a low voice, 'Small beer, small beer!' They said, 'Give him small beer or anything!' Accordingly a great silver cup was brought, which held two quarts of small beer. Pulteney drank off the whole at a draught, and demanded another. Another cupful was administered to him, and soon after that he fell into a profuse perspiration and a profound slumber for nearly twenty-four hours. In this case the saying was verified, 'If he sleep he will do well.' From that time forth he recovered wonderfully, insomuch that in a few days the physicians took leave of him."

To the memory of a seventeenth-century warrior there is an epitaph in Winchester Cathedral churchyard, which runs, as lawyers say, "to the contrary" :—

"Here lies in peace a Hampshire Grenadier,
Who met his death from drinking cold, small beer.
Soldiers ! Take warning from a comrade's fall,
And when you're hot, drink strong, or none at all."

This stone, falling into ruin, was replaced in the following century by the officers of a regiment quartered in the town, who added the explanatory couplet :—

"A gallant soldier never is forgot,
Whether he die by musket or by pot."

And since then it has had to be restored a second time.

Small beer as brewed nowadays is the second extract obtained from the malt, after the ale has been drained off. It was formerly called the "second shut." In the Black Country it is called "pit beer," because it is given to the colliers, just as in some counties cider is given to farm labourers ; or sometimes miners call it the "allowance beer," though perhaps more frequently it is contemptuously dubbed " rot stocking" and " starve gut."

Broken beer was soured beer, and the designation was used somewhat in the same sense as we use the term "broken" victuals.

The Englishman's preference was undoubtedly for strong ale. An old custom once honoured in many families of standing was to brew a special ale on the birth of the eldest son, and broach it twenty-one years after, at the heir's " coming of age."

Old strong ale was known, particularly in Yorkshire, as "stingo." It would be difficult to say what town or countryside in England had not, at some period or other, claimed a special excellence for its brews. London malt liquors, brown and black, have long claimed pre-eminence ; Burton's reputation is world-wide ; and when national reputation gives place to local fame, it is perplexing to know where to leave off enumerating ; for a wide popularity has been claimed for Nottingham ales and Wrexham ales, for Newcastle beers and Birmingham beers, and the brews of many other towns and centres. Even college brews have acquired reputations for excellence, as at Brasenose and Trinity.

> "Oh, in truth, it gladdens the heart to see
> What may spring from the ale of Trinitie."

Manchester has long been reputed for a fine assortment of ales and beers ; in the eighteenth century the praises of another local brew were thus sung :—

> "I've been ˌcrammed with good things like a wallet,
> And I've guzzled more drink than a whale ;
> But the very best stuff to my palate
> Was a glass of your Warrington ale."

At the present day light beers are found to be growing steadily in public favour ; but it may be that the traditional Englishman of the old fighting days preferred a strong ale because he found it increased his native bull-dog pugnacity. A Boniface of old Wednesbury, when asked what were the ingredients of his strong ale, which so invariably set his customers a-quarrelling, replied that he " brewed it of women's tongues and men's fisses " (fists). Norfolk Nog was the name given to the strong ale of that county. Banbury ale was accounted so strong that even the tinkers and cobblers were floored by it ; and as the old proverb says :—

> " Cobblers and tinkers
> Are your true ale drinkers."

A draught of sound Derby ale, according to an Elizabethan playwright, was calculated to bring a flush of colour into the cheeks of the most pallid maiden. But different drinks, different effects.

> "Never tell me of liquors from Spain or from France,
> They may get in your heels and inspire you to dance ;
> But the ale of Old Burton, if mellow and right,
> Will get in your heads and inspire you to fight."

"The chief thing about Nottingham ale," according to an old Dictionary of Agriculture published in 1726, " is in the making of it, which is only when 'tis working to let it stand in a tub four or five days before it is put into the cask; stirring it twice a day and beating down the head or yest into it, which gives it the sweet aleish taste. If ale or beer do not fine well," proceeds our ancient authority, "pour into a hogshead two or three bottles of old stale ale or beer, and it will much promote its clearness."

A Birmingham rhymester in 1763 composed a song in praise of the local brew, but in one stanza appears this significant admission :—

"I grant that fair Nottingham once bore the bell
For our grandsires that tasted the sweets of good ale "—

though in another he gives vent to his local patriotism thus :—

"Ye mortals who never in all your wild trips
With good humming liquor saluted your lips
Give ear to my story, ye strangers to cheer,
The pleasure I sing of is Birmingham beer ;
'Tis here the salutis of Life's to be found ;
For merchants who circuit the kingdom around
Declare, on their travels from Thames to the Tweed,
That Birmingham stingo all others exceed."

So much for the once famous local brews we have found space to notice. But mention of a once popular imported ale cannot be omitted.

Mum was a strong ale brewed from wheat malt and flavoured with a number of aromatic herbs. According to a receipt recorded and preserved in the old town-house of Brunswick, it was "a wholesome drink" brewed from wheat malt, boiled down to a third of its original quantity, to which were added oatmeal and ground beans, and after the working, quite a number of herbs and other vegetable products, including the tops of fir and birch, handfuls of burnet, betony, marjoram, avens, pennyroyal, wild-thyme, and elder-flowers, and a few ounces of cardamum seeds, and barberries. The details of preparation are too lengthy to quote, but the receipt ends thus : " Fill up at last, and when 'tis stopt, put into the hogshead two new-laid eggs unbroken or crackt, stop it up close, and drink it at two years' end."

An old writer, commenting upon the English adaptation of this imported beverage, says : " Our English brewers use cardamum, ginger and sassafras, which serve instead of the inner rind of firr ; also walnut rinds, madder, red sanders, and ellecampane. Some make it of strong beer and spruce beer ; and where it is designed chiefly for its physical virtues, some add watercresses, brooke-lime, and wild parsley, with six handfuls of horse-radish rasped to every hogshead."

Brunswickian Mum, however, does not seem to have retained the favour of Englishmen for any length of time ; as a matter of fact, in a petition to Parliament of 1673, it was classed with tea, coffee, and brandy as detrimental to the bodily health of those who habitually used it instead of the national beverage, sound barley beer.

It was about the year 1750 that the beverage called Porter was introduced. Previously the malt liquors in general use were ale, beer, and twopenny. It was very customary to call for half-and-half, that is, half beer and half twopenny ; and sometimes for three-thread, meaning a third of ale, beer, and twopenny. Then the publican was compelled to draw from three casks to serve one customer. To avoid this trouble and waste, a brewer of the name of Harwood conceived the idea of making a liquor which should partake of the united flavours of ale, beer, and twopenny : this he called *entire*, or entire butt beer, meaning that it was drawn from one butt or cask. It was soon found to be a very hearty, nourishing liquor, suitable to porters and other hard-working people, or at any rate it became the favourite drink of London porters, and from this fact it obtained the name of *porter*.

Stout was a name given to porter of extra strength—a brew for which Dublin subsequently became famous. A classical use of the term by Tennyson is to be found in " Will Waterproof's Lyrical Monologue," "made at the Cock Tavern," the famous chop-house to which the poet was wont to resort ; a piece fitting, though too long, to be quoted here in its entirety. Our illustration is taken from the fifteenth stanza :—

> " The waiter's hands that reach
> To each his perfect pint of stout,
> His proper chop to each."

The universality of ale, even to the earlier decades of the nineteenth century, is well illustrated by an extract from the writings of the free-living George Borrow :—

"On arriving at Chester," he says in his 'Wild Wales,' chapter ii., "at which place we intended to spend two or three days, we put up at an old-fashioned inn in Northgate Street to which we had been recommended. My wife and daughter ordered tea and its accompaniments ; and I ordered ale and that which should always accompany it, cheese. The ale I shall find bad, said I ; Chester ale had a bad reputation since the time of old Sion Tudor, who made a first-rate Englyn about it, but I shall have a treat in the cheese ; Chester cheese has always been reckoned excellent."

To his great delight he found the ale as bad as it was in the days of Sion Tudor, and therefore he hilariously threw it out of the window. Then tasting the cheese, he found the cheese bad also and promptly threw that after the ale. " Well," he said, " if I have been deceived in the cheese, at any rate I have not been deceived in the ale, which I expected to find execrable. Patience ! I shall not fall into a passion, more especially as there are things I can fall back upon. Wife ! I will trouble you for a cup of tea. Henrietta, have the kindness to cut me a slice of bread and butter."

Sion Tudor, the ale expert here alluded to, lived about the fourteenth century. He was a bard, and as such had to turn out Englyns, which are odes or quatrains composed mainly for "eistedfoddic purposes." Perhaps work turned out under such conditions cannot be expected to have too strict an adherence to truth ; anyway, Chester at the present day rather boasts itself on the excellent quality of its ales. And Wrexham, near by, has long had quite a national reputation for the products of its breweries.

If William IV. ever lived in the popular heart it was, perhaps, first because he was a sailor, and secondly on account of legislation in his reign having the tendency to cheapen the price of ale. The people sang his praises in this strain :—

> " So ' Long,' we'll sing,
> ' Live Billy the King,
> Who bated the tax upon beer.' "

Among the many customary drinkings of olden times were the Leet Ale, given by the lord of the manor to the jurymen assembled to transact the business of the Leet Court ; and the Tithe Ale, the entertainment given to the tithe-payers by the tithe-owner on the day he, or his steward, received the tithes from them.

Every one has heard of Foot Ale, and the custom of paying one's "footing," the fine of beer which an apprentice always paid on entering his trade or calling ; and which was also at one time almost as frequently paid by a workman commencing work at any fresh place of employment.

Mr. William Ryland, giving a history of the Plated Wares Trade for the British Association in 1865, says of the Birmingham workshops during the early decades of the nineteenth century :—

"The masters were not very strict in the discipline of their works—'foot ales' and 'marriage ales' and 'child ales, 'walking-stick ales,' 'change of place ales,' 'ales charged for making a new article,' 'journey ales,' with numerous others, supplied a constant excuse for extending the five o'clock rest ; for 'tea' was scarcely known as a beverage in any works. This was often carried on with the master's knowledge, if not with his sanction. The man who 'paid his ale' paid a shilling, the shopmates putting down threepence each. All this is now changed, at least, in the writer's experience."

VIII

ANCIENT RESTRICTIONS ON BREWING AND SELLING ALE

The common law requires that persons shall not stay at inns too long—No monopoly in brewing and selling ale—And water the only adulterant—Manorial Ale-conners—The three desiderata : adequate supply, sound quality, and fixed price—Assize of Bread and Ale—" Sealed quarts "—Ale-tasters in City, Manor, and University—"The lord of the tap "—The Ale-taster—Curious test for sugar adulteration—A Pure Beer Bill called for—Introduction of State licensing, 1552—Moral obligations recognised —First-fruit of the Reformation.

THE business of brewing and selling ale called for regulation by the authorities almost from the earliest period ; it was the nature of such a business to challenge restrictive legislation.

As the inns of ancient Rome were regulated by law, it is not unfair to suppose that the taverns or posting-houses of Britain, mentioned in Chapter I., were under Imperial regulation. Restrictive regulations, as we have seen in the same chapter, grew up in the Saxon era ; and by the time of Henry II. it was found necessary to bring all inns under State supervision as a check upon their becoming the haunts of criminals. It was this necessity, and also possibly the great scarcity of inns, through which the common law of the land demanded that persons should not stay too long at an inn—they were to sleep there for a night or two only, and then pass on to make way for fresh comers.

In mediæval times any one might brew beer without tax or licence ; and everybody who was before the world did brew his own beer, and according to his own taste. Although different stuff from that brewed at the present time, the ale of those days was certainly purer, if not better. It was possibly less palatable, but it was free from chemicals and every other kind of adulterant— except, perhaps, water.

There was no such monopoly as there is now. The lords of the manors seem to have granted permits or licences for the sale of ale very freely ; and there were probably more people who sold beer then than sell it now. Beer-sellers, too, seem to have been in trouble in those times as often as those of the present day. For the manorial authorities appointed special officers, called Ale-conners, whose duty was, not only to assay the beer, but to inspect the measures in which it was sold ; and of all the offences punished by fine in the manorial courts, none was so common as that of selling ale in false measures. So that "in the good old times" it was entirely a man's own fault if he drank bad beer or failed to obtain his money's worth.

In the "Cobler of Canterburie" (1608), the Ale-conner is thus described :—

> "A nose he had that gan show
> What liquor he loved I trow ;
> For he had before long seven yeare
> Been of the towne the Ale-conner."

In those times governments and local authorities concerned themselves mainly in renewed and persistent attempts to ensure three great desiderata : first, an adequate supply of ale ; secondly, that it should be of good quality; and thirdly, that it should be procurable at a reasonable price.

By the Assize of Bread and Ale of Henry III.'s reign, the prices of these two commodities of universal consumption were duly fixed by statute ; fines and even corporal punishment were inflicted on brewers who failed to observe the law, and juries inquired into its administration, particularly as to the strength and quality of the liquor vended, and whether the pots in which it was vended bore the official stamp.

To prevent fraud on the consumer there was a standard measurement known as the " sealed quarts." These were generally pewter measures bearing the Ale-taster's mark, which mark varied according to locality, in the boroughs often consisting of the borough arms, and in many places being merely the Ale-taster's initials. Sealed quarts were sometimes hung up outside the alehouses doors, as signs to typify that good ale was to be had within, just as a bush typified the sale of good wine. When topers challenged each other's drinking capacity, the use of sealed quarts was usually stipulated with the gravest punctilio.

In every ancient Court Leet the Ale-taster was an officer of considerable importance, appointed and sworn to look to the assize and goodness of all the ale and beer brewed within the jurisdiction of the lordship. London and other old cities had their special Ale-conners, properly and similarly authorised officers, to taste and approve of the beers and ales produced within their respective city limits.

There was also a recognised Ale-taster to the University of Oxford, duly licensed to his office by the Vice-Chancellor. It was his duty to go round to every ale-brewer to taste the ale on the day it was brewed. For approving and passing the brew he was entitled to a fee of "one gallon of strong ale, and two gallons of small wort, worth a penny."

In the latter half of the eighteenth century, it was the practice of the municipal authorities of Cambridge to appoint during the period of the great annual fair an officer known as "the lord of the tap," whose duty was to visit all the booths to test the quality of the ale sold in them.

This later period produced ale-testers instead of ale-tasters. In England and Scotland a couple of hundred of years ago ale was tested for no other impurity than sugar. If it had no sugar in it, it was regarded as unimpeachable.

" The official ale-tester," we are informed by an authority, " wore leather breeches. He would enter an inn unexpectedly, draw a glass of ale, pour it on a wooden bench, and then sit down in the little puddle he had made. There he would sit for thirty minutes by the clock. He would converse, he would smoke, he would drink with all who asked him to, but he would be very careful not to change his position any way. At the end of the half-hour he would make as if to rise, and this was the test of the ale ; for, if the ale was impure, if it had sugar in it, the tester's leather breeches would stick fast to the bench, but if there was no sugar in the liquor no impression would be present—in other words, the tester would not stick to the seat."

Not a few critics of our chaotic licensing laws hold the opinion that the only reform called for now is something in the nature of a revival of the ancient Assize of Bread and Beer—that is, so far as the latter commodity is concerned—as, for instance, would be accomplished by the passing of a drastic and thoroughgoing Pure Beer Bill.

An epoch-making date was reached in 1552, when at last the regulation of all this corrosive trafficking was taken from the control of the local manorial jurisdictions and elevated to the higher plane of national State control.

The licensing of public-houses may be regarded as one of the first-fruits of the Reformation.

In the old days of free trade in ale, abuses probably prevailed to a larger extent than will ever be known. Even in the royal forests drinking huts, known as "Ale Shots," were kept by forest officers. In the City of London some sort of control was set up, those who kept ale-houses paying to the Lord Mayor an annual tribute known as "Ale-silver," but even here the supervision was very lax.

In a work of this character, which is purely one of historic review, it would perhaps be out of place to discuss the ethics of licensing legislation. But it may be pointed out that after the earlier efforts of legislation which, as we have seen, concerned themselves with the protection of the consumer against the producer, there came a time when the law sought to protect the consumer against himself. And immediately the law recognised tippling or drunkenness in any form as an offence, the same moral considerations insisted that the facilities for obtaining strong drink should no longer go unrestricted and unregulated. It marked the dawn of a more enlightened age when the interests of public peace and good order were admitted to call for some amount of State control. It is noteworthy that the creation of the licensed monopoly in the vending of intoxicants synchronises with, if indeed it did not result from, the recognition by the State of its moral obligations; and hence, as will be here seen, the legislative efforts which followed are divided almost equally between the suppression of illicit houses and the devising of punishments for drunkenness.

IX

EARLY LICENSING AND LEGISLATIVE REPRESSION

Ale-house keepers provide sureties for good behaviour in 1495—The
first Licensing Act (1552)—Directed against tippling houses—
Stubbs' testimony against the "malt-worms" in 1583—Spirit of
Puritanism aroused against the prevalence of excessive drinking
—The prolific legislation of James I.—Directed against sotting
and tippling—Severity of law overreaches itself—Tipplers driven
into unlicensed houses which spring up (1604–1606)—The
fearful condition of society described—Extract from Dekker's
"Seven Deadly Sins of London"—The number of licensed
houses in 1621—A monopoly of licensing granted to Sir Giles
Mompesson and others—The tippling townsman fined and condemned to the stocks—Conviction obtained through common
informers—Strangers and travellers also penalised for drunkenness—Punishments extended from ale-house keepers to innkeepers, vintners, and victuallers—Whipping imposed as penalty
for the keeping of illicit houses—How ale-houses were suppressed
—Seven repressive enactments between 1604 and 1627—The
reaction from Puritanism after the Restoration (1660).

HALF or three-quarters of a century before the influence
of what is generally known as Puritanism made itself felt
there was a strong feeling in the country that there were
already too many ale-houses ; and the first law by which
it was sought to keep some sort of a check upon those
who carried on the trade of retailing ale was the enactment of 1495—the earliest licensing law on the statute
book, 11 Henry VII.—empowering any two justices "to
put away common ale-selling in towns and places where

they should think convenient, and to take sureties of keepers of ale-houses in their good behaving."

The Act of Edward VI. (1552) was but a confirmation of the preceding law for the suppression of unnecessary ale-houses. It enacted that no one should be allowed to keep an ale-house unless he had obtained the authority of two justices, who were to take sureties for the due observance of the regulations for the proper conduct of the houses, to try offenders for the breach of the rules, and to punish persons who kept ale-houses without being licensed so to do.

"Forasmuch" (says the Act of 1552) "as intolerable hurts and troubles to the Commonwealth of this Realm do daily grow and increase through such abuses and disorders as are had and used in common Alehouses, and other houses called Tippling Houses "; and on grounds of public policy the justices were empowered " to remove, discharge, and put away the common selling of ale and beer in such towns or places where they shall think meet and convenient."

The moral condition of the country in relation to the prevalence of drunkenness is clearly set forth in "The Anatomie of Abuses," published in 1583 by the Elizabethan moralist, Stubbs, who says : "Every country, city, town, village, and other places hath abundance of alehouses, taverns, and inns, which are so fraught with malt-worms, night and day, that you would wonder to see them."

In the following reign, excessive drinking reached its climax in the degraded Court of James I. ; but it has been pleaded that in these high quarters the vice was not altogether of native growth. "That's as may be." It is certain the spirit of Puritan England was roused against the prevailing vice. In Devonshire the Justices of the Peace in 1607 made an order that no more Church Ales or similar carousals under Church auspices were to be held in that county. The order seems to have had little

MR. WILLIAM GROVES.

The Famous Punch-maker.

[*Page* 158.

TAVERN LIFE—THE BOXING FRATERNITY.

[*Page* 177.

effect, for in 1622 these ecclesiastical merrymakings were reported as rife as ever.

In the reign of James I. the legislative machinery was set in force from time to time against the prevalent practice of sotting and tippling. There were four enactments in this reign, each successive one becoming more stringent in its provisions. Any ale-house keeper who permitted a townsman—not a stranger or a traveller, be it noted—to sit tippling in his house forfeited ten shillings to the poor of the place in which the offence was committed. Constable or churchwarden might levy it by distress, and if after six days the sum could not be raised the offender might be committed to gaol till it was paid. An amending enactment disabled the offender from keeping an ale-house for three years afterwards.

The Act of 1604 was intended "to restrain inordinate haunting and tippling in inns, alehouses, and other victualling houses." An innkeeper was forbidden to allow drink to any one unless he were a lodger in the house, or was invited by a traveller staying in the house, or was a labouring man there only in his dinner-hour.

The severity of this law rather overreached itself by driving the tipplers into unlicensed houses, and two amending Acts had to be passed in 1606. The preamble to the second of these is worth reproducing here. It ran :—

"Whereas the loathsome and odious sin of drunkenness is of late grown into common use in this realm, being the root and foundation of many other enormous sins, as bloodshed, stabbing, murder, swearing, fornication, adultery, and such like, to the great dishonour of God and of our nation, the overthrow of many good acts and manual trades, the dishonour of divers workmen, and the general impoverishing of many good subjects, and wasting the good creatures of God "; and so on, in the usual Puritanical strain.

But that there was good cause for the delivery of this homily is evident from a description of the average citizen of the time, given by the Elizabethan poet, Thomas Dekker (1570–1637), in his "Seven Deadly Sins of London," thus :—

"The damask-coated citizen, that sat in his shop both forenoon and afternoon, and lookt more sowerly on his poore neighbours than if he had drunk a quart of vinegar at a draught, sneakes out of his own doores, and slips into a taverne, where, either alone or with some other th battles their money together, they soe ply them-selves with penny pots, which (like small shot) goe off powring into their fat paunches, that at length they have not an eye to see withal nor a good legge to stand upon. In which pickle if ainye of them happen to be justled downe by a post (that in spite of them will take the wall, and so reeles them into the kennell), who takes them up or leades them home ? Who has them to bed and with a pillow smoothes this stealing so of good liquour, but that brazen-face Candle Light ? Nay more he entices their very prentices to make their desperate sallies out, and quicke retyres in (contrarie to the oath of their indentures which they are seven yeares a swearing), only for their pintes and away."

As to the facilities for obtaining intoxicating liquors at that period, it was calculated in 1621, when the population of England and Wales was probably under five millions, that there were no less than 13,000 licensed premises in the country. This was the year in which James I. (for a consideration, of course) granted the power of licensing to Sir Giles Mompesson and Sir Francis Mitchell, an incident treated very interestingly by Harrison Ainsworth in his novel, entitled "The Star Chamber," the scene of which opens, appropriately enough, in the Vintry.

There is something anomalous about the action of the monarch making the licensing of public-houses into a monopoly, while his Parliament is engaged so assiduously in devising measures for the restriction of the drink traffic.

The growing influence of the Puritan party during the time of James I. followed up the tippler himself, and presently the tippling townsman was made to forfeit 3s. 4d. to the use of the poor, and if unable to pay was placed in the stocks for four hours. Very soon the penalty was increased, and any one convicted of drunkenness was to forfeit 5s., or sit for six hours in the stocks ; while the penalty for a second conviction was made more severe still. Apparently some difficulty had been found in obtaining evidence in these cases ; the law was therefore next amended, so as to make one witness sufficient to secure a conviction ; or if one of a party of guilty sots confessed, the oath of this confessed drunkard was accepted as sufficient to convict the others, his whilom boon companions.

An Act of 1623 also charged every town or village official on their oaths to act as common informers against any tipsy man ; and not only townsmen, but any stranger, even "the bonâ-fide traveller," was brought within the meshes of this newer and more stringent measure. Such overweening anxiety to secure a conviction is scarcely creditable to the otherwise commendable wave of Puritanism which was then sweeping over the country. It argues the failure, so far, of all this repressive legislation.

By a new Act passed on the accession of Charles I. (1625), the penalties incurred by ale-house keepers for permitting tippling were now imposed on innkeepers, vintners, and victuallers. Two years later any one keeping an ale-house without a licence was to forfeit 21s., or in default to be whipped, while a second conviction for the offence was punishable by a commitment to the House of Correction for one month.

At the same time we find the usual indulgence allowed for merrymakings at public assemblies was still permitted, for any person was free to sell malt liquor in a booth during a fair.

The penalty of whipping seems to have become a necessary alternative, because the generality of the persons charged with this offence were found too poor for any fine to be levied upon them ; so also as these illicit houses were often kept by "Ale-wives," it was further enacted that if the offender were a married woman, her husband might suffer the punishment ordained. From which provisions it may be gathered that the ale-houses of the period were frequently little better than poverty-stricken hovels, while not a few were low-class dens of infamy.

With regard to the disabling clause, it was held that if a suppressed ale-house should, within the three years, be licensed by two other justices out of session, the first two justices who suppressed it might do so again, and commit the party for disobeying their order. But there was some difference in suppressing an ale-house which was licensed, and one which was not ; for in the first case the common nuisance of its disorderly character had to be proved on an indictment at sessions; while an unlicensed ale-house might be suppressed by the justices at their discretion, and no appeal lay for refusing a licence to premises already condemned as illicit.

In the two dozen years from 1604 to 1627 no less than seven Acts of Parliament were directed against drunkenness and the drink trade. But it cannot be said that much improvement in the social and moral condition of the people had been effected thereby. There had been rather an actual increase of drunkenness, and there was unmistakable evidence that an enormous increase in the number of unlicensed and illegal drinking-shops had taken place. And when it came to the flogging of delinquent ale-house keepers it may safely be inferred that only the most worthless characters engaged in this kind of tavern-keeping ; as a matter of fact, it is set forth that the whipping clause was introduced because so many of those convicted of the offence could neither pay the fines nor bear the cost of being conveyed to prison, "and moreover do leave a great charge of wife and children upon the parish wherein they live." So that, on the face of it, the last stage of these legislative efforts was worse than the first.

After the Restoration, and with the consequent reaction from Puritanism, the drinking habits of the nation were as bad as ever ; all the punishments devised by the authorities proved in effect as non-deterrent as the teaching of the age was spiritless and uninspiring. "If upon Sunday the church doors be shut, the ale-houses will be open," was the reproach levelled at the English clergy in 1670.

Here is a picture of the ale-house and the Ale-wife during the Puritan period :—

"If these houses haue a boxe-bush, or an old post, it is enough to show their profeshion. But if they bee graced with a signe compleat, it's a signe of good custome : In these houses you shall see the history of Judeth, Susanna, Daniel in the Lyons Den, or Diues and Lazarus painted vpon the wall. It may bee reckoned a wonder to see, or find the house empty, for either the parson, churchwarden, or clark, or all, are doing some church or court businesse vsually in this place. They thriue best where there are fewest ; It is the host's chiefest pride to bee speaking of such a gentleman, or such a gallant that was here, and will bee againe ere long : Hot weather and thunder, and want of company are the hostesses griefe, for then her ale sowres : Your drinke vsually is very young, two daies olde : her chiefest wealth is seene, if she can haue one brewing vnder another : if either the hostesse, or her daughter, or maide will kisse handsomely at parting, it is a good shooing-horne or bird-lime to draw the company thither againe the sooner. Shee must bee courteous to all, though not by nature, yet by her profession ; for shee must entertaine all, good and bad ; tag, and rag ; cut, and long-tayle : She suspects tinkers and poore souldiers most, not that they will not drinke soundly, but that they will not lustily. Shee must keepe touch with three sorts of men, that is ; the maltman, the baker, and the justices clarkes. Shee is merry, and half mad, upon Shroue-tuesday, May-daies, feast-dayes, and morrice-dances : A good ring of bells in the parish helpes her to many a tester, she prayes the parson may not be a puritan : a bag-piper, and a puppet-play brings her in birds that are flush, shee defies a wine-tauerne as an vpstart outlandish fellow, and suspects the wine to bee poysoned. Her ale, if new, lookes like a misty morning, all thicke ; well, if her ale bee strong, her reckoning right, her house cleane, her fire good, her face faire, and the towne great or rich ; shee shall seldome or neuer fit without chirping birds to beare her company, and at the next church-ing or christning, shee is sure to be ridd of two or three dozen of cakes and ale by gossipping neighbours."

X

RESTRICTIVE PUNISHMENTS IN THE OLDEN TIME

Licensing laws under jurisdiction of Quarter Sessions—The many
and various indictments presented by Grand Jury—Some
curious examples—Ale sometimes too strong—And landlords
themselves disorderly—Illegal exactions on the ale sold in a
county gaol—The Stocks as punishment—for drunkards and
sundry tipplers—Used as late as 1872—The quaint punishment
of the Drunkard's Coat—And a jocular penalty for not drinking
—Manorial jurisdiction—and town bylaws to regulate the
trade—Examples from records of Sutton—Hertfordshire—and
Market Drayton—Complaints of Sunday tippling—and unlawful games—At Birmingham as late as 1798—Penalties levied
by churchwardens and constables.

AFTER the introduction of the system of licensing houses
by the Justices of the Peace, every breach of the licensing
laws naturally went before the Courts of Quarter Session
for consideration and punishment.

Typical examples of the restrictive punishments inflicted for breach of licensing laws are to be found in
the published records of Worcestershire County Sessions
for the years 1591 to 1643. Over and over again occur
presentments by the Grand Jury of this county of offenders
for selling ale without a licence, and for keeping unlicensed ale-houses ; for the selling of ale by other
than victuallers' measure, and for selling less than a full
quart of best beer for one penny ; for keeping ale-houses

with unlawful games; for keeping common tippling houses, and for breaking the Assize of Bread and Ale.

Sometimes it is the sworn ale-tasters of the Leet who present offenders for keeping disorderly houses, or for selling by unlawful measure. Lengthy lists of those guilty of selling ale without licences are presented at most Quarter Sessions.

In 1612 a petition was presented to the justices complaining of the disorders, assaults, and misdemeanours occasioned through certain ale-house keepers selling extraordinary strong ale at a penny a pint. In 1619 complaint is made of one landlord gambling and drinking all night, and calling his neighbours cowards if they will not "carouse and drink full cups with him." But perhaps the most curious complaint is that against Marjery Moore, who has been permitted to succeed to the post of her late husband as keeper of the county prison. The widow Moore is accused of practising many wrongs, hard usages, and exactions upon the prisoners under her charge. It was not only that she failed to separate the felons from the debtors (among the latter being many "poor prisoners"), but that although bound under a penalty of £100 to "sell an ale quart of beer for a penny," her exactions reached the enormity of obtaining from her tapster thirty-two shillings for every hogshead of ale drawn in the prison, the price she paid to the brewer for the same being only twelve shillings.

For the punishment of drunkards it was enacted in 1605, and again in 1623, that every offender, upon conviction, should be fined five shillings and spend six hours in the stocks. Tippling on Sunday during the hours of divine service was punished by the stocks till quite a late period. In 1790 nine men were locked in the stocks at Sheffield all at one time for this offence.

More than half a century later it was still the practice in some old-fashioned places—at Beverley, for instance, in 1853—for the churchwardens to go round the parish looking in at the various public-houses to detect any one drinking during these prohibited hours. Perhaps the last recorded case of an offender being placed in the stocks for drunkenness occurred at Newbury in 1872.

If the punishments for drunkenness were not deterrent, they were sometimes quaint. During the Commonwealth a special form of punishment was devised for the correction of drunkards. This was a contrivance called the Drunkard's Coat, and consisted of a wooden barrel; the culprit had to put his head through a hole in the top end, and bear the weight of the tub on his shoulders, two holes in his wooden coat allowing him to thrust out his hands, one on each side. This form of punishment is said to have been general at that period, but the evidence is satisfactory only so far as it relates to the magistracy of Newcastle-on-Tyne. Mr. William Andrews, in his well-known work, "Bygone Punishments," has an interesting record of what we may call "something contrariwise." He says that at Haddon Hall, in Derbyshire, there was a curious relic of bygone manners, in the shape of an iron handcuff, or ring, which was fixed in the banqueting-room there.

"If any person refused to drink the liquor assigned to him, or committed any offence against the convivial customs at the festive gatherings for which this ancient mansion was so famous, his wrist was locked in an upright position in the iron ring, and the liquor he had declined, or else a quantity of cold water, was poured down the sleeve of his doublet."

We can imagine the merriment when this humorous form of punishment was administered before a full court of carousers, and the smirk of self-sufficiency which it occasioned among the seasoned topers.

A wealth of information on the social and economic conditions which prevailed when ale was regarded as the national beverage, and when ale-houses entered more largely into the everyday life of the people, may be obtained from the study of ancient manorial and municipal records.

These bylaws and local ordinances were directed towards the usual points of restriction—the suppression of gaming on licensed premises, the fixing of a closing-time for public-houses, the prevention of Sunday drinking during the hours of divine service, and the maintenance of a standard price for ale. As to the last-named point, a statute of 1603 had declared that " none shall sell less than one quart of best beer or ale for a penny, and two quarts of the smaller sort for a penny."

At Sutton Coldfield, the town bylaws in olden times for the regulation of Trinity Fair there, ordered that " no brewer sell into the fair a barrel of good ale above ten shillings, no long ale, no red ale, no ropye ale, but good and holsome for man's body, under ye payne of forfeyture."

Again, the Court Leet of Sutton Coldfield in 1548 ordered "that no Victuallers allow servants or boys of anyone to play at unlawful games in their houses in the time of divine service or at any other time under a penalty for each default of 20s."

In Hertfordshire, at the close of the sixteenth century, an order prevailed " that ale-house keepers and vittlers" shall close at eight in winter and nine in summer, and " that none of them shall sell any ale or beare above the rate of fourpence a gallon, and that everyone of them shall have a second sort of ale and beare, which they shall sell for twopence a gallon, which they shall from time to time sell out of their houses to their poor neighbours."

The Court Leet of the manor of Great Drayton (Market

Drayton), like many others, empannelled a jury to discover not only who had been " guilty of high treason, rebellion, murder, and robbery," but to inquire if any " brewer had made ale and beer hurtful to man's body."

Even so late as the end of the eighteenth century, the authorities at Birmingham seem to have experienced great difficulties in controlling licensed houses sufficiently to preserve the " decorum fitting to the Lord's Day." A public notice issued in 1798 states that—

"Great complaints had lately been made by many serious and well-disposed inhabitants that, notwithstanding the repeated Admonition of the Church & Chapel Wardens, many Butchers, Hucksters, and Others continue to exercise their Trades on the Lord's Day ; that many Publicans suffer Tippling in their houses during Divine Service ; and many riotous and disorderly persons assemble themselves and practice unlawful Sports and Pastimes."

So more stringent rules were drawn up by the magistrates respecting the issue of licences ; applicants were to appear personally and show that they were of strict honour and integrity, and free from every kind of profligacy, and give assurance that they would " discourage all Tippling and Irregularity, particularly in the labouring people." The penalties proclaimed, however, seem rather inadequate after this preamble. For instance :—

"An Ale-house keeper encouraging Tippling forfeits 10s., to be levied by the Churchwardens or Constables." . . . "An Ale-house keeper encouraging Gaming forfeits for the first offence 40s., and for every subsequent one £10, three-fourths to the Poor, one-fourth to the Informer. . . . Individuals guilty of Tippling forfeit 3s. 4d., and in the case of non-payment, to be confined 4 hours in the Stocks. . . . An Ale-house keeper for drunkenness forfeits his licence for three years."

XI

INTRODUCTION OF ARDENT SPIRITS AND ADVENT OF THE EXCISE

English said to have acquired habit of spirit-drinking from the Dutch—"Dutch courage"—Brandy sold in England as a cordial—*Eau de vie*—Consumption of malt liquors decreased through spirit-drinking—A petition of 1673 to prohibit brandy and encourage native malt beverages—Ale and beer declared to be strength-giving to the laborious classes—The Revolutionary Parliament of 1643 first imposes Excise duties—Levied on ale, beer, cider, and perry—The signification of the term "Excise"—The new impost continued and increased after the Restoration—Dr. Johnson's bitter definition of "Excise"—National hostility to the Excise—An incentive to smuggling and fraud—Price of malt liquors raised through high duties (1692)—Beer duties take place of the ancient baronial dues which provided the national army—High price of ale and beer—A cheaper substitute sought—Fall in the output of the breweries (1690-2)—Only small duties on the distilling and sale of spirituous liquors—Gin-drinking thus encouraged at the expense of the consumption of ale.

TILL the moral awakening of the nation to the enormity of the prevailing vice of drunkenness, as denoted by the passing of the first Licensing Act in 1552, and the numerous subsequent Acts, directed in the main against tippling, which followed on each other so closely till the end of James I.'s reign, the offending intoxicant had been either ale or wine. We now approach the period when the consumption of spirituous liquors began to

make itself felt. And with the advent of distilled spirits
to a place among the food adjuncts of the English
people, we have to note the introduction of the Excise
system.

By the end of the fifteenth century brandy had become
an important article of manufacture in the wine-pro-
ducing countries of the Continent, and the habit of
drinking spirits began to spread through Europe. It is
asserted by the antiquary Camden that the English
troops employed in the Low Countries were mainly
responsible for introducing the habit of drinking spirits
into England—probably the habit of drinking schnapps
had been acquired during the hardships of severe cam-
paigning. The phrase "Dutch courage," as an equivalent
for being pot valiant, is a well-known slang term reflecting
on the drinking habits of Dutch fighting men of old time.
International jealousies may more likely account for its
use than any characteristic weakness in the Dutch
character.

In the sixteenth century the use of distilled spirits
spread over the continent of Europe, and thence was
introduced into the American colonies. Under the
name of "brandy" it had previously been introduced
into Ireland with such disastrous effects that the Government had been compelled to prohibit its manufacture.
On the Continent it was prepared from grapes, and in
Spain and Italy was sold as a medicine. In England it
was sold as a cordial. The Genoese prepared it from
grain, and as a medicament it was sold by apothecaries
under the name "water of life."

The appropriation of *eau de vie* ("water of life")—a
name borrowed from one of the most precious of the
divine promises (John iv. 14 and Rev. xxii. 17)—to a
strong drink of this description has been regarded as
nothing less than a profanation ; the untutored savage,

with a truer instinct, has named such drink "fire-water."
In Tahiti it is known as "British water," but wherever it
has been taken among savages, it would be a blasphemous
irony to call it "water of life." This by the way.

The increasing consumption of ardent spirits in place
of the comparatively harmless malt beverages hitherto in
vogue among the people of this country, led to social
and economic changes of no little import, and which
were indeed far-reaching in their consequences.

A petition was presented to Parliament in 1673 praying
that tea, coffee, and brandy should be prohibited, as the
use of these newer beverages interfered with the consumption of barley, malt, and wheat, the native products
of the country. The petitioners boldly asserted that the
"laborious people," who constituted the majority of the
population, required to drink "good strong beer and
ale," which greatly refreshed their bodies after their hard
labours ; and that the pot of ale or flagon of strong beer
with which they refreshed themselves every morning and
every evening, did them no great prejudice, hindered not
their work, nor took away their senses, and while it cost
them little money it greatly promoted the consumption
of home-grown grain ; whereas the drinking of brandy
destroyed many of his Majesty's subjects, "not agreeing
with their constitution."

Till the Revolutionary period of the seventeenth
century, Englishmen had been content to drink malt
liquor. It may be said that through the centuries till
then, ale had been "the wine of the country," the
national beverage all-sufficient for the taste and temperament of the Englishman. On the outbreak of the
Civil War, in 1643, Parliament, with a view to increasing
the national revenue, imposed Excise duties on ale and
beer, cider and perry. The imposition of these duties,
in that they eventually tended to alter the drinking habits

of the people, will be found to be epoch-marking and far-reaching in its effects.

The word "Excise" literally means "a piece cut off" (from the Latin, *excido*), being a toll levied on articles of home consumption, or a slice cut off from those things for the national purse.

The Royalists raised money by a similar tax, and after the Restoration these duties were continued with additional imposts on the new luxuries of tea and coffee. In the reign of James II. there was a temporary Excise on wine, vinegar, tobacco, and sugar; in the following reign salt, malt, and distilled liquors were similarly taxed; and then came a Customs duty on tobacco, tea, brandy, and wine. Little wonder that Dr. Johnson defined Excise as "a hateful tax" upon our home-produced commodities; that the very name always excited the anger of Englishmen—and for the matter of that, of Scotchmen, too; for in 1725 a riot broke out against the tax of 3d. a barrel on ale in Glasgow, while in Edinburgh opposition to the tax took the form of the brewers refusing to brew. Nor must the fact be lost sight of, that shameful and gigantic frauds were systematically practised on the revenue by smuggling, forgery, and collusion.

Confining our observation for the moment to that old English commodity, ale, not only were the Excise duties maintained, but from time to time they were substantially increased. Thus the tax of 2s. 6d. per barrel on strong beer in 1650 had become 5s. in 1692, with the inevitable result of raising the price of malt liquor to the consumer.

Compensation was made to Charles II. for the abolition of all the ancient feudal dues, by voting him an Excise duty on beer. Beer duties thus took the place of baronial dues—those dues which once provided the nation with a standing army. (To-day we rely for thirty-six millions

of public revenue on the Excise, derived from the
" noxious trade.")   In the next reign—William III.—the
price of ale was fixed by law at 3d. per quart.

Naturally enough, ordinary people demurred to paying
such enhanced prices for their accustomed beverage, and
also, naturally enough, public attention was directed
towards providing some cheap substitute.

Between 1690 and 1692 the output of the licensed
London breweries fell from 2,088,000 barrels to
1,523,000, while at the same time a great impetus was
given to the manufacture and consumption of spirituous
liquors.   It was not long ere the working classes were
found to be discarding honest old-fashioned English
beer, and to be acquiring a passion for English gin.   No
doubt there were contributory causes to the sudden and
wonderful rise in public favour won by the juniper-
flavoured spirit.   Parliament, to spite the French, prohibited the importation of brandy and other foreign
spirits, while at the same time they encouraged home
industries, by granting permission to all persons, on payment of small duties, to distil and retail spirits made from
English-grown corn.   Whether this was considered a set-
off to the heavy duties which had been placed on beer,
the effect was to encourage the drinking of gin at the
expense of the consumption of ale.   It was the avowed
purpose of the Government to encourage the distillation
and sale of British spirits.   How well they succeeded will
be seen in the next chapter.

THE OLD BULL AND MOUTH INN.

[*Page* 184.

"THE TABARD," SOUTHWARK.

[*Page* 213.

THE GIN FEVER

DISTILLERIES now sprang up everywhere, whereas
previous to the Revolution there had been exceedingly
few British distilleries in existence. The Brewers'
Company obtained charters, both from Charles II. and
James II., conferring upon them the right to distil;
while between 1690 and 1701 a number of statutes gave
direct encouragement to the distilling industry. The half-
million gallons of spirits produced in 1684 grew to two
millions in 1714, and was still rapidly on the increase.

The Act which was first passed with a view to checking this growing evil was the one which originated the present system of licensing public-houses at a general annual meeting of the justices (1729).

In 1736 the " drinking of Geneva," it was alleged, had become constant and excessive among the lower orders of the population, destroying thousands and rendering tens of thousands unfit to labour ; it was debauching the morals of the nation and leading to increase of crime.

In London one house in every four was a gin-shop, for the spirit was retailed by tradesmen who dealt in other commodities ; it was even sold from stables, sheds, and wheelbarrows ; gin was so cheap it was not uncommon for a sign to read—"Here a man may get drunk for a penny, and dead drunk for twopence."

The madness for gin-drinking attained such a height the Government became seriously alarmed, and set about devising legislation for checking it. In 1736 a tax of twenty shillings a gallon was put on gin, and every retailer of it was compelled to pay £50 for a licence. Compliance with the statute was to be enforced by the machinery of the common informer. On the day the Act came into force, September 29th, the signs of all the liquor-shops were put into mourning. Hooting mobs assembled round the dens where they could no longer get drunk for a copper, and the last rag was pawned to obtain a drink of the beloved liquor.

Such was the height of popular resentment against the Gin Act of September 29, 1736, it was thought advisable for some days after to mount a double guard at Kensington Palace, while the guards at St. James's Palace and at the Horse Guards in Whitehall were reinforced, a guard was placed at the Rolls Court in Chancery Lane, and a detachment of guards paraded

in and around Covent Garden in readiness to suppress
any tumult which might arise.

Several distillers took out licences to sell wine, and
others made preparations to take to the brewing trade ;
others again went down to Oxford and Cambridge to
open taverns there. The University of Oxford, however,
contested the right to do so, as the privilege of licensing
vintners had been granted to it by a charter of
Henry VIII., and subsequently confirmed by an Act of
Parliament in 13 Elizabeth.

According to one tradition, it was during the prohibition of gin being sold in less than two-gallon quantities
that the famous brand of London gin, known as " Old
Tom," came into vogue. An old Government spy,
calling himself Captain Dudley Bradsheet, is said to have
set up an illicit establishment outside which was the sign
of an old tom cat, cut out in wood or metal, and project-
ing into the street. By depositing a penny through a slot
in the figure, a supply of gin to that value could be made
to trickle from a pipe concealed in the cat's fore-paw.
This was in 1755, and if the story be true, the contrivance was an early anticipation of the penny-in-the-
slot machines now so largely used for the automatic
supply of sweetmeats and other small commodities. Dr.
Brewer, however, in " Phrase and Fable," gives another
origin for the name of this popular cordial gin. He says
that one Thomas Norris, formerly employed in the
distillery of Messrs. Hodges, opened a gin palace in
Great Russell Street, Covent Garden, and called the gin
concocted by Thomas Chamberlain, one of the firm of
Hodges, " Old Tom," in compliment to his former
master.

As had been foreseen by some, the Act was evaded ;
just as the 5s. duty in 1728 had given an impetus to
illicit trading. Hawkers in the streets sold a coloured

"mixture," and pretended chemists opened shops for the sale of what they called "Cholick Water." Fond, playful names attracted customers to their old haunts, where they could purchase " Tom Row," " Make Shift," " Ladies' Delight," and other strangely named beverages. Informers were rolled in the mud or thrown into the Thames. Thus were high duties and prohibitory enactments met by evasion if not by open defiance.

For several years Gin Riots were constantly taking place ; broadside and ballad were freely used by both sides in the great gin struggle.

> "Good lack, good lack, and Well-a-day
> That Madam Gin should fall ;
> Superior power she must obey—
> This Act will starve us all."

By 1743 the consumption of gin had actually increased, and it was then thought advisable to reduce the excessive duty.

Licences for the retailing of spirituous liquors and strong waters were now to be granted only to those who kept public victualling houses, inns, coffee-houses, ale-houses, or brandy-shops, and to no other traders whatever.

It may not be out of place here to mention that one rejected clause of the famous Prohibition Act of 1736 had sought to protect the sugar colonies by encouraging the consumption of rum, and proposed to exempt punch-houses from the operation of the Gin Act, provided the agreeable liquor so retailed was made one-third spirit and two-thirds water, and so mixed in the presence of the buyer. If the liquor were stronger than what sailors call "two-water-grog," the tippler might pay for his bowl by laying an information !

The Act had been designed to suppress the sale of spirits in small quantities, the £50 licence being considered prohibitive to those selling but a few gallons. The penalty for selling without a licence was £100, and the intention was to clear out of existence all the hucksters and small traders who sold gin, as well as the barrow-women and itinerant salesmen who went round with it. In this direction the evil had been in some degree mitigated. Whereas there had been 7,044 gin-shops in London in 1725, by 1750 some 1,700 of them had been suppressed.

Illicit trading had made the Act an utter failure, for while there was at first an apparent decrease of consumption, the evil was found to be actually augmented. In two years twelve thousand persons were punished for infringing the law. Distillers took out wine licences and sold a concoction of gin, sugar, and spice as wine; chemists put gin into physic bottles and sold it as medicine, while in the taverns everywhere gin was sold under other names. Between 1733 and 1742 the consumption of gin in England and Wales rose from eleven millions to twenty millions of gallons. Well might the Rev. James Townley write—

> "Gin, cursed fiend, with fury fraught,
> Makes human race a prey;
> It enters by a deadly draught
> And steals our life away."

The repealing Act of 1743 reduced the retail licence duty from £50 to 20s., and abolished the duty of 20s. on each gallon. Suppression of the traffic was abandoned as hopeless; but it was thought that retailers who had refused to take out licences at the prohibitive figure would not fail to do so when licences could be had for a reasonable sum. But here again legislators were mistaken, and conditions became, if possible, worse than ever.

XIII

LINGERING EFFECTS OF THE GIN POLICY

FROM the effects of the mistaken "gin policy," and of
the mass of blundering legislation which has accumulated since, the country can hardly be said, even now, to
have more than begun to make any real recovery.

Henry Fielding's treatise, published 1750, entitled,

" Inquiry into the Causes of the late Increase of Robbers,"
treats of two matters within the present purview. The
first section was aimed at Public Houses, Public
Gardens, Public " Wells," and similar places of entertainment " licensed for music under Act of 25
George II." Fielding was a London magistrate as well
as a novelist, and he proposed to stop the progress of
vice by removing the temptation. He condemns the
numberless places which had been opened to the public
where the eyes were feasted with show, the ears with
music, where drunkenness and gluttony were allured by
every dainty, where the finest women flaunted themselves, and " where the meanest person who could dress
himself clean might mix with his betters." London was
full of such resorts.

The second section of the treatise is directed against
drunkenness ; and of the evils of gin, as the parent of
crime, he adduces his experience as a magistrate, dealing
constantly with the wretches brought before him through
succumbing to the great gin epidemic of the period.

When, in 1751, a member of Parliament proposed to
attack the evil by again increasing the duty, Mr. Pelham
gave forth the opinion that no possible remedy could be
found for it. But in the time of George II. drunkenness
was the vice of the high as well as the low, of statesmen
and politicians as of the proletariat.

In the same year, prompted by the agitation in connection with the Gin Act, and on the side of restricting
the sale of this pernicious liquor, appeared a pair of
Hogarth's caricatures, which are the best known among
his minor works. These are the " Gin Lane " and
" Beer Street " cartoons. In the latter every lusty beer-
drinker is made to appear prosperous, the only exception
being the impoverished pawnbroker, whose dilapidated
premises are barricaded against the bailiffs, while he

himself is receiving through a hole in the door a pot of
the beverage to which his bankruptcy is due. The
satire is keen. In " Gin Lane," on the other hand,
everything is the reverse of prosperous with the drinkers
of " Bung-your-eye " and " Strip-me-naked " ; everywhere
is poverty, vice, and misery, the figures of the itinerant
gin-seller, and the gin-sodden maudlin mother whose
infant is dropping from her helpless arms, being appal-
ling in their ghastliness. Charles Lamb has admirably
described " Gin Lane "; and Dickens, in commenting
upon the picture, says the very houses seem to be absolutely reeling, and though the church is handsome and
prominent, no one seems to be interfering for the prevention or the cure of the generation going out, or the
one coming in, while the only sober men in the
composition appear to be the beadle and the undertaker.

Gin still continued to be, in the words of Fielding,
" the principal sustenance (if so it may be called) of more
than a hundred thousand persons in the metropolis " ;
and if these words of a contemporary writer, or the
pictures of a satirist of his times like Hogarth, exaggerate
the condition of things then existing, there can be no
doubt scenes were to be witnessed in the daily life of
London which were a disgrace to a civilised community.
A system of prohibition and high licence having thus
failed so signally, the Legislature, in 1751, made fresh
efforts, and an Act was passed forbidding distillers to sell
either retail or to unlicensed publicans, and enacting that
debts for drink should not be recoverable at law.

According to that eminent historian, Mr. Lecky, these
propositions being essentially more reasonable, had a real
and very considerable effect for good ; and with some
newer regulations in regard to licensing which set up a
more reasonable system of control, a greater measure of
success was secured than in all the previous years during

which the Legislature had blundered along in their ill-considered attempts with restrictions which were impracticable of enforcement.

There was a reversion, if not a complete one, from gin to malt liquors, although it was very long indeed ere the country recovered from the harm which the "gin policy" had inflicted upon the habits of the lower orders of society.,

Much of the brutality, ignorance, and degradation of the eighteenth century was attributable to excessive drinking. Everybody drank, and nobody drank moderately; the vice was common to all, rich and poor alike. At social parties no gentleman ever thought of leaving the table sober; the host would have considered it a slight on his hospitality. Even ladies and clergymen sometimes got drunk, and intoxication was so common a thing it passed without remark. The upper classes drank wine, and every man among them liked to boast himself a "two-bottle man"; and even if he could not consume that quantity, he could at least drink till he fell beneath the table.

The lower classes drank beer when they did not drink gin, and it was a common thing among working men to drink three or four quarts of strong, heavy ale each day of their lives. In 1761 an attempt to raise the price of ale to 3½d. a quart was successfully resisted by the public.

Perhaps the Ale-house Act of 1828 was intended to remove some of the lingering effects of the long-discredited "gin policy," and to restore to its ancient popularity the national beverage; it was certainly believed by many that free trade in ale would check the growing consumption in spirits. Then the Beer Act of 1830 went a step further; it enabled any householder whose name was on the rate-book to sell beer, but no other intoxicating liquor, by retail, without obtaining a licence from the justices, and free from any control, by merely paying the small sum of two guineas to the Excise. The effect of this laxity was immediate and alarming. Within the first three months of the Act's coming into force nearly twenty-five thousand persons had paid this nominal fee of two guineas, and obtained their beer licence from the Excise authorities. In Liverpool alone fifty new beer-shops were opened every day for a period of several weeks, and some of the places where beer was sold were mere cellars and places similarly unfit. It was clear from the excessive number of licensed houses, and the increased difficulties of control, that the licensing problem instead of being solved, was entering upon a newer, a more difficult phase than ever. As one way out of the difficulty, holders of beer licences were encouraged by the magistrates to take out spirit licences as well, so that their houses might be brought under proper magisterial control. Then the holders of full licences endeavoured to meet the competition of the cheaply conducted beer-houses by enlarging their premises and increasing the attraction of their houses; and in the end the net result of it all was a steady increase in the consumption of spirits—a result the very reverse of that which the Legislature had set out to attain.

From 1830 to 1869 any person of good character could obtain a beer-house licence for a tenement of certain ratable value. There was no power to refuse them, and they were not forfeitable except on certain specific conditions. Also, as just stated, full licences for selling spirits as well were readily granted, some magistrates preferring to grant full licences for better-class premises rather than create more beer-houses. Licences were granted so freely that it is not difficult to find even now a number of public-houses close together in one street, if not indeed next door to each other.

During the middle decades of the nineteenth century, when the number of beer-houses was multiplied so enormously by the easy licensing conditions then prevailing, ale was retailed not only by many struggling shopkeepers, but by numbers of really small householders. In countless cases the premises of a licensed beer-seller were of the humblest description, and the room in which customers were accommodated would frequently be a medley of kitchen, parlour, and hall—all in the most primitive style of English cottage life.

Avoiding as far as possible the controversial, and keeping to the historical aspect of the subject, the legislative alterations made subsequently to 1830 must be briefly summarised.   In 1834 "off" licences were granted for the sale of beer "not to be consumed on the premises"; in 1860 licences were granted to wine- and refreshment-houses; in 1869 wine- and beer-houses were brought under magisterial control, like other licensed houses subject to inquiry at annual Licensing Sessions, although the beer-houses already in existence retained some of the privileges and immunities so foolishly granted them in 1830.   And lastly, in 1872, a great reform was achieved when public-houses were no longer allowed to keep open their doors all night long.

Here it may be advisable to give the different grades and classes of licensed houses.

An ale-house is defined as a place where ale, beer, &c., are drunk. An inn differs from an ale-house in this—that the former is a place intended for the lodging as well as the entertainment of guests, whereas the latter is intended for their entertainment only. If, however, ale or beer is commonly sold in an inn—as is almost invariably the case—it also is an ale-house, and if travellers be furnished with beds, lodged, and entertained in an ale-house, it also is an inn.

The Ale-house Act, 1828, required the issue of justices' licences for inns, ale-houses, and victualling houses, and the licence authorises the sale by retail of any kind of excisable liquor.

A privilege enjoyed by the keeper of an ale-house is that he may keep a billiard-table for public use without any licence from the justices.

An inn is a house for the accommodation of travellers in general. All persons are deemed innkeepers who keep houses where a traveller is furnished for profit with everything which he has occasion for whilst on his way. To the keeping of an inn certain obligations attach.

Innkeepers are bound to take in all travellers and wayfaring persons and to entertain them at a reasonable charge, provided they behave themselves properly ; they have a lien upon the goods of their guests for board and lodging, &c., but not on their persons or personal clothing in actual wear. They are bound to take not merely ordinary care of the goods, money, and baggage of their guests, to an amount not exceeding £30, excepting where the goods have been stolen or lost through the wilful act, default, or neglect of the innkeeper or his servant, when the goods have been deposited with him expressly for safe custody.

By 27 & 28 Vict. c. 18 "inn" means any hotel, inn, tavern, public-house, or other place of refreshment, the keeper of which is responsible for the goods of his guest.

Then there is the obligation of billeting soldiers. The following houses are liable to be listed for this purpose : Victualling houses, inns, hotels, livery stables, ale-houses ; also the houses of sellers of wine by retail (whether British or foreign) to be drunk on the premises, and all houses of persons selling brandy, spirits, strong-waters, cider, or metheglin by retail. The legalised exemptions to this are private houses, canteens held or occupied under the authority of a Secretary of State, vintners, distillers (who do not permit tippling in their houses), shopkeepers whose principal dealing is more in other goods than brandy, &c., houses where beer and cider are sold not to be consumed on the premises; and the house of any foreign consul.

In 1830 it was deemed "expedient for the better supplying of the public in England to give greater facilities for the sale thereof than are at present afforded by licences to keepers of inns, ale-houses, and victualling houses." The Beer-house Act, 1830, was accordingly passed, authorising any person being a householder assessed to the poor rate, except Sheriffs' officers, &c., to obtain from the Excise on payment of two guineas a year a licence to sell beer by retail. This licence authorised the holder to sell beer by retail in his dwelling-house whether for consumption on the premises or not, but was issued subject to certain penalties expressed on the face of it, for the breach of any of which he was subject to heavy penalties. The Act of 1869 provided that this licence should not be renewed by the Excise without the production of a certificate of the justices assembled at the General Annual Licensing Meeting, or some adjournment thereof.

The line of reform at the present day appears to lie in two directions—a statutory reduction of public-houses by the gradual extinction of licences on some economic plan of a non-confiscatory nature, and a scheme of high licence duties. It is but necessary to set out the existing scale of licence duties to show its inadequacy. While a modest country inn, with a ratable value of but £20 a year, pays a licence duty of £8, a flaming East End gin palace, with a ratable value of £200 a year, pays but £30 a year, or say, 11s. 6d. a week, for its valuable monopoly.

That the pernicious "gin habit" has not entirely disappeared at the present day is painfully evident to any one acquainted with the slum life of modern London. How much worse it was three generations ago, ere the gospel of total abstinence had made its appearance, may be gleaned from the works of Cruikshank.

George Cruikshank, no doubt deeply moved by the social conditions of his time, produced a powerful cartoon entitled "The Gin Juggernaut, or the worship of the Great Spirit—Its devotees destroying themselves—Its progress is marked with desolation, misery, and crime." This was a weird production of the "hungry forties," when drinking was made more horrible in its effects by the scarcity of good solid food with which to stay the stomachs of the labouring poor. In 1848, by which date Cruikshank had become a total abstainer, he produced "The Bottle," and its sequel, "The Drunkard's Children," both of which deal vigorous blows at the flaring gin palaces and the low, dirty beer-shops. "The Bottle" pictures were instantly a huge success and sold in immense numbers, no less than 100,000 copies at a shilling each being sold within the space of a few days. "The Bottle" was at once dramatised, and played simultaneously at eight London theatres. The sixteen plates of the other series trace with graphic detail the progress of the drunkard and his family from comfort and respectability to the beer-house, the pawnshop, the asylum, the court, the hulks, and the river.

XIV

DRINKING CUSTOMS

Drinking healths—Legend of Rowena and Vortigern—Origin of the
Wassail Bowl—A Twelfth Night custom—The Loving Cup—
Poculum charitatis, or Grace Cup—The Lichfield ceremonial—
Ceremony of the cup—Origin of "Toasts"—Another account
from the *Tatler*—Literary allusions—The Toast-master—Pegged
tankards—Derived phrases and literary allusions—The Stirrup
Cup — Hobnobbing — Bumpers — Heel taps — The Sneaker's
penalty—"Ting"—Rummers—Toddy—Tumblers—Local and
seasonal customs—Clerkenwell Christmas custom—A Cornish
custom on St. Paul's Eve—A custom at Barnstaple Fair—
Treating the parson—Seal drinks—"Seals and meals"—Standing
treat—Drinks round—Literary allusion.

THE practice of drinking one another's health at banquets was practised by the ancient Assyrians, Egyptians,
Greeks, and Romans.

The first recorded instance in this country is that
mentioned as occurring in the year 450 A.D. at a feast
given by the British King Vortigern to his Saxon allies.
On that occasion, according to a commonly accepted
tradition, Rowena, the beautiful daughter of the Saxon
chief Hengist, took a golden goblet filled with wine, and
on her knees drank to the health of their royal host,
" Liever Kyning, Wass-hael ! "—that is, " Lord King,
your health ! " Not understanding the custom, Vortigern
had it explained to him by the attendants, and was as

much charmed by the compliment as bewitched by the
fair Saxon damsel who had thus pledged him :—

" ' Health, my lord King," the sweet Rowena said ;
' Health,' cried the chieftain to the Saxon maid ;
Then gaily rose, and 'mid the concourse wide
Kiss'd her pale lips, and placed her by his side.
At the soft scene, such gentle thoughts abound
That healths and kisses 'mongst the guests went round."

The Saxons never had a feast without handing round
the drinking or pledge cup, or Wassail Bowl, and in
course of time this practice became transferred to the
Christmas festivities, and is now only recognised in
the custom of drinking healths or toasts at public
dinners.

The ancient folk custom was for the Wassail Bowl,
filled with spiced ale, to be carried about by young
women on New Year's Eve, who went from door to
door in their several parishes singing a few couplets of
homely verses composed for the purpose, and presenting
the liquor to the inhabitants of the houses where they
called, expecting a small gratuity in return for a proffered
drink of their slabby stuff. The custom of wassailing is
now quite obsolete, and has been for upwards of a
century ; Cornwall was the latest place in which the
practice obtained, though even there the time of the
performance had been changed to Twelfth Day.

The origin of the Loving Cup, a large drinking vessel
passed round from guest to guest at State banquets and
City feasts, is peculiar. During the Danish occupation of
England, if an Englishman presumed to drink in the
presence of a Dane, without his express permission, it
was esteemed so great a mark of disrespect that nothing
but his instant death could expiate it. The English
became so intimidated that they would not venture to
drink, even when they were invited, until the Danes had

GEORGE HOTEL (AN ANCIENT PILGRIMS' INN), GLASTONBURY.

[*Page* 214.

THE OLD GEORGE INN, SALISBURY.
(From the Garden.)

[*Page* 214.

pledged their honour for their safety. Whence arose the custom of pledging each other in drinking—the one sitting next the drinker would stand with uplifted sword to guard his friend whilst engaged in the act of drinking.

Another account of the origin of the Loving Cup is given. On the introduction of Christianity among the Anglo-Saxons, the custom of wassailing was not abolished, but it assumed a religious aspect. The monks called the Wassail Bowl *Poculum charitatis* (Loving Cup), a term still retained by the London City companies, though in the Universities the term Grace Cup is more general.

Miss Strickland says that Margaret Atheling, wife of Malcolm Canmore, in order to induce the Scotch to remain for grace, devised the Grace Cup, which was filled with the choicest wine, and of which each guest was allowed to drink *ad libitum*, after Grace had been said. But by whichever name known, Loving Cup or Grace Cup, the custom of drinking from it at public banquets is still preserved—two adjacent persons always stand up together, one to drink and the other to pledge his safety whilst doing so.

The ceremonial as anciently observed in Lichfield was described by the learned antiquary of that city, Elias Ashmole, in 1666. The first two toasts always were, first, the reigning monarch, and then " Weale and worship," drunk from a massive embossed goblet holding three or four quarts. " The Mayor drinks first, and on his rising, the persons on his right and left also rise. He then hands the cup to the person on his right side, when the one next to him rises, the one on the left of the Mayor still standing. Then the cup is passed across the table to him, when *his* left-hand neighbour rises ; so that there are always three standing at the same time— one next the person who drinks, and one opposite to him." At Oxford it was customary at some of the college banquets for the two who waited upon the drinker to place their thumbs upon the table.

The passing round of a Loving Cup was practised in this country from the earliest times ; it was an indispensable feature at every banquet, and gave us the time-honoured custom of drinking toasts.

The cup was filled to the brim with wine, ale, or mead, on the top of which would float a piece of toasted bread. After putting his lips thereto, the host would pass the cup to the guest of honour on his right, and he after drinking would pass it on to the neighbour on his right hand.   In this manner the cup would circulate round the table, in barbarous times each drinker in turn being protected from the possibility of sudden and treacherous assault by his neighbour courteously standing at his back while both his hands were occupied in holding the two-handled cup.

Every one having taken a sip, the cup came back finally to the host, who drained it, and then swallowed the piece of toast in honour of all his guests.

Such was the origin of " toasts."   Somewhat similarly we obtained the term " Wassail," signifying the pledging of health.   This was at first a New Year's custom among the Saxons, who, upon drinking in honour of a friend, first saluted him with the words, " Wes hal ! "—that is, " Be hale ! " or more freely, " Health be to you ! "

This is one derivation of the word " toast " as applied to the drinking of one's health.   But according to the *Tatler* the term did not originate till the reign of Charles II., and under these circumstances :—

" It happened that on a public day, a celebrated beauty of those times was in the Cross Bath, and one of the crowd of her admirers took a glass of the water in which the fair one stood, and drank her health to the company.   There was in the place a gay fellow, half fuddled, who offered to jump in, and swore though he liked not the liquor he would have the toast. He was opposed in the resolution, yet the whim gave foundation to the present honour which is done to the lady we mention in our liquor, which has ever since been called a toast."

The sacramental significance given by the Jacobites to their method of drinking the usual loyal toast is well known. When challenged they always responded to the toast of " The King " by undemonstratively holding their glasses over the water-bottle, thereby signifying to those in the secret that they drank to " The King over the Water "—to the exiled Stuart, not to the usurping Hanoverian.

Butler, in his " Hudibras," makes a somewhat obscure allusion to the practice of toasting. It is in the passage (Canto I.) in which the lady tries to persuade her lover to whip himself for her sake, and is made to say :—

"It is an easier way to make
Love by, than that which many take,
Who would not rather suffer whipping
Than swallow toasts of bits of ribbin."

In the drinking of toasts ladies have the modest custom of excusing themselves, which is thus delicately described by Goldsmith in his " Deserted Village" :—

"Nor the coy maid, half willing to be prest,
Shall kiss the cup to pass it to the rest."

The office of Toast-master can be traced to that of the master of the feast, who, at Roman banquets, prescribed, under certain penalties, regulations for the whole company, ordering singing, drinking, dancing, or the exercise of any talent an individual was known to possess, and which he thought would entertain the company. The modern toast-master acts under the instructions of the founder of the feast in giving the toasts, and officiates generally in regulating the order and all formalities of a convivial meeting.

Two well-known phrases grew out of a drinking custom which legendary lore has attributed to St. Dunstan. This great Saxon reformer, in order to check the intemperate drinking habits of the early English, introduced the custom of pegging the tankards. The Saxon drinking tankard held two quarts, which by Dunstan's precept were divided into eight equal parts, each marked with a silver pin or peg, so that from one mark to the next measured half a Winchester pint. By the rules of good fellowship the drinker was supposed to stop drinking only at a pin ; if he drank beyond it, he was expected to drink on to the next. As it was always difficult to gauge the draught, the vain efforts to stop at a pin gave rise to much mirth, and generally ended in the drinker's draining the tankard, by which time he was in merry mood, or, as the phrase ran, "in merry pin." Thus in Longfellow's "Golden Legend" we have the allusion :—

> "Come, old fellow, drink down to your peg,
> But do not drink any farther, I beg."

In the same connection we derive the saying, "I'm a peg too low," meaning "I want another drink to cheer me up." The drinking capacity, or power to stand strong drink, varies very much with different men, according to their varying constitutions. When the poet Cowper says of "John Gilpin" that he was "in merry pin," we are to infer that he was elated, as one who had drunk down to the "pin" or mark which rendered him less sedate than usual.

The "Stirrup Cup" was the name given to the parting drink which was handed to a guest upon his departure, and when his feet were in the stirrups. The custom was

chiefly practised in the North, as thus in Scott's famous
poem :—

> "Lord Marmion's bugles blew to horse ;
> Then came the stirrup cup in course ;
> Between the baron and his host
> No point of courtesy was lost."

Then as to South Britain. Is it not a matter of history
that Edward the Martyr was treacherously stabbed in the
back while mounted on his horse and drinking the parting cup at the gates of Corfe Castle in the year 979 ?
Some would trace the Stirrup Cup to a Roman origin,
but on the face of it, it looks more like the manifestation
of the hospitality so characteristic of our Saxon ancestors ;
it was a last effort of the reluctance to part with a guest.

To hobnob is to drink familiarly with another—"hab
nab" was used as a call in drinking, and is supposed to
be derived from the Anglo-Saxon *habban*, "to have," and
nabban (for *ne habban*), " not to have." The ceremonial
at hobnobbing was to clink cups together before drinking
to each other.

A bever—the term is connected with our word "beverage"—was a drink between meals. At Eton College they
had bever days, when extra beer was served to the students.
Beaumont and Fletcher's " Woman Hater " contains the
allusion :—

" He will devour three breakfasts without prejudice to his bevers."

Another Bacchanalian extravagance was the drinking
of bumpers.

" Bumpers all round and no heel taps " is the convivial
call to do special honour in drinking a toast. The term
" bumper " has been traced to two sources, both
doubtful : first, to the custom of monks drinking to the
head of their fraternity as *au bon père;* the second
derivation, purely English, has been given as signifying

a glass or cup so filled that it "bumps" up in the middle, the liquid being higher in the centre than at the brim. The heartiness of the drinking is expressed not only in the filling but in the emptying of the vessel, as the drinker is expected to turn it upside down afterwards to show that it has been enthusiastically emptied of its contents ; the term "heel-taps" being derived from the peg in the heel of a shoe, which is only removed by the shoemaker when his work on it has been quite completed. This is the usual explanation of the term, but it is by no means convincing.

In the hard-drinking days of the eighteenth century, whenever the votaries of Bacchus were in full revel assembled, any "sneaker" who failed to keep pace with the rest of the company, as soon as detected, was compelled to offer a special libation to the rosy god.

It was once a common drinking custom to knock the glass on the thumb, to give it an ostentatious fillip and make it cry *ting;* this was to show that the drinker had performed his duty. To the term "bumper" Dryden makes the following allusion :—

> "Then Rhenish rummers walk the round—
> In bumpers every king is crowned."

As to the term "rummer," which the poet also introduces to our notice, it may be explained as a word of German origin—perhaps in original form it was " Roman glass "—to name a tall, cylindrical glass with a stem, and used in the seventeenth century for drinking toddy. "Toddy," again, is a name for spirits mixed with hot water, sweetened and flavoured ; it will be found mentioned in "Noctes Ambrosianæ," that delightful record of pleasant evenings spent by "Christopher North" in the congenial company he was wont to find at Ambrose's Tavern in Edinburgh.

The term "tumbler," as applied to a drinking glass, originated in an old drinking custom. The original tumbler was a drinking horn, the bottom of which was weighted with a bulbous mass of lead. The purpose of this was twofold ; as Saxon custom demanded that the entire contents should be drunk at one draught, the vessel in its first stage was made so that it could not be set on its bottom without tumbling over and spilling the contents ; then some ingenious individual developed the second stage by adding the weight to the rounded bottom, which by the law of physics preserved the upright position in equilibrium. There was said to have been another advantage in these weighty vessels —if they fell off the table during an orgie they could not roll very far away out of the obfuscated drinker's reach.

Of quaint old drinking customs pertaining to particular seasons, or peculiar to certain localities— customs associated with trading, and bargaining, or in some way to be classified as special rather than general—there are many to be met with up and down the length and breadth of the country. A selected few must suffice here.

There was a curious Christmas custom in ancient times connected with the "Pied Bull" at Clerkenwell. The landlord of this hostelry for some reason or other— probably traceable to one of those jocular tenures of which we may read in Blount—was under an obligation to bestow on every woman who came into his house on Christmas Day before noon, and kissed him, a given measure of ale. Whether he honoured the custom in fear of the forfeit, or because he found it pleasant, his tenancy seems to have depended upon its observance.

There is a drinking custom in Cornwall which has given rise to many speculations as to its real origin. On St. Paul's Eve the tin miners used to leave their work and shy stones at a pitcher filled with water until it was broken. The moment it fell shattered to the ground the company adjourned to the nearest inn, filled another pitcher—but this time with beer—and drank it up, presumably to save it from the fate of the water.

Although St. Paul, according to the local legend, landed in Cornwall and preached the gospel there, it is not probable the custom has anything to do with the great Apostle of the Gentiles. It is more likely the custom is a survival of an old-time protest against the compulsory drinking of water in the mines.

At Barnstaple is still practised an ancient custom which dates back to the reign of Athelstan. At the opening of the annual fair a stuffed white glove is fixed up outside the town hall, and there it remains during the whole time the fair is open, to symbolise freedom from arrest ; while inside the building the mayor regales a company of invited guests with toast and ale. For this occasion a brave display of the Corporation plate is always made, the spiced ales being dispensed from silver punch-bowls and a service of silver-gilt flagons and goblets.

Most newspaper readers will remember " Beer and Bible " as a political outcry of recent times ; but no one would have been scandalised in the good old days by an equally incongruous association of " Beer and Bishop." For in those times it seems to have been a custom for a visiting clergyman to be hospitably entertained at the church with beer or some other strong drink. Thus at Bewdley the church accounts for 1593 contain this item —" Paid for a galland of beere given to the Beishopp of Hereford...iiij*d*."

In 1724 the Bishop of Lincoln seems to have been similarly regaled at St. Mary's, Nottingham ; and the custom of " treating the parson " who had come to preach on some special occasion was apparently widespread and regularly honoured at that period.

It was formerly a common practice at markets and fairs, and at no distant date either, for all bargains of any magnitude to be "sealed" or clenched by vendor or purchaser—either the one or the other, whichever was mutually agreed to have secured the advantage—paying for drinks. Hence no doubt was derived the term "seal drink" given to the liquor gratuitously handed round at auction sales. This practice, however, of freely dispensing copious and expensive drinks to all and sundry assembled in a sale-room on licensed premises, not five per cent. of whom were legitimate bidders for the property at auction, is now rapidly falling into desuetude.

The term "sealed quarts" has been explained in Chapter V.; and it is not improbable that another old use of the word "seal" had some connection with one or other of those explained. Thus in the days of statute hiring fairs, a servant letting himself out, generally asked his master if he would be allowed "seals and meals," meaning the usual time for rest and refreshment, of which liquid refreshment was not considered the least important part.

The practice of treating another person to drinks, or as it is variously called, "standing treat" and "standing Sam," is too well known and too commonly prevalent at the present day to call for much comment here. It is the English practice of all others which is characteristically stupid, in that it leads to so much unnecessary drinking; for a meeting of friends on the common ground of a public-house is invariably celebrated by their drinking together, and, as a rule, an end cannot be put to the celebration till each man has acquitted himself by paying for "drinks round"—and therefore the larger the party the larger the number of drinks taken, and probably all of them except the first quite unnecessary, either for the quenching of thirst or the celebration of a happy meeting. To most reasonable men the custom presents itself in the light of an unmitigated nuisance, though one which needs some amount of moral courage to resist, its approach always being made in so pleasant a guise. It is an old custom, too; but time-honoured as it may be, its irksomeness has always been felt; for that roystering poet, Ben Jonson, a veritable prince at all merrymakings, was constrained to say—

"As the fund of our pleasure, let us each pay his shot."

The term "shot," by the way, is commonly used to signify a reckoning at an inn—it is good old tavern slang.

XV

DRUNKENNESS THE NATIONAL VICE

English drinking matches—The drinking habit copied from the
Dutch during Elizabethan Wars—The drunken London of
Shakespeare's time—Notorious London taverns—Country
taverns crowded with determined drunkards (1583)—The
"wicked folks" of Newcastle-under-Lyme (1638)—An Englishman's drinking capacity—The butt of the old playwrights—
Puritan crusade against tippling clergymen—The drink-
drenched "Merrie England" of the Restoration—Pledging
of healths a danger to sobriety—The custom decried by Chief
Justice Hale, but defended by a divine—Charles II.'s proclamation against drinking his royal health—Annean era—Drinking
as a recognised amusement—A magniloquent excuse for getting
drunk—Apologists for the drinking habit—Leigh Hunt's views
—Drink stimulants a human necessity—Alcohol unsuspectingly
taken in other forms—W. E. Gladstone's attitude on the subject
—An Order of Temperance founded (1600)—The moderation
of a philosopher—Earliest temperance poem known (1656)—
Drunkenness no disgrace in early nineteenth century—Total
abstinence pledge (1832)—Origin of the word "teetotal"—
G. K. Chesterton's condemnation of our national insobriety—
The nastiness of temperance drinks—Their unsuitability as food
accompaniments—Traces of alcohol in temperance drinks.

IT cannot be denied that the custom of hard drinking had
long to be reckoned as one of our national vices. While
the Frenchman, the Italian, and the Spaniard enjoyed the
luxury of the grape, they never indulged in the set
convivial parties, or drinking matches, which have
characterised the social habits of the Northern peoples.

" As drunk as an Englishman," occurs in the works of Rabelais.

The custom, which lasted quite two centuries in England, was a borrowed one; for nations, like individuals, in their intercourse are often great imitators. Camden's " History of Queen Elizabeth " states that " The English in their long wars in the Netherlands first learnt to drown themselves with immoderate drinking, and by drinking others' healths to impair their own. Of all the Northern nations, they had been before the most commended for their sobriety."

The London of Shakespeare's time was a drunken London. Whether the increase of drunkenness among the citizens of the sixteenth century was attributable, as Camden asserts, to their familiarity with the Flemings, it is certain they regularly spent too much time in taverns. An old bard has favoured us with a list of the most popular and most frequented taverns; his black-letter poem, entitled " Newes from Bartholomew Fayere," runs in this enlivening strain :—

" There hath been great sale and utterance of wine,
  Besides beere, and ale, and ipocras fine,
  In every country, region, and nation,
  But chiefly in Billingsgate, at the Salutation;
  And the Bore's Head, near London Stone,
  The Swan at Dowgate, a taverne well known;
  The Mitre in Cheape; and then the Bull's Head,
  And many like places that make noses red;
  Th' Bore's Head in Old Fish Street, Three Cranes in the Vintry,
  And now, of late, St. Martin's in the Sentree;
  The Windmill in Lothbury; the Ship at th' Exchange,
  King's Head in New Street, where roysters do range;
  The Mermaid in Cornhill, Red Lion in the Strand,
  Three Tuns, Newgate Market; Old Fish Street, at the Swan."

Not only was drunkenness rife in the sixteenth century among the citizens of London, as we have already learnt, but it was equally prevalent in the country; for if Stubbes, that bitter writer of the period, may find credit, we are to believe from his "Anatomie of Abuses" that every public-house was crowded from morn till night with determined drunkards (1583).

In Drunken Barnaby's Itinerary we have an allusion to the wicked folks of Newcastle-under-Lyme, which seems to suggest that in his day (1638) there was some common-place rhyme on the subject, but which has long been lost. The passage we allude to runs thus :—

> " Newcastle-under-Line—a
> There I trounced it in burnt wine—a ;
> None o' th' wicked there remained,
> Weekly lectures were proclaimed."

Massinger, in his *Grand Duke of Florence* (act ii. scene 2) has a tilt at the drinking capacity of the Englishman :—

> " *Bernardo.* Have they (*i.e.*, the English) not store of wine there?
> *Caponi.* Yes, and drink more in two hours
> Than the Dutchman or the Dane in four-and-twenty ! "

A bit of dialogue from another old playwright forces home the same truth :—

> "Believe it? Believe anything ! No swallow like an Englishman's. A man in a quart bottle, or a victory, it's all one—down it goes ! "

It will be seen that the national vice had become the butt of the satirists and other contemporary writers.

For a century or so after the Reformation the Puritans indicted, in thousands of parishes up and down the country, the beneficed clergy of the newly-established Church of England for being tipplers and frequenters of taverns in which they gamed with cards, even upon " the

Lord's day." But these attempts at repression, as we have seen, had little or no real and lasting effect. The futility of it all was seen at the Restoration.

With the removal of all the absurd restrictions upon the ancient amusements of the people, with the setting up again of the Maypoles in the villages, and the reopening of the theatres in the towns, the pendulum perhaps swung too far to the opposite side, and reprehensible excesses of pleasure were indulged in. And there was little to choose between the carding and the dicing and other dissolute pursuits of the upper classes, and the cock-fighting, animal baiting, and other brutalities of the common people. This cannot be accepted as the real "Merrie England"—the pleasures of the people lacked innocent Arcadian simplicity, and the vine-leaf was too much in evidence.

The danger to sobriety and temperate habits which lurked in the old English practice of drinking healths, was recognised by that illustrious Chief Justice of the seventeenth century, Sir Matthew Hale. To his grandchildren he left this injunction :—

"I will not have you to begin or pledge any health, for it is become one of the great artifices of drinking and occasions of quarrelling in the kingdom. If you pledge one health, you oblige yourself to pledge another, and a third, and so onwards ; and if you pledge as many as will be drank, you must be debauched and drunk. If they will needs know the reason of your refusal, it is a fair answer, That your grandfather that brought you up, from whom under God you have the estate you enjoy or expect, left this in command with you, that you should never begin or pledge a health."

While the custom of pledging each other in drink has found defenders, it has also been bitterly attacked by the more thoughtful commentators on many occasions. Among the former may be noted a solemn passage found

in Ward's " Living Speeches of Dying Christians " : " My
Saviour began to mee in a bitter cup ; and shall I not
pledge Him ? " On the other side, again, a tract of
" William Prynne, Gent.," published in 1628, hurled
anathemas at the practice, and distinctly declared " the
pledging of healths to be sinful, and utterly unlawful
unto Christians." But more remarkable was the royal
proclamation issued soon after the Restoration, owing to
the excessive indulgence of the people in this cheap form
of loyalty. Subjoined is an extract from this extraordinary
proclamation :—

" C.R.

" Our dislike of those, who under pretence of affection for us,
and our service, assume to themselves a Liberty of Reviling,
Threatening and Reproaching of others. There are likewise
another sort of men, of whom we have heard much, and are
sufficiently ashamed, who spend their lives in Taverns, Tippling-
houses, and Debauches, giving no other evidence of their affection
for us but in Drinking our Health."

The frequency of drinking the King's health had
actually threatened to disturb the peace of the realm,
and the issue of the proclamation positively became
a public necessity.

In the Annean period, drinking was looked upon by
" young gentlemen of quality " as a recognised amusement. Hear Dean Swift on the vice in his time : " I
dined with Mr. Addison and Dick Stuart, lord Mountjoy's
brother, a treat of Addison's. They were half fuddled,
but not I ; for I mixed water with my wine, and left
them between nine and ten." An early hour to leave
gentlemen half drunk, surely, and those having a claim
to be taken as men of breeding and men of intellect, too.

In the eighteenth century, when drinking and classi-
calism were both in vogue together, a writer (in the

magniloquence of the period) thus attempts to excuse, even to justify, the prevailing vice :—

" Drunkenness was so habitual and national a Vice, that *Pergracari* signifies to be mad with Drunkenness : The Romans were so addicted to this latter Vice of the Grecians, that they instituted their *Leges Compotandi*, their Laws for Drinking, which they commonly observ'd; the one was, to be *ad Diurnam Stellam Matutinam potantes*, to drink down the Evening Star, and drink up the Morning Star ; the other was to drink so many Bumpers as there were Letters in their Mistress's Name ; for Martial tells us,

> Nœvia sex cyathis, septem Justina bibatur,
> Quinque Lycas, Lyde quatuor, Ida tribus.

> With six full Bumpers Nœvia's Health be crown'd,
> Let seven at Justina's Name go round,
> Let five at Lycas, four at Lyde be ;
> But at the Name of Ida fill but three.

Nor were the Gentlemen only distinguish'd among the Romans for Drinking ; but, for the Consolation of our Modern Ladies, the Ladies of Rome were not free from this Excess: Seneca assures us, that in Drinking they even outdid the Men, and Juvenal's Description of them exceeds all that a modern vitiated Fancy could imagine."

It is perfectly characteristic of the early Georgian period that a man should establish a reputation, which was almost national, merely as a maker and a drinker of punch. Among the "remarkable persons" of George II.'s reign was one William Groves, accounted "the very essence of a good fellow." Punch was his favourite liquor, and in the preparation of that celebrated mixture his reputation was said to have equalled that of the famous Ashley, who set up the first regular punch-house in London, on Ludgate Hill. Like him, too, Groves turned to advantage his expert knowledge of the then popular beverage, by commencing business as a publican.

THE BELL INN, FINEDON.

[Page 224.

THE OLD WHITE HART INN, NEWARK.
(From an old print, by kind permission of G. Sheppard, Esq., Borough Surveyor,
Newark-on-Trent.)

[*Page* 225.

Though he condescended to deal in other liquors, yet his punch was famed above the rest of his choice drinks, and a club was formed at his house, under the title of the "Honourable Society of Non-Common Pleas," of which he was elected president, and became the first Grand Master. The fame and reputation of this club gave rise to similar assemblies, as the "Old Codgers," the "Odd Fellows," and other eccentric societies. Such was the eminence attained in this line of social intercourse by Groves, portraits of him were engraved and published in 1734, one by P. Fremont and the other by J. Williams. Under the latter these lines were printed :—

> "Non-Common Groves ! Grand Master of the Rolls ;
> The Prince of Topers, and of merry souls ;
> An utter enemy to sordid pelf ;
> And friend to every mortal but himself :
> Give him a flowing bowl to take his swill—
> 'Hang Care ! 'twill kill a Cat !' cries honest Will."

The drinking habit has not been without its apologists and defenders, even in more recent times. Leigh Hunt said that "a tavern and coffee-house is a pleasant sight from its sociality, not to mention the illustrious club members of the times of Shakespeare and the Tatlers." Presently the essayist proceeds in this tolerant strain : "We confess that the commonest public-house in town is not such an eyesore to us as it is with some. It may not be very genteel, but neither is everything that is rich . . . Before we object to public-houses, and above all to their Saturday evening recreations, we must alter the systems that make them a necessary comfort to the poor and laborious."

In a recently published survey of the licensed trade, the writer expresses the view that the natural man has in all ages demanded stimulants, that the demand is reason-

able, and for the vast majority of men innocuous. He
says :—

> " The human race itself has long since decided that the most
> convenient, as well as the most acceptable form which the
> apparently indispensable stimulant can take is alcohol. The pro-
> hibitionists set up alcohol as a bogey which everyone should avoid.
> They would have the world believe that not even the smallest
> possible quantity of alcohol can be taken without doing harm. . . .
> To this it may be replied, on the authority of Dr. Max Schottelius,
> Professor of Hygiene at Freiburg University, that 'everyone,
> including the strictest teetotalers, takes alcohol daily. Fresh bread
> contains ½ per cent. of alcohol, and that is why fresh bread tastes so
> good.' "

Dealing with the question of prohibitive legislation the
author of the work (Mr. Pratt) quotes the late Mr. Gladstone as saying—

> " How can I, who drink good wine and bitter beer every day of
> my life, coolly stand up and advise hard-working fellow-creatures to
> take the pledge ? "

Another apologist boldly claims that abstention from
alcohol does not tend to race culture, does not produce
a dominant race ; and instances the Scotch who dominate
Great Britain, the Irish who dominate America, and the
Jews (who have never been a nation of teetotalers) who
dominate the policy of civilisation.   This writer laments
the " drab propriety of abstention," and says the world
is duller to-day than in " the old days of (drinking)
freedom."

The line of progress generally proceeds from cure to
prevention.   The earliest recorded movement towards
drinking reform was the institution of the Order of
Temperance, by the Landgrave of Hesse, December 25,
1600.   The rules of this Order cannot be regarded as
very stringent, for members merely undertook not to

drink more than seven glasses of alcoholic liquor at one time, and that not oftener than twice a day. Seventy years later, our English philosopher, Hobbes, whose ethical system ranks with that of Bacon and Locke, evidently thought himself a miracle of moderation when he boasted he had "not been drunk above a hundred times" in the whole of his long life.

Even two centuries ago the prevailing vice of drunkenness had evidently forced itself on the public notice ; for a composition of 1,500 lines was recently discovered in an old book (from which these few have been selected as a fair sample of the whole), the earliest of teetotal poems known :—

THE DRUNKARD'S PROSPECTIVE, OR BURNING GLASSE.

Composed by Joseph Rigbie, Gentleman, Clerke of the Peace of the
County Palatine of Lancaster.

London : Printed for the Author, and are to be sold at the Brazen
Serpent in St. Paul's Churchyard, 1656.

Drink beastiates the heart, and spoils the brains,
Exiles all reason, all good graces stains,
Infatuates judgement, understanding blinds,
Perverts the wits, and doth corrupt the minds.
It doth surprize the thoughts, and it doth all
The powers and faculties of soul enthrall.
    *   *   *   *   *
Drunkards for nothing that is good are fit,
In all the world of earth, the barens't bit,
Like to a dumb Jack in a virginall,
They have no voice in commonwealth at all.
They've no more use of them throughout the land,
Than Jeroboam had of his withered hand.
    *   *   *   *   *
Health out o' the body, wit out of the head,
Strength out o' th' joints, and every one to bed.
All money's out a purse ; drink out o' th' barrels,
Wife, children, out of doors, all into quarrels.
    *   *   *   *   *

To you churchwardens, constables, and others
That love the Lord, the Church, the State, your brothers,
Your selves, your sons, the people of the land,
Put forth against this sin your helping hand.
Help, help the Lord, the lawes, some ground to win,
Against I say, against this mighty sinne.

In the early part of the nineteenth century it was not an unknown incident for an intoxicated member of Parliament to attempt to address the House, when he was scarcely able to utter a word; even Cabinet Ministers of the period lie under this imputation. Such conduct was not considered disgraceful, till the era of temperance set in, when drunkenness among all classes of society began slowly to decline in the face of a newer and higher standard of morality.

It was in 1832 that a number of gentlemen of Preston formed themselves into a society pledged to abstain entirely from intoxicating liquors. There were many who urged that temperance did not mean total abstinence, but one of the members created a new and famous word when he declared that half-and-half measures were of no use, that "nothing but te-te-total would do." This is claimed to have been the origin of the term "teetotaler."

Since that time the progress of temperance has been remarkable, though it might certainly have been greater had it been promoted with more discretion, with a truer insight into the temperamental qualities of the English people.

Mr. G. K. Chesterton, in declaring that the English democracy cannot claim to repose on a basis of sobriety, recently said :—

"We are justly renowned throughout the world as the one specially and almost permanently drunken nation. If we suggest that we are more sober than Frenchmen we might really just as well say that we are more musical than Germans."

One of the chief obstacles to temperance, according to a speech recently delivered in the House of Commons, is "the extraordinary nastiness of temperance drinks." Instead of direct repressive measures, a speaker advocated legislation for encouraging the consumption of light alcoholic liquids, such as thin claret and hock, or lager and light beers. The so-called temperance beverages never do compare favourably with grape or malt liquids, in palatability and general acceptableness, while such mixtures as "lemon-squash" and "soda-and-milk" miserably fail to harmonise as table drinks with a solid meal of any pretensions. While rigid teetotalers always seem frightened to admit the use, even to others, of alcoholic beverages of light strength, it is curious to observe that the most popular and perhaps the most palatable of temperance drinks contain an appreciable percentage of alcohol. This is the brewed "stone beer" —a ginger-beer, the palatable qualities of which are obtained by the fermenation of sugar. The *Lancet* has examined samples of stone beer very popular among teetotalers, which proved to contain more alcohol than light beer, and very nearly as much as is contained in good cider. As the *Lancet* says, in deciding on what may or may not be drunk, it would seem to be a question of nomenclature with some people. "Some teetotalers in their innocence, while aghast at the idea of drinking a light hock or claret, do not object to ginger-wine, which relatively is highly alcoholic."

Artemus Ward said, "I prefer temperance hotels— although they sell worse liquor than any other kind of hotels." But then we may incline to believe "this was rote Sarcastikul."

XVI

SOME MYSTERIES OF THE DRINKING CULT

Drinking terms imported from the Netherlands—" Half-seas-over "
—" Upsee Dutch "—" Upsee freeze," &c., &c.—*Super nagulum*
—Carousals—Hooped pots—The vocabulary of drink—extensive in the sixteenth century—Later examples—University
slang—Other drinking colloquialisms—Five reasons for drinking—Degrees of drunkenness—The seven stages of drunkenness
—A modern expert's division into five stages—Degrees of
drunkenness expressed by similes—Gascoigne's quaint com-
parisons (1576)—Antidotes to intoxication—And provocatives
of thirst—" Shoeing-horns " and other " pullers-on "—Robert
Greene's inglorious death—" Flap-dragons," the last resort of
the toper.

A TOWN wit of Elizabeth's reign—one Tom Nash, in his
" Pierce Pennilesse "—gives the same origin as Camden
for the national habit of drunkenness. "Superfluity in
drink," he says, " is a sin that ever since we have mixed
ourselves with the Low Countries is counted honourable ;
but before we knew their lingering wars, was held in the
highest degree of hatred. Then, if we had seen a man
wallowing in the streets we should have spet at him."
  This imported folly of hard drinking introduced a
variety of modes and customs, freaks and extravagances,
and enough technical language, to raise it almost to an
art. It was against this bestial indulgence, this national
drunkenness, that the numerous severe statutes passed in
the reign of James I. were aimed.

Drinking terms derived from Dutch, Danish, and German sources abounded in the language of the period. Some of them are interesting because met with in the literature of the time.

Half-seas-over, signifying " nearly drunk," is a phrase said to be derived from the maritime Dutch. *Op-zee*, in their language, means literally " over-sea," and was a name given to a stupefying beer introduced into England from the Low Countries. *Freezen*, in German, signifies to " swallow greedily." Thus, in Ben Jonson's *Alchemist*—

> " I do not like the dulness of your eye,
> It hath a heavy cast, 'tis *upsee Dutch*."

Another dramatist of the period, Fletcher, uses the term *upsee freeze* to signify " a tipsy draught," " a swallowing of liquor till drunk." Another commentator, while deriving this term from Frieseland beer, agrees that the meaning was " to drink swinishly like a Dutchman."

Our spirited Tom Nash in another passage discloses a few other mysteries of the drinking craft. " Now, he is nobody that cannot drink *super nagulum ; carouse* the hunter's *hoope ;* quaff *upse freze crosse ;* with *healths, gloves, mumpes, frolickes*, and a thousand such domineering inventions." For many of these terms of jollity we are indebted to the Danes, and some of them need rather elaborate explanation — " healths," " frolickes," and " mumpes," however, being good English, the last-named meaning grimaces.

Super nagulum literally means " on the nail," and relates to the custom of turning upside down the cup, from which the drinker has quaffed the whole contents, to make a pearl, with the last drop left in the vessel, upon his thumb-nail; if more than a spot remained the drinker was to drink again as a penance. In the observance of this Bacchic freak the cry of the challenger

would be, " Supernaculum, supernaculum !" A drinking
ceremony embodying the same idea, was that in which
the host filled a silver cup to the brim, held it
towards the guest sitting next him, and desired him
to take off the cover and assure himself that the cup was
quite full, before drinking the health of the company.
Each guest in turn went through the same ceremony,
emptying the cup and inverting it, placing the edge upon
his thumb-nail to prove he had swallowed every drop ;
any defaulter having to fill the cup again and drink it off
a second time.

Carouse and *rouse* are terms derived from the Danes.
A rouse was a large glass, in which a health was given,
the drinking of which by the rest of the company formed
a carouse.   There could be no carouse unless the glasses
were emptied ; and though we have lost the terms we
have not lost the practice, as we are reminded in the
time-honoured call of the chairman of a present-day
banquet, " Gentlemen, charge your glasses !"

The " hunter's hoop" alludes to the practice of marking a drinking-pot with hoops by which each successive
drinker could measure his draught.   The practice would
seem to be very much older than the Protestant Wars.
Does not that Shakespearean demagogue, Jack Cade,
promise his supporters furious reformation in this direction ?   "There shall be in England," he exclaims, "seven
halfpenny loaves sold for a penny ; the three-hooped pot
shall have ten hoops ; and I will make it felony to drink
small beer."

In the sixteenth century a seasoned and practised
tippler was hailed as "a good fellow," "a boon companion," "a mad Greek," "a true Trojan," "a stiff
blade," "one that is steel to the back," "a Low Country
soldier," "one who drinks deep though it be a mile to
the bottom," " one that knows how the cards are dealt,"

" one that will be aflush of all four," " one that bears up stiff," " one whom the brewer's horse hath bit," " one that drinks upsefreeze," " one that lays down his ears and drinks," and so on, and so on ; as a lively wit and a fecund fancifulness inspired. "Ale-knight" is perhaps one of the oldest of these nicknames. When old " Sir John Sack-and-Sugar " compares himself to a brewer's horse (i *Henry IV.*, act iii. scene 2), he no doubt has in his mind the slang phrase about being bitten by a brewer's horse. The language is certainly more appropriate to the period than the many allusions to Sack—which seems to have been an anachronism, and perhaps an intentional one, on Shakespeare's part.

The vocabulary of conviviality is extensive, and does infinite credit to the inventiveness of the band of good fellows to whom we are indebted for this great wealth of figurative language. One who is intoxicated is said to be fuddled or flustered ; tipsy, top-heavy, or boozy ; to be chockfull or pot valiant ; in drink, or in his cups ; to be elevated or overtaken ; under the table, or in a merry pin ; to be a little in the suds, or in a quandary. At Oxford he is said to be cup-sprung, or if he has taken liquor till it seems to run out of his eyes in tears, to be maudlin—which is allusive to Magdalen the Penitent. At Cambridge the affected one is said to have business on both sides of the street, or to be unable to sport a right line. The sailor says of him that he is groggy, or breezy ; that he is slewed (in his hammock) or cast away (if dead drunk) ; that he heels a little (as a boat in a rough sea), or has been in a storm. With the sportsman the obfuscated individual is winged, or has got a spur in his head ; he shows his hobnails, or he chases geese. Among other phrases expressive of the same idea, and common to all classes, are those which tell that the drunken person sees double, or cannot see a hole through a ladder ; that he has had a drop too much, or (in a phrase of more recent coinage) that he has copped the brewer. These few specimens by no means exhaust the list of equivalent colloquialisms.

"There are five reasons why men drink," says Dean Aldrich—

> "Good wine, a friend, or being dry ;
> Or lest you should be by-and-by ;
> Or any other reason why."

We all know the old rule :—

> "Not drunk is he who from the floor
> Can rise again and still drink more,
> But drunk is he who prostrate lies,
> Without the power to drink or rise."

Seven stages in the state of drunkenness have been noted and commented upon by a certain London police-court magistrate, who is as well known for his wit and the keenness of his observation as for his common-sense judgments.

First, says our authority, is the " Perky " period ; then comes the Irritable succeeded by the Mellow ; then alternate the Pugnacious with the Affectionate ; sixthly comes the Lachrymose, and finally the Collapse.

Commenting upon this the *British Medical Journal* said :—

" Dr. Magnan, who was one of the first to begin the scientific study of the physiological action of alcohol, distinguished five stages : First, slight excitement and a feeling of well-being, in which speech and gestures became more animated ; in the second stage ideas become crowded together and confused, the mood being, without any very obvious reason for the difference, gay, or sad, or full of tender emotion ; in the third stage the confusion of ideas was greater, and accompanied by incoherence, perversion of taste and smell, illusions, thick speech, vacant countenance, and stagger-ing gait ; the fourth stage was coma, and the fifth death."

If the degree of inebriation needs to be indicated colloquially he is three sheets in the wind; he may be as drunk as an owl or as drunk as a pig; as drunk as a beggar or as drunk as a lord, as drunk as a piper or as drunk as a fiddler, or again as drunk as a tinker; he may be as fuddled as a ape, as merry as a grig, or as happy as a king.

A curious treatise was written by "George Gascoigne, Esquier," in 1576, to prove "all dronkardes are beasts"; and his contemporary, the satirist Nash, has left a fanciful sketch very similar in its humour.

"The first is *ape-drunk*, and he leaps and sings and hollows and danceth for the heavens; the second is *lyon-drunk*, and he flings the pots about the house, calles the hostess w——e, breaks the glass windows with his dagger, and is apt to quarrel with any man that speaks to him; the third is *swine-drunk*, heavy, lumpish and sleepy, and cries for a little more drink and a few more clothes; the fourth is *sheep-drunk*, wise in his own conceit when he cannot bring forth a right word; the fifth is *maudlin-drunk*, when a fellow will weep for kindness in the midst of his drink, and kiss you, saying, "By God, Captain, I love thee; go thy ways; thou dost not think so often of me as I do of thee," and then he puts his finger in his eye and cries. The sixth is *martin-drunk*, when a man is drunk, and drinks himself so sober ere he stir; the seventh is *goat-drunk*, when in his drunkenness he hath no mind but on lechery. The eighth is *fox-drunk*, when he is crafty drunk, as many of the Dutchmen be, which will never bargain but when they are drunk."

On the frontispiece of this old work the beast-drunkards are represented as men with the heads of apes, swine, and so on.

Antidotes to intoxication and provocatives of thirst have been employed from the earliest days of civilisation Horace informs us that—

"Stew'd shrimps and Afric cockles shall excite
The jaded drinker's languid appetite."

Says the inimitable " Ingoldsby " :—

> "We bore him home and put him to bed
> And we told his wife and daughter
> To give him, next morning, a couple of red
> Herrings, with soda-water."

Shoeing-horns, sometimes called *gloves*, were the means resorted to for renewing or increasing a toper's waning thirst. Says Bishop Hall in " Mundus alter et idem " : " Then, sir, comes up a service of shoeing-horns of all sorts; salt cakes, red herrings, anchovies, and gammon of bacon, and abundance of such pullers-on." It was through a surfeit of Rhenish and pickled herrings and such-like shoeing-horns or drawers-on, as these incitements to appetite were called, that Robert Greene, the Elizabethan dramatist and congenial wit, lost his life so ingloriously.

Curious contrivances for exciting the flagging efforts of the accomplished bibber of olden days were *flap-dragons*, small combustible bodies fired at one end and floated in a glass of liquor, which an experienced toper deftly swallowed unharmed while it was yet blazing. Falstaff in describing Poins's dexterity in ingratiating himself with the prince, says that, " he drinks off candle-ends for flap-dragons." Beaumont and Fletcher in " Monsieur Thomas " have—

> "Carouse her health in cans
> And candle's ends."

Shakespeare again in *Love's Labour Lost* says—

> "Thou art easier swallow'd than a flap-dragon."

Surely a display of dexterity and prowess in the manipulation of flap-dragons was the *dernier ressort* of the accomplished boozer.

XVII

OLD TAVERN LIFE

Attractions of the tavern—The various reasons for resorting thereto
—How social history is reflected in old tavern life—Taverns the
meeting-ground for wits, poets, and other old-time literary
heroes—The Shakespeare tavern-haunting legend—" Drunken
Bidford "—Robert Greene's drunken end—Celebrated taverns
of Shakespeare's time—The Mermaid Club—Milton outside the
tavern influence—Ben Jonson—At the " Mermaid "—At the
Devil's Tavern—Influence of tavern life on English literature—
Tavern life frowned down by the Puritans—Revived at the
Restoration—Taverns used for business transactions—Literary
allusions and associations — Steele, Coleridge, and Lamb—
Dickens and Forster—Thackeray, Wilkie Collins, Edmund
Yates, and other recent writers of Bohemian habits.

A TAVERN (says an old writer), "is a common consumption of the afternoon and the murderer or making away of a rainy day. To give you the total reckoning of it, it is the busy man's recreation, the idle man's business, the melancholy man's sanctuary, the stranger's welcome, the scholar's kindness, and the citizen's country. It is the study of sparkling wits, and a cup of canary their book" —which last sentence shows that the term "tavern" was once equivalent to wine-shop, a fact to be kept steadily in mind. The rule, however, was not universal; in mediæval times, though ale was the beverage of the household, the "Good Wyf taughte her Daughter" that "she must not visit the tavern" (here meaning an ale-house), and that always she was to partake "measurably" of the good ale.

A large field for the study of national manners is opened out by the tavern life of old London ; for these public resorts were the recognised rendezvous of politicians and traders, they were the only places of convenient sojourn and pleasant sociality.

The taverns of old England have played no unimportant part in the social history of the country ; they were the meeting-places of poets and wits from the days of Shakespeare to those of Addison and Johnson ; and, says a recent writer on the subject, English literature to-day would be all the poorer if it had missed the sayings and writings inspired by the "flowing bowl" at such gatherings. "The flow of soul and the feast of reason" which characterised some of those convivial meetings of our greatest literary heroes constituted a phase of English tavern life which has left an indelible mark on the literary history of the English people. "A tavern," says another authority, "is a rendezvous, the exchange, the staple of good fellows."

Was not the immortal Shakespeare traditionally reckoned among the pot-house roysterers ? Does not the old doggrel of the period inform us how he attended the fairs, the Church Ales, and all the merrymakings at the neighbouring villages around Stratford-on-Avon ? —The local Shakespearean legend is to the effect that in the days of Good Queen Bess the small Warwickshire town of Bidford possessed two teams of drinkers, the first team being called the topers and the second the sippers, both remarkable for their prowess in the drinking contests of those days. A team from Stratford, in which Shakespeare was included, journeyed to Bidford to challenge the topers. The topers had gone to Evesham, but the sippers offered to defend the honour of the little

town, and they easily defeated the Stratfordians, who
made for home, but were forced to spend the night
under a crab-tree a mile outside Bidford. In the morning some were for returning to the charge, but Shakespeare said he had had enough, the sequel to it all being
the epigram : " I have drunk with

> " Piping Pebworth, Dancing Marston,
> Haunted Hillborough, Hungry Grafton ;
> Dodging Exhall, Papist Wixford
> Beggarly Broom, and Drunken Bidford."

It is a well-known tradition that the crab-tree when
cut down served to supply mementos of Shakespeare in
the shape of snuff-boxes and other articles. The Falcon
Inn at Bidford is claimed as the scene of these legendary
drinking bouts. Robert Greene also, the talented but unhappy dramatist, could not keep away from the ale-
houses and the drinking-booths, and died from his
excesses in 1592.

In the time of Shakespeare, the places principally
honoured by genius were the Sun and Moon Tavern,
in Aldersgate Street ; the Devil Tavern in Fleet Street,
close to Temple Bar ; and the famous one called the
" Mermaid," which was situated in Cornhill.
There, as Beaumont tells us—

> " Hath been shown,
> Wit able enough to justify the town
> For three days past—wit that might warrant
> For the whole city to talk foolishly
> Till that were cancelled ; and when that was gone,
> We left an air behind us, which alone
> Was able to make the two next companies
> Right witty ; though but downright fools, more wise."

The celebrated club at the " Mermaid," originated with
Sir Walter Raleigh ; and, as that eminent man of letters,
William Gifford, has truly observed, " combined more

talents and genius, perhaps, than ever met with, before
or since." Here, for many years, regularly repaired
Shakespeare, Ben Jonson, Beaumont, Fletcher, Selden,
Cotton, Carew, Martin, Donne, and many others, whose
names, even at this distant period call up a mingled feeling of reverence and respect. Here, in the full flow and
confidence of friendship the lively and interesting " wit
combats " as Fuller calls them, took place between
Shakespeare and Jonson ; and hither, in probable allusion
to them, Beaumont let his thoughts wander, in his letter
to Jonson, from the country :—

> " What things have we seen
> Done at the Mermaid ! heard words that have been
> So nimble, and so full of subtle flame,
> As if that every one from whom they came,
> Had meant to put his whole wit in jest," &c.

There were temperamental reasons why the great
Puritan poet would not have been found among this
tavern-haunting crew, even supposing he had been
precisely contemporaneous with them. But though
Milton was quite a small boy when Shakespeare was a
frequenter of the Mermaid Tavern, a meeting between
the two poets was not altogether impossible. John
Milton lived with his parents, close by the tavern, in
Bread Street ; and a conjectural encounter has been
thus surmised by Professor Masson :—

"Any time between 1608 and 1614, while Milton was a child,
we may fancy those meetings going on close to his father's house, at
which, over a board covered with cups of Canary, and in a room
well filled, surely, with tobacco-smoke, the seated gods exchanged
their flashes. Nay, and if we will imagine the precise amount of
personal contact that there was or could have been between
Shakespeare and our poet, how else can we do so but by supposing that, in that very year 1614 when the dramatist paid his last
known visit to London, he may have spent an evening with his old

THE OLD COURT YARD, SARACEN'S HEAD HOTEL, SOUTHWELL.

PUBLISHED BY HOWARD BARRETT, SOUTHWELL

Photo, Howard Barrett]

COURTYARD OF THE "SARACEN'S HEAD," SOUTHWELL.

[Southwell.

[Page 226.

"THE FEATHERS," LUDLOW.

[*Page* 226.

comrades at the Mermaid, and, going down Bread Street with Ben Jonson on his way, may have passed a fair child of six playing at his father's door, and, looking down at him kindly, have thought of a little grave in Stratford Churchyard and the face of his own dead Hamnet?"

The sallies of the wit combatants are not unfrequently placed on record by their admiring auditors. Jonson confesses he kept a note-book, in which he regularly entered every good thing he heard, with a view to future use. Some repartees there are on record, which are said to have been launched at the "Mermaid"; but none of them have the least pretension to the character of wit; and the authenticity of the whole is most doubtful. One example may suffice : "Mr. Ben Jonson and Mr. William Shakespeare being merrie at a tavern, Mr. Jonson begins this for his epitaph—

> "Here lies Ben Jonson,
> Who was once one——"

He gives it to Mr. Shakespeare to make up, who presently writ—

> "That while he lived was a slow thing,
> And now, being dead, is nothing."

This lacks the true ring, certainly.

The Devil's Tavern, near Temple Bar, has been immortalised by Ben Jonson, who wrote his "Leges Conviviales" for a club of wits that assembled in its chief room, an apartment he dedicated to Apollo, and over the chimney-piece of which the laws of the club were preserved. As an example of the extent to which tavern life has influenced literature, here are a few extracts from an old manuscript of the poet, preserved at Dulwich College.

"Mem.—I laid the plot of my *Volpone* and wrote most of it, after a present of ten dozen of palm sack from my very good lord T—— ;

that play I am positive will last to posterity and be acted when I and envy be friends, with applause."

"MEM.—The first speech in my *Cataline,* spoken by Sylla's ghost, was writ after I parted with my friends at the Devil's Tavern ; I had drank well that night, and had brave notions. There is one scene in that play which I think is flat—I resolve to drink no more water in my wine."

"MEM.—Upon the 20th May the King (heaven reward him) sent me a hundred pounds. At that time I went oftentimes to the Devil ; and before I had spent forty of it, wrote my *Alchymist.*"

"MEM.—*The Devil an Asse,* the *Tale of a Tub,* and some other comedies which did not succeed (written by me) ; in the winter honest Ralph died ; when I and my boys drank bad wine at the Devil."

Ben Jonson candidly confesses he owes some inspiration to the wine and conviviality of the tavern.

Among other well-frequented taverns of the Metropolis of Tudor times few were more renowned than the " White Rose " (the symbol of the York party) in Old Palace Yard, Westminster, which stood near the chapel of our Lady, behind the high altar of the abbey church.

The gloomy manners of Puritanism gave a severe check to these temples of jollity ; but the restoration of Charles again revived their popularity. The cavaliers and adherents of the Royal party, for joy of that event, were, for a time, incessantly drunk ; and from a picture of their manners, in Cowley's comedy of *The Cutter of Coleman Street,* it may be collected that taverns were places of much more frequent resort than churches and conventicles. When the frenzy of the times was, however, abated, taverns, especially those in the City, became places for the transaction of almost all descriptions of business. There accounts were settled, conveyances executed ; and there attorneys sat, as at inns in the country on market-days, to receive their clients. In the space near the Royal Exchange, which is encumbered by Lombard, Gracechurch, part of Bishopsgate, and Thread-needle Streets, the number of taverns exceeded twenty ; and on the site of the Bank there stood no less than four. At the "Crown," which was one of them, it was not unusual, in the course of a single morning, to draw a "butt of mountain" (120 gallons) in gills.

How much taverns were frequented by the *literati* in the early part of the eighteenth century, the *Spectator*, the *Tatler*, and other British essayists, bear abundant evidence ; and there is little doubt but many of these papers were produced at a tavern, or originated at the "wit combats" that frequently took place within the walls of such.

Although Sir Richard Steele was extravagant in his uxoriousness, yet who has not admired that passage in one of his letters to his wife, written from a tavern, in which he assures her that he will be with her "within half a bottle of wine " ?

By the close of the eighteenth century, when boxing and pugilism had taken so remarkably a firm hold on the sporting section of the community, many taverns became the recognised resorts of the fighting fraternity, among whom there was no higher hall-mark of good-fellowship than a pair of black eyes. Not the least famous of these resorts was the Castle Tavern (known later as the Napier Tavern) in Holborn. It was kept by a succession of well-known heroes of the prize-ring— Belcher, Tom Cribb, and Tom Spring—and till its demolition in quite recent times, the marks were shown on the floor of the " back parlour " where the ring-posts used to be set up for the pugilistic encounters for which the house was once so famous.

Dr. Robert Farquharson, writing in *Blackwood's Magazine* of June, 1892, says :—

"We may be certain that Coleridge and Lamb did not toil up Hampstead Hill to drink water at the ' Salutation ' and ' Cat,' and the merry coffee-housing of the club was mellowed by potations which stimulated the talk of Burke and Goldsmith and the appreciation of Reynolds.

"We see Dickens and Forster and Stanfield and Maclise at their early dinners before the play, or at their suppers after the curtain fell, and we know that there was just enough liquor among them to warm, but not heat, and to set their tongues going with free but decorous elasticity."

Tavern life in its latest and final phase was not unknown to Charles Dickens. One of his finest characters, Charles Darnay, is said to have been founded on a real personage whom he met, in the crowded life of London, at "The Grotto"—a clever writer of Bohemian habits named Whitehead, who haunted that resort in the "forties."

Another famous night haunt at that time was the Cider Cellars in Maiden Lane, frequented by the fast young "swells" of the City and the West End after the theatres were closed ; rivalling as a place of low, if not immoral, resort, the "Coal Hole" in Drury Lane, and the notorious "Judge and Jury." The Cider Cellar is still to be found, and its spacious and fine saloon, little changed from its old form, is let for concerts and entertainments.

"In the same building," says Mr. J. Ashby-Sterry, "was at one time a notable institution, namely, the Fielding Club (which must not be confused with another short-lived but select circle of modern times in King Street, bearing the same name), whereat Thackeray, Albert Smith, W. H. Russell, Wilkie Collins, Beverley, Shirley Brooks, Edmund Yates, Peter Cunningham, John Leech, Leigh Murray, Robert Keeley, Benjamin Webster, and other notable people of that time used to assemble of an evening and frequently remain until the small hours."

The tavern life of old London opens a large field for the study of our national manners and customs ; more than mere places of sojourn for travellers and traders, they became the rendezvous of politicians and publicists,

the recognised meeting-places for much social intercourse, and especially for that pleasant form of sociability
which is accompanied by friendly entertainment. How
useful they were in the days when travelling was difficult
and newspapers scarce, and all means of intercom-
munication were correspondingly slow, is indicated by
the extraordinary number of taverns with which the
main thoroughfares of old London were lined.

XVIII

THE OLD-TIME POPULARITY OF INNS

"Inns" in figurative language—An "inn" defined—Its uses specified
—A public-house found near to every church !—The wayside inn
—A place for rest and refreshment—Always necessary in the
days of the pack-horse—and the stage-wagon—Inn-yards—The
necessity for stabling in olden times—The "ostler" also indispensable—Roads turnpiked—Fast mail-coaches introduced (1784)
—From post-boys to mail guards—Coach-yards—"Putting to"
the horses—The coachman and his whip—The guard and his
horn—The "laws" of the inn-yard—Coach-yard scenes of
animation and bustle—Mr. Alfred Jingle's anecdote of an archway tragedy—The yard of the "White Hart" described by
Dickens—Advent of the railway hotel—Revival of the wayside
inns by cycling and motoring—"Bait and Livery Stables."

IN Dryden's time everybody who travelled used inns, for
travelling was impossible without them. Hence the poet's
figure of speech in the line—

"The world's an inn, and death the journey's end."

The use of inns has even entered into the imagery of
the epitaph writer, as thus at Richmond in Yorkshire an
epitaph on an infant runs—

"Into this world as strangers to an inn
    This infant came, guest-wise ;
Where, when 't had been and found no entertainment
    worth her stay,
    She only broke her fast and went away."

180

The Act passed in the first year of James I. (1603) defined "the antient, true, and principal use of inns, ale-houses, and victualling houses" to be for the "resort, relief, and lodging of wayfaring people, travelling from place to place, and for such supply of the wants of such people as are not able by greater quantities to make provision of victual." The preamble then proceeds to lay down that such inns "are not meant for entertainment and harbouring of lewd idle people, to spend and consume their time and their money in lewd and drunken manner."

Every one has heard the old gibe about the village inn being close to the church, and that the thirsty wayfarer in search of a place whereat to quench his thirst has only to look out for the nearest steeple. There is much truth in the scoff. The old inn and the weather-beaten church often enough stand close together on the village green, while some village inns stand almost within the churchyard ; and at such public-houses not only did "ringers" or "singers" of a bygone generation obtain surreptitious drinks during divine service, but at not a few of them vestry meetings and other official gatherings of the congregation were commonly held as a mere matter of course.

In England the public-house is as universal as the place of worship ; and under healthy conditions is a natural and a useful institution.

These old inns gave a relish to travel ; the stoppages made at them for the reasonable refreshment of man and horse were always pleasurable interludes in the journey ; and not unfrequently the welcome of the cheery host amidst novel and pleasant surroundings made the traveller almost forget the comforts of home.

This was the heyday of the English inn. The roads were then good. But previous to this era, when the lumbering stage-wagon and the carrier's van monopolised the roads—which they did for almost two centuries, in succession to the pack-horse of the unbeaten, unstraightened, and often unlevelled bridle-path—the wayside inn was but a rude kind of halting-place, and generally comfortless in its sleeping accommodation if not in all other respects.

Notwithstanding this, if the old ballad is to be believed, one could make himself jolly in an old wayside inn.

"When first I went a-waggoning, a-waggoning did go,
I filled my parents' hearts with grief, with sorrow and with woe,
And many are the hardships that I have since gone thro',
    And say wo, my lads, say wo !
    Drive on, my lads, heigh-ho !
And who won't lead the merry life we jolly waggoners do ?

It is a cold and stormy night, I'm wetted to the skin,
But I'll bear it with contentment until I reach the inn,
And then I'll get a drinking with the landlord and his kin,
    And say," &c.

The inn-yards assumed greater importance when wheeled vehicles took the place of pack-horses for road traffic ; and they were further improved both as regards accommodation and security when the roads were turn-piked and made fit for the fast coaches which superseded the old slow coaches and carriers' wagons.

Till a century ago, or less, travelling was very different from what it is now. Long journeys on horseback, in post-chaises, or in stage-coaches, all had a smack of the open air in them, involved a certain measure of hardi-hood, and occasionally were not without a spice of adventure and romance. That was the time when the old English hostel of the superior kind, with its solid comforts, its old English cheer, dispensed by a genial landlord of the ideal John Bull type, was truly a national institution.

In the times when all travelling that was not done afoot was accomplished on horseback, the yard with its stabling was an adjunct indispensable to every inn on the road. "As soon as a passenger comes to an inn," says an old writer, "the servants run to him, and one takes his horse and walks him till he be cold, then rubs him, and gives him meate—while another servant gives the passenger his private chamber"—and so both man and beast were properly cared for at every well-regulated inn. That humble functionary, the ostler, was then indispensable to the traveller.

The word "ostler" was derived by Dr. Johnson from the French *hostelier*, which signified the host of the inn or hostel, and not the ostler or stableman. This use of the term, it will be seen, came from the time before people travelled in carriages, and when the innkeeper was required not only to tend his guests, but to take care of their horses, and when, therefore, the "hosteller" was actually the horse-keeper as well as the host. The wits have derived ostler from "oat stealer!"

When a road was turnpiked, inns sprang up along its route almost as a matter of course. And inns played a very important part in the evolution of the mails. Not till 1784 did the condition of the roads permit the introduction of the fast mail-coach, as distinct from the older and much slower stage-coach; previous to this the mails had been carried by post-boys, the "boys" often enough being men of fifty or sixty years of age. Mounted on ponies, these weather-beaten messengers jogged along the roads as fast as their animals would carry them, always as ready for the snug welcome of an inn fire as their jaded beasts were for the warm stable; the post-office generally being a stable as well, the term "post-master" often bearing a double significance.

The coming of the fast coach, with its scarlet-coated

mail guard, gave that impetus which raised the status of the better class of inn, as previously described. There were a number of celebrated houses along every main coach-road ; and a ballad, or more correctly a popular song of the period, entitled " The Mail Coach Guard," introduced the names of all the famous coaching inns, very cleverly hitting off the propensities of the mail guards for carrying gossip as well as news.

Where could have been found a finer or more typical specimen of the old coaching-house than the " Bull and Mouth " in Aldersgate Street ?

The scene presented by a coach-yard in full activity was always an animated and interesting one. The coach, a handsome, well-built vehicle, in all the brilliancy of a highly-varnished claret ground, or it may be of bright yellow, when ready, would stand well in the middle of the drive. The four beautiful, spirited animals attached to it, with their glossy, velvety skins, covered with cloths till the moment of "putting to," would be under the charge of two stablemen in corduroy breeches and heavy boots—men typical of "Robin Ostler," with slouching gait, the complexion of dried rosy apples, and rasping voices such as men get by habitually talking to horses through their teeth. Then the coachman, mounted on the box, getting his whip and his ribbons adjusted exactly to his mind. He is well buttoned up to the throat in an enormous box-coat of whitish drab colour, fastened with immense mother-o'-pearl buttons ; and having muffled round his neck a red silk handkerchief, reaching up to his nether lip and covering well the tips of his ears. There is a rakish brim to his hat, which goes well with the air of nonchalance he affects—for is he not the skipper, as it were, not only in command of the gallant equipage, but controlling, for the time at least, the destiny of all his passengers ? To see him gather up the reins in that leisurely, masterful way, as he signals the ostlers to "give 'em their head," is to inspire confidence in every breast. And when the impatient animals are released, clear the gateway in a few brisk steps, and break into a good round pace immediately they turn on to the road, every one feels as the coach bowls away to the lively tooting of the guard's horn, that they have assisted at one of the day's "events." Such were the daily scenes in a busy inn-yard during the coaching period, which after all was a brief one, in the long history of travel.

A taking sign to hang out when stage-coaches and post-chaises were in vogue was—

> "In this tavern you may find
> Everything to suit your mind—
> Good wine, good fish, and flesh in courses;
> Coaches, chaises, harness, horses."

The inn-yard was by no means an unimportant part of the establishment, and still observed the code of rules which had come down through generations of hosts and ostlers. It can readily be understood that the "laws of the inn-yard" would call, among other things, for protection against fire, and the preservation of the purity of the household water-supply. In fact the rules started off with enumerating the forfeits imposed on any who "dabbled the water cistern" or "carried lighted candles about the stables"—and so on.

But while that period lasted, the yard of a coaching-house was always interesting if not picturesque. At many hours of the day, as in a modern railway station, it was a scene of animation and bustle, with the arrival and departure of each coach that used it. Typical of its kind was that of the "Golden Cross" in the Strand, the great coaching-house from which the illustrious Pickwickians, in company with their newly-made acquaintance, Mr. Jingle, started that bright May morning

in 1827, by the Commodore coach, for Rochester. It
had the usual low archway over the entrance, against
which Mr. J. kindly cautioned the passengers when
they started—" Heads ! Heads ! Take care of your
heads ! "—after which that voluble and irrepressible
gentleman proceeded to relate the tragic episode of the
" head of the family " being removed "through unfortunately forgetting the arch." . . . " Dangerous work
—other day—five children—mother—tall lady eating
sandwiches—forgot the arch—crash—knock—children
looked round—mother's head off—sandwich in her
hand—no place to put it in—shocking ! shocking ! "
It was thus the talkative passenger would mark the
beginning and end of each stage, even when volubility
failed to beguile the tedium of the whole distance.

Here is Dickens's description of the yard of the
" White Hart," in Southwark, when the novelist first
introduces Sam Weller to our notice :—

" The yard presented none of that bustle and activity which are
the usual characteristics of a large coach inn. Three or four
lumbering wagons, each with a pile of goods beneath its ample
canopy, about the height of a second-floor window of an ordinary
house, were stowed away beneath a lofty roof, which extended over
one end of the yard ; and another, which was probably to com-
mence its journey that morning, was drawn out into the open
space. A double tier of bedroom galleries, with old clumsy
balustrades, ran round two sides of the straggling area, and a
double row of bells to correspond, sheltered from the weather
by a little sloping roof, hung over the door leading to the bar
and coffee-room. Two or three gigs and chaise-carts were wheeled
up under different little sheds and pent-houses ; and the occasional
heavy tread of a cart-horse, or rattling of a chain, at the further
end of the yard, announced to anybody who cared about the
matter that the stable lay in that direction. When we add that
a few boys in smock frocks were lying asleep on heavy packages,
woolpacks, and other articles that were scattered about on heaps
of straw, we have described as fully as need be the general
appearance of the yard."

This inn-yard may be regarded as typical of its class, and the verbal picture here given us of it is just as vivid as words can make it.

Then for upwards of another half-century after the extinction of the stage-coach and the post-chaise, the high-roads of the country were practically deserted, the wayside inn was neglected, and the once-flourishing posting-house languished till it fell gradually into decay. The railway hotel took the place of both.

A new era of prosperity for roadside inns and hotels with commodious yards is manifestly dawning with the ever-growing popularity of the pneumatic-tyred wheel. The bicycle begets thirst and the motor-car fills the mouth and the nostrils with dust; the house of call, particularly the one which offers garage accommodation as the old inns once provided stabling, promises to be in greater demand than ever.

There may occasionally be seen, even at the present day when the cycle and the motor-car have all but superseded the traveller on horseback or in horsed vehicle, on the walls of wayside inns, the once familiar legend, "Bait and Livery Stables." The word "bait" is derived from the Anglo-Saxon *bæton*, "to feed," and was used to designate a meal taken by travellers to refresh them on a journey. "Livery" is connected with the word *delivery*, and stood for the stabling accommodation to which a traveller delivered his horse. A passage in the writings of Edmund Spencer well illustrates this point. "What livery is we know well enough; it is the allowance of horse-meate to keep horses at livery; the which word, I guess, is derived from delivering forth their nightly food."

The use of the other word is well illustrated in the couplet from Jenyns:—

"A Fair, where thousands meet, but none can stay;
An Inn, where travellers bait, then post away."

IN PRAISE OF INNS

THE social status of the inn in the eighteenth century,
the position it then held in the estimation of the public,
is clearly indicated by that oft-quoted quatrain of the
poet Shenstone, which he is said to have scratched on
the window-pane of an inn at Henley. The " Red
Lion " at Henley-on-Thames has contended for the
honour of having inspired the verse, and at a recent
sale of the property it was announced that " the window
and record were still in existence "; but the famous
stanza was really written on the window of the " White
Swan " at Henley-in-Arden, which was not many miles
from the poet's home at Halesowen, near Birmingham.

Shenstone was not unknown in London, where his
favourite haunt was George's Coffee House, near

Temple Bar. Here is the whole poem "Written at
an Inn," of which the last stanza is by far the best
known :—

> "To thee, fair Freedom ! I retire,
>   From flattery, feasting, dice and din ;
> Nor art thou found in domes much higher
>   Than the lone cot or humble Inn.
>
> 'Tis here with boundless power I reign,
>   And every health which I begin,
> Converts dull port to bright champagne ;
>   For Freedom crowns it, at an Inn.
>
> I fly from pomp, I fly from plate,
>   I fly from falsehood's specious grin ;
> Freedom I love, and form I hate,
>   And choose my lodgings at an Inn.
>
> Here, waiter ! take my sordid ore,
>   Which lacqueys else might hope to win ;
> It buys what Courts have not in store,
>   It buys me Freedom, at an Inn.
>
> And now once more I shape my way
>   Through rain or shine, through thick or thin,
> Secure to meet, at close of day,
>   With kind reception at an Inn.
>
> *Whoe'er has travelled life's dull round,*
>   *Where'er his stages may have been,*
> *May sigh to think how oft he found*
>   *The warmest welcome—at an Inn."*

"He goes not out of his way who goes to a good
inn," says the proverb of our great-grandfathers' days.

How the Colonial of early times, in his new-made
country across the Atlantic, imitated the old English
inn, almost with a detail which bespoke his affection
for it, is eloquently told in the words of the American

poet. Longfellow's description of "The Wayside Inn"
begins :—

"One Autumn night, in Sudbury Town,
Across the meadows bare and brown
The windows of the wayside inn
Gleamed red with firelight through the leaves
Of woodbine hanging from the eaves,
Their crimson curtains rent and thin.
As ancient is this hostelry
As any in the land may be,
Built in the old Colonial days
When men lived in a grander way,
With ampler hospitality.
A kind of old Hobgoblin Hall,
Now somewhat fallen to decay,
With weather-stains upon the wall
And stairways worn, and crazy doors,
And creaking and uneven floors,
And chimneys huge and tiled and tall,
A region of repose, it seems
A place of slumber and of dreams,
Remote among the wooded hills !
Across the road the barns display
Their lines of stalls, their mows of hay ;
Through the wide doors the breezes blow ;
The wattled cocks strut to and fro ;
And, half effaced by rain and shine,
The Red Horse prances on the sign."

Some hundred years or more ago, Dr. Johnson, at
Chapel House, expatiated to Boswell "on the felicity of
England in taverns and inns, and triumphed over the
French for not having in any perfection the tavern life."
He dwelt on the independence of the place, the alacrity
of the attendance, the oblivion of care and freedom from
solicitude which he himself enjoyed whenever he entered
a tavern door.   "There is nothing," he concluded,
"which has yet been contrived by man by which so
much happiness has been produced as by a good tavern
or inn."

THE "FIGHTING COCKS," ST. ALBANS.

[Page 227.

NEW INN, GLOUCESTER.

[Page 228.

And when the tired traveller does take his ease within
the comfortable walls of the hospitable inn, he becomes
the undisputed monarch of all he surveys, arrayed in
slippered state, an armchair his throne, and the poker
his sceptre.

The whole secret of the success, the attractiveness
of the inn, is revealed in this panegyric of the "Great
Cham." The disclosure should remove from the minds
of many misguided persons the notion that men are
drawn to the public-houses primarily by a taste for
strong drink. This is a mistake too many would-be
reformers have made in the past and which some
continue to make. Men are mainly attracted to the
public-houses by the cheerfulness, light, and warmth
which are invariably offered there, and which too many of
the lower class miss at home ; by a longing for congenial
society, and by a desire to be free, if only for a little
while, from the pressure of domestic worries and daily
cares.

> "How oft doth man, by care oppressed,
> Find in an inn a place of rest!"

These simple wants are still met in some remote country
inns which, preserving the traditions of the past, leave
their guests to spend the evening over a single jug of
beer, if they so please ; but it is to be feared that in many
others, and certainly in the gin palaces of the towns, the
repeated order is the condition of a continued welcome.
This attitude of the management is betrayed by the
inhospitable seatless bar, specially designed for "perpendicular drinking."

In a work entitled, " As We Are and As We May Be,"
that great social reformer, the late Sir Walter Besant,
than whom no man was more intimately acquainted with
the working classes, has said of the modern public-

house, in its relationship to the daily lives of the people :—

"Perhaps the workman spends, night after night, more than he should upon beer. Let us remember, if he needs excuse, that his employers have found him no better place and no better amusement than to sit in a tavern, drink beer (generally in moderation), and talk and smoke tobacco. Why not? A respectable tavern is a very harmless place; the society which meets there is the society of the workman; it is his life; without it he might as well have been a factory hand of the good old time—such as hands were forty years ago; and then he should have made but two journeys a day—one from bed to mill, and the other from mill to bed."

Commodious hotels of a newer type, fitted with every up-to-date convenience, and adapted to all present-day requirements, have risen up in most large towns and places of resort, because they have become a necessity in an age of travel. The importance of a good hotel system in these day of touring clubs cannot be denied. Everywhere, as tourists and travellers, the home-loving English people are daily becoming more and more reconciled to hotel life and are no longer shy, as they once were, of eating in public.

But admirable as a good hotel system may be, there is something after all in the personality which directs the management of any house of public entertainment in which one has to make a temporary sojourn. A well-travelled Englishman has recently said, "A good inn-keeper is worth more than a big hotel. A prepossessing appearance, a cordial reception, is better than all the modern improvements of the big caravanserais, whose steam heat does not suffice to warm up the heart."

A magazine writer, treating the same subject, contrasts the inns of the old days with the hotels of the present day.

"The cosy inns of the coaching days—which went out about the middle of last century, and experienced a revival lately through

cyclist and motorist—with smiling host and hostess, blazing fires
and substantial good cheer, has developed in some cases into the
smart modern hotel, where one loses individuality, and becomes a
number, and where the telegraph and telephone and bustling ways
of modern life have killed old-fashioned leisure."

Yet a more recent writer, although treating of London
only, expresses himself with anything but tenderness for
the hotels the last generation of travellers had to put up
at—or with.   Describing the metropolitan hotels at the
"sixties" and "seventies," he says their disappearance
calls for but few regrets.   Notwithstanding the halo of
romance which Dickens had thrown over the country
inns of a few decades earlier, this writer declares the
London hotels of his own time were dingy and in reality
none too comfortable—but then he is obviously com-
paring them with the palatial and luxuriously appointed
hotels of the present day.

"An old-world air of quaintness certainly hung over them," says
our critic, " but this was poor compensation for the dinginess and
dirt which were its occasional concomitants.   The old-world
English waiter, too, though a character in his way, was, as a rule,
none too temperate ; whilst the rest of the staff was usually of a
somewhat happy-go-lucky disposition, more or less addicted to
tolerated inebriety.   Bath-rooms" (he continues), " such as abound
in modern hotels were, for the most part, non-existent ; and where
one did exist, it was usually of a none too efficient kind ; besides
which it was often the receptacle of brooms, mops, and the like
articles of domestic necessity."

In London the providing of a public midday dinner,
commonly known as an "ordinary," and so very
different from the French *table d'hôte*, never became
quite naturalised as it did in the country.   There was
till recent times a good ordinary at the "Saracen's Head"
in Snow Hill, at which the landlord presided ; and there
were the famous "fish dinners" at Billingsgate.   It was
more of a success in the suburbs among the retired City

tradesmen—such as had used the City chop-houses,
perhaps—and Goldsmith is recorded to have frequented
one of these. "There was a very good ordinary of two
dishes and a pastry, kept at this time at Highbury Barn,
at tenpence per head, including a penny for the waiter."
Which allusion to that venerable institution, the waiter's
tip, is not the least interesting item in this extract, which
is taken from Forster's Life of the poet.

A great change is now taking place in the character of
the accommodation provided at the larger hotels.   The
old-fashioned hotel drawing-room has long been without
occupants.   Modern ladies away from home dislike the
coldness and formality of a public drawing-room ; they
prefer to assemble with their men-folk, and so we now
have the hotel lounge, where the men may smoke—and
the ladies, too, may take their cigarettes, if they affect the
habit—while they enjoy each other's society, listen to
music, chat, take their coffee, or even receive their
visitors, under the most luxurious conditions that
modern furnishing permits of.   Another great change
the student of hotel life may observe in the commercial
houses.   When the commercial traveller was a power in
the land and railway facilities were much less than they
are now, compelling him to spend more nights as well as
days in hotels, the commercial-room of the hotel was
sacred to him.   He had the best of living at the cheapest
of rates, and a sort of divinity hedged him and his pre-
rogatives around in every well-conducted commercial
hotel.   His status was far above that of the ordinary
uncommercial traveller, who was relegated to the coffee-
room ; or who, if permitted within the sacred precincts
of the commercial-room, was graciously allowed to pay
for his share of the wine, whether he consumed any or
not, was expected to pay great deference to the chair—
occupied by a seniority calculated on length of stay in

the house—to contribute to various table collections, and altogether to feel the honour conferred by being permitted to sit at table in such august company. The " Commercial " of those days was a well-salaried man, with an allowance of thirty shillings a day for expenses, and he always sat down to a " wine dinner "—a pint of sherry to each man. But where is the old-fashioned commercial-room now ? At some establishments those old-time institutions, the " Bar " and the " Tap " are also being abolished ; and everywhere the employment of waiters, invariably looking out for tips, is becoming more universal.

This time-honoured inn custom of " tipping" has survived to modern hotels, restaurants, and tea-rooms ; has, in fact, become practically universal wherever guests or patrons have need to utilise the services of the under-paid staff of a caterer. The origin of the custom is said to be traceable to the practice in old coaching inns of having a money-box displayed on the sideboard of the chief guest-room for customers to drop in their gratuities intended for the servants. This box was labelled " To Insure Promptitude," the initials of these three words being always painted in large capitals and forming the word TIP. In Japan, where inn tariffs are exceedingly low by force of law, it is the practice to give the largest tip to the innkeeper himself !

XX

INNS AS PUBLIC INSTITUTIONS, AND SERVING MANY PUBLIC PURPOSES

Ancient inns serving as public institutions—The galleried inn-yard, the prototype of the tiered theatre—From "free and easy" to music-hall—Exhibitions held in inns—Daniel Lambert exhibited at a chop-house—Inns as museums—As sporting centres—And places of assembly for recreation—As homes of musical societies—The Cogers Debating Society—As homes of the Geological Club—Philosophical societies—And book clubs —As a printing and publishing office—As headquarters of the Friendly Societies—"Wet rents"—As political meeting-houses —Birmingham Jacobin and Anti-Jacobin taverns—The Priestley Riots—The Birmingham "Caucus"—Smoke-room politicians— Local government carried on at an inn—As meeting-places for conspirators and agitators—The Gunpowder Plot (1605)—The Revolution House (1688)—London Mug-houses—Inns as courts of law—Coroners' courts—Magistrates' courts—As prisons—At Greenwich—At Coventry—At Lewes—At Southwark—Inns as religious centres—The founding of the Swedenborgian Church —A Methodist Sunday School—And a mission service held on licensed premises—A commemoration feast by "The Merry Undertakers"—As a post-office—As a "cure-house"—The earliest proposal to municipalise public-houses (1662).

ONLY a few centuries ago the inn played many parts in the social economy of this country. In a more primitive state of society, when public buildings other than those devoted to ecclesiastical or military purposes were few and far between, the inn as a place of resort, as a common meeting ground open to the community at large, was used for a variety of public purposes. The theatre, with its tier of boxes, was an architectural arrangement copied from the old inn-yards, in which travelling mountebacks and strolling performers of all kinds were wont, four or five centuries ago, to give their shows in the presence of the inn guests assembled in the galleries which ran round the yard on every bedroom floor.

The ancient inns having the open courts with bed-chambers round them, gallery above gallery, are supposed to have been constructed in the Roman fashion. Specimens of this form of inn architecture were plentiful enough in London a century ago. There were the " Belle Sauvage " in Ludgate Hill, the " Saracen's Head " in Snow Hill, the " George " and the " Ram " in Smith-field, the " Swan with Two Necks," the " Green Dragon " in Bishopsgate Street, and others. Fragments of these spacious old hostelries remained latest in Aldgate, Holborn, and Southwark. In Southwark the " King's Head," the " Queen's Head," the " Catherine Wheel," and the " George " particularly deserve mention.

The music-hall is a direct product of the tavern. Before music licences had to be taken out numbers of public-houses in every part of the country utilised their large club-rooms for the holding of concerts on some regular evening in each week, every item of which was volunteered by members of the company present. Whether such meeting was called a " free-and-easy," or what not, it was usually under the direction of a sort of perpetual chairman, who was either the host himself or some regular *habitué* of the house with a talent for presiding at such convivial assemblages. He was generally a loud-voiced gentleman, and one not only quick to discern latent talent, but an autocrat to whom it could not be denied. And then the heartiness—or the loudness

—with which, at the conclusion of the novice's performance, he led the applause, was always in itself a sufficient
reward.

The intermediate stage, between the tavern "sing-song"
and the modern music-hall, arrived when the platform
came to be occupied by professional instead of amateur
performers ; but it was with the dominating presence of
the chairman still in the rostrum to announce the "turns"
in stentorian tones, and to hammer the applause at the
beginning and end of each effort. Members of the
audience if not then allowed to contribute to the har-
mony, always had the privilege of asking the chairman
to drink with them ; an honour he seldom refused—"for
the good of the house."

The use of licensed houses as exhibitions and show
places is still common enough. Bird Shows, Bird
Singing Contests, Pipe Smoking Competitions, Dog and
Poultry Shows, and similar exhibitions, although now
frowned upon by licensing authorities, have long been
held on licensed premises in some parts of the country.

The use of licensed premises for markets, exchanges,
and other forms of trading is an ancient one, and one
not altogether obsolete.

Adjacent to the entrance to Stationers Hall Court, in
London, is a doorway upon which few passers-by would
bestow a second glance. Through this door is a long
passage, at the end of which was to be found a roomy
old tavern with quaint corners, and originally known by
the sign of the " King's Head," at which time it was
a fashionable coffee and chop-house. At the beginning
of the nineteenth century the famous fat man, Daniel
Lambert, took up his lodgings at this house, and here he
held public receptions, at which visitors, for a modest
fee, might look upon his fifty-two stone of human flesh.
For years after Lambert had departed this life his portrait

in oils hung upon the tavern walls, and his walking-stick was also preserved as a curiosity. From that time this house, which had been used as his show place, became known as the " Daniel Lambert." Recently the premises of this once famous chop-house have been acquired by a well-known firm of caterers for a modern *café*, and the old portrait, put up at auction, fetched the sum of £5 10s.

The conversion of public-houses into "side shows" has been a very common practice during the past century; but under the stricter *régime* of the present day, licensing magistrates look upon it as a mere device to attract customers to drink, and a persistence in it would probably endanger the licence of the house.

Numbers of public-houses have acquired local fame as museums of antiquities, or museums of natural history specimens, or other collections. No doubt the primary object of these collections was to attract customers rather than visitors; but they were none the less useful or instructive on that account, being frequently the best-conducted houses in the neighbourhood, and the neighbourhood generally too poor to boast of, or hope for, publicly supported institutions of like character. At Wednesbury and at Birmingham respectively were " museum " taverns, which obtained the name because when first opened, their walls were lined with cases of stuffed birds and other trophies of the taxidermist's art. At Sutton Coldfield there was also a good public-house museum of natural history. But perhaps the best example of this type of licensed house was the " Black Horse," at Birdlip, in Gloucestershire, which had a most interesting collection, since dispersed, of fossils, ancient flint weapons, old coins, pictures, and a perfect medley of curiosities.

The association of sport with public-houses is too well

known to need more than a passing reference here. Within living memory most old inns and taverns, even in the towns, provided their customers with material and accommodation for the playing of some sort of game. Some had Skittle Alleys, some Marble Alleys, and those of the more pretentious kind provided expensively built and well-appointed Racket Courts.   But since the more stringent administration of the licensing laws, all those games which tended to encourage gambling have been frowned out of existence.   Happily many public-houses still retain their bowling-greens or their quoit pitches. And although cards and dominoes are generally taboo on licensed premises, billiards and bagatelle are allowed to be played without let or hindrance.   The simpler and less expensive the game, the more jealously the authorities regard it ; so that in this country the labouring man seeking recreation at a house of public entertainment— less happy than his *confrère* on the Continent—is debarred participation in a cheap and simple game, such as dominoes, and is restricted severely to the only pleasure permitted him—that of imbibing drink.   This is as the wisdom of our rulers ordains.

The facilities offered by licensed houses for public meetings have caused them long to be utilised as educational and recreative institutions.   Countless numbers of musical societies have met, and still meet, at public-houses, not a few of which have become famous for their glee parties and their philharmonic unions.   Similarly they have often been the birthplace of literary, scientific, or philosophical debating societies. Birmingham, for instance, as becomes the foremost city in Warwickshire, has some of its finest Shakespeare reading societies attached to licensed premises; as also many northern towns have their Burns Societies similarly housed.

The oldest debating society in London—probably the oldest in the world—Ye Antient Society of Cogers, is in session all the year round on Saturday evenings at the Rainbow Tavern, at the top of Fleet Street. The society was established in 1755 at the sign of the "White Bear," 15, Bride Lane, and has only changed its home twice in the century and a half of its existence. The name—which must not be pronounced "Codgers"—is derived from the first word of its motto, "Cogito ergo sum" ("I think, and therefore must have existence").

It was within the walls of that famous old tavern, which stood at the bottom of St. James' Street, close to the site of what is now the Thatched House Club, that the Geological Club was founded in the year 1824. The original Thatched House Tavern, which was the resort of all the wits, politicians, and men of fashion of the day, was demolished in the early "forties" in order to make room for the Conservative Club. It was then removed to another house a little lower down, and on its site again there was erected, in 1865, the present Thatched House Club, which was known in the earlier years of its existence as the Civil Service Club. The Thatched House Tavern was the headquarters from time to time of many bodies similar to the Geological Club. Among these were the Catch Club, the Royal Academy Club, the Royal Society Club, the Johnson Club, the Dilettanti Society, the Linnæan Society, the Farmers' Club, the Philosophical Club, the Star Club, the Institute of Actuaries, and many others.

In a history of the Dudley Book Club, written by Mr. Joseph Ridgway, we read :—

"As our forefathers had their social evenings at the most respectable hostelry of the towns in which they resided—among kindred spirits—so we find Dudley no exception. The chief

townsmen of that time met at the 'Saracen's Head,' at least the
Nonconforming portion, where they smoked their pipes over a
quiet tankard of home-brewed; talking over the events of the
day, business, politics, and religion. It was in such a region and
under such circumstances that this society germed. This con-
jecture bears strong confirmation from the fact that from the
beginning of the nineteenth century to the present day this
society has been located in the hotel mentioned, with only some
small interims—one at the 'Dudley Arms,' and again at the
Bush Hotel. Their meetings were monthly. In the first decade
of this century it flourished as a society that had existed a long
time before. The ministers of the Old Meeting have generally
been presidents. The society, however, is not a close one; it
has received into its company most sorts and conditions of men.
The circulation list of members comprehends every shade of
creed and politics. In that cosy meeting-room of the society
many schemes for the advancement of education, reforms (municipal and Parliamentary), have been hatched. Church rates were
opposed, and some of the members suffered their goods to be
sold on principle."

There is more than one instance of an inn's being used
as a printing and publishing office. In the early part of
the sixteenth century a foreigner named Peter Treviris
set up a printing press at the Three Widows Inn, Southwark, and for several years issued therefrom a number of
books, as their title-pages testify. Then there was the
"King's Head," at the corner of Chancery Lane, dating
from the time of Edward VI.—a picturesque pile which,
as the residence of Izaak Walton, appears in all his illustrated editions of the "Compleat Angler," which he
advertised to be "sold at his shopp in Fleet Street,
under the King's Head tavern."

The flourishing condition of Friendly Societies and
similar institutions, established for the welfare of the
industrial classes, is a monument to the business capacity
of English working men, and the history of these clubs
and societies shows how much such beneficent institutions owe to public-houses. In thousands of cases the

lodges and branches have found their only home in the club-room of an inn. Successful as the working has been, and creditable to all parties concerned, there was just one practice to which objection could be raised.

This custom, which is now rapidly giving way before the force of a more enlightened public opinion, was that known as "wet rents." For almost a century it was customary for the landlord of a public-house where Friendly Societies held their regular meetings and carried on their routine office work to charge no fixed money rent, but to have an agreement with the club management that so much of each member's contribution should be spent in drink. Each of the members attending a weekly, fortnightly, or monthly lodge meeting was expected to consume a pint or so of ale "for the good of the house." In consideration of this the landlord could well afford to forego a cash rent if the lodge were at all a flourishing institution. The term "wet rents" has also been applied to the income derivable from the sale of exciseable drinks at a music-hall or any similar place of entertainment. Metal checks or tokens, often of the face value of the price paid for admission, were often given at some of the lower-class Music-halls and Beer Gardens, such checks being negotiable in the purchase of refreshments inside the show. Further allusion to public-house checks will be found in a later chapter.

Of the holding of political meetings in public-houses it may perhaps be better to say as little as possible in these days when the law of the land penalises corrupt practices at election times so severely. The use of licensed premises for political assemblages is not unknown at the present time, and in the intervals between the excitements of electoral contests practically little harm comes of the practice.

It is not very wide of the truth to assert that to a too

intimate connection between public-houses and politics in the past, may be attributed the present-day policy of attempting to sever that alliance. This intimacy is illustrated in many of its salient features by Hogarth's " Election " series. The first plate shows an election entertainment at a country inn ; the second plate (which is here reproduced as our frontispiece) is entitled "Canvassing." In this scene we see the candidates' agents scattering bribes almost openly, and with no niggardly hands. One agent, with a subtlety that does him credit, is presenting, from the box of a travelling Jew, those ribbons and baubles which are often more effective in gaining the favour of the ladies than even the coin of the realm. He is supposed to entertain the village with a puppet-show, the tickets for admission to which have just been delivered for distribution by a kneeling porter, and the pictorial advertisement of which is seen thrown over the inn-sign—the upper part of the cloth depicts a treasury loading a wagon with money, while the lower half, equally appropriate to the occasion, shows Punchinello scattering money among the populace with right royal profusion. The landlady of the inn is seated on the old figure-head of a ship (such as were commonly fixed at inn-doors in those days), a carving of a British Lion swallowing the Flower-de-luce, and emblematical of the old-standing animosity between England and France ; she is counting, under the wistful eyes of a grenadier, the coins which have removed all her scruples against one of the candidates. In the centre we see the besetting and corrupting of voters ; and also in the foreground, seated at a table, two ale-house politicians, the barber and the cobbler, planning sieges and settling the affairs of state with small coins and bits of tobacco-pipe. In the window of the inn may be seen that copious eating and drinking so inseparable from all election proceedings. In the distance is seen another public-house, of which a rival mob is trying to tear down the sign—"The Crown," be it observed—and so intent upon their purpose that they pay no regard even to the discharge of firearms.

In the old days, particularly at the period when the fever of the French Revolution had spread to England, political clubs of all sorts came to be held regularly in taverns and other licensed houses. The fact is, there were available no public rooms suitable for such purposes other than those to be found at taverns and coffee-houses.

The history of Birmingham affords one or two good illustrations of this practice. In Bell Street of that town was the "Leicester Arms," commonly known as The Poet Freeth's Coffee House, which was the resort and acknowledged headquarters of the townsmen who, holding advanced opinions as to the rights of man to civil and religious liberty, were dubbed Jacobins ; and where they fraternised nightly, encouraged not a little in their propaganda by mine host's singing of suitable ballads of his own composing. At the Minerva Tavern in Peck Lane, not far away, was a house kept by another popular landlord, Joe Lindon, the resort of their political opponents, the Anti-Jacobins, or Tories. The notorious Priestley Riots of 1791 originated through a dinner held in celebration of the French Revolution at the Royal Hotel, Birmingham, the disturbances on that occasion commencing with the smashing of the hotel windows. A caricature by Gilray, entitled "A Birmingham Toast," depicts the leading men of the Jacobin party, who were said to be ready "to sell their King for a jug of ale, and demolish the church for a bottle of gin," seated at the table heartily endorsing these revolutionary sentiments in their favourite liquor.

Birmingham, as a political Mecca of times more recent, is known as the home of the " Caucus." It is interesting to note that Dr. Murray, in his new dictionary, derives the term "Caucus," meaning an electioneering machine, from the Greek *kaukos,* "a cup," perhaps because the flowing bowl was once a regular feature at all assemblages for the engineering of political victories.

How much of the local government and public business of a parish has been conducted within the walls of its public-houses in times past it would be impossible to estimate. At one time the village inn was often, for all practical purposes, the parish council chamber. A generation or two back the smoke-room company of a respectable inn included all the leading spirits of the place, and they assembled nightly—for manufacturers and professional men then lived on their business premises within the confines of the city, and did not retire every evening to a residence in the suburbs or some more distant country place—not merely for conviviality, but to discuss, if not to arrange, the public affairs of the town. Even of Birmingham, which has since boasted itself "the best-governed town in the kingdom," it is said that before the Chamberlain era the business of the Town Council was regularly arranged, and indeed all but transacted, at the "Wool Pack," or at some other hostelry, popular for the time being with the ruling *coterie* that happened to be in power. Nowadays "pot-house politics" do not carry much weight—at least in an enlightened community.

At Darlaston the White Lion Inn was for many years used practically as the town hall and municipal offices of the parish, and only ceased to be so used some twenty years ago, when the public spirit of the place demanded the erection of its first town hall. There are still in the villages old inns at which Parish Councils hold their

THE "OLD BOAR'S HEAD," EASTCHEAP.

[*Page* 239.

LIBERTIES ARE TAKEN WITH JOHN WILLET'S BAR.

(A scene depicted in "Barnaby Rudge.")

[*Page* 248.

meetings, just as the Vestry meetings of a former generation were wont to be held in them.

History aided by topography would reveal the repeated
use of inns as meeting-places for conspirators and political
agitators.   The Gunpowder Plot conspirators of 1605
arranged to meet, under pretence of holding a hunting
party, at the "Red Lion," a pack-horse inn, kept by one
Morrison, at Dunsmoor Heath, on the London Road, near
to Dunchurch ; while others of the party assembled at
the Bull Inn, Coventry.   Perhaps even more important,
because of its far-reaching consequences, was the private
meeting held at a Derbyshire public-house one morning
in 1688.   On this momentous occasion William Cavendish,
Earl of Devonshire, Thomas Osborne, Earl of Danby,
and Thomas D'Arcy met at Whittington, a quiet spot mid-
way between their three residences, to consult as to the
Revolution which was then in progress, and which that
year brought William of Orange to the throne of England.
Their meeting-place was the little village inn, which was
known by the sign of the "Cock and Pynot" (*pynot* is
the local name for the magpie), situated where the road
from Chesterfield branches for Sheffield and Rotherham.
"Plotting Parlour" of the Revolution House, as it was
dubbed, afterwards became a great show place.

The London "Mug-houses" of the early eighteenth
century were practically political clubs.   They were distinguished by the rows of pewter mugs placed in the
windows or hung up outside the houses.   They were all
practically in the hands of the loyalist faction favourable
to the "Protestant Succession" of the House of Hanover ;
and in those times of political disturbance, when riot and
tumult were frequent enough, bodies of men armed with
stout cudgels would issue from the Mug-houses to put
down the Tory mobs.

The inn as a court of law is well known.   At the

present day many coroners still hold their courts of inquest at the public-house nearest the place where the dead body which forms the subject of inquiry lies.[1]

As a petty sessional court for the transaction of magisterial business the inn is scarcely obsolete. And naturally enough in this connection there are many records of inns being used as prisons, some of them historic. According to L'Estrange, in his "Chronicles of Greenwich," the Ship Inn at that place was used in 1664 to keep a number of "the Lancashire Witches" in confinement. In 1569 Mary Queen of Scots was brought into Coventry and there kept a prisoner at the Bull Inn (on the site of which the barracks now stand) in the custody of the Earls of Shrewsbury and Huntingdon.

It was at this same inn that the Gunpowder Plot conspirators proposed to seize the person of the little Princess Elizabeth, then eight years of age : a plan which miscarried, as did their pretended "hunting party" at the "Red Lion," where they dispersed in affright, as just related.

Harrison Ainsworth, in his "Cardinal Pole," informs us—and doubtless on good authority—how one of the victims of the Marian persecution was imprisoned in a vault beneath the Star Inn, at Lewes, the night before he was burnt at the stake in the year 1554. It is an historical fact that the "White Lion," opposite the "Tabard" in Southwark, was once a prison for felons and other notorious offenders. Stow, writing in 1598, says the "White Lion" was "first used as a gaol these forty years last past." In 1640, we are told by Laud in his " History of the Troubles," the rabble apprentices

---

[1] The place where the inquest is to be held rests entirely in the discretion of the coroner, but by 2 Edward VII. c. 28 (Licensing Act, 1902) no coroner's inquest shall be held on licensed premises where other suitable premises have been provided for such inquest.

released the whole of the prisoners in the "White Lion."

Well known as it is that the licensed houses of the eighteenth century were commonly used for all sorts of public meetings, even for the purposes of religion as well as high politics, it is not so generally known that the founding of one of our Christian denominations may be traced to a public-house meeting. It was in 1783 that four men of Clerkenwell took to meeting together regularly for the study of the works of Swedenborg. Presently they called a public meeting in a public-house, and from that meeting an organised Church was formed. To-day the new Church then formed has sixty-eight meeting-places and forty ministers, and is not the least influential among the English denominations.

In "Sedgley Researches," the history of a Staffordshire parish in the Black Country, it is recorded that previously to the building of the Methodist New Connexion Chapel, at Woodsetton, in 1859, the members of the congregation used to meet in the club-room at the Swan Inn, then kept by a very worthy host named Isaac Richards. It was in this room, on licensed premises, that the first Sunday-school Anniversary in connection with this Church was held.

As recently as 1907, during the special efforts of a Church Mission at Scarborough, a service was held in the smoke-room of a public-house. And why not?

In olden times one use of public inns was to hold therein an annual feast in commemoration of some deceased person who had bequeathed money for that specific purpose. The ancient "Give Ales," which have been previously noted, were of a very similar origin. In the last quarter of the eighteenth century a sprightly and playful artist, named Nixon, once came across a party of undertakers celebrating such a memorial feast in the grounds of the Falcon Inn, between Wandsworth and Battersea. Observing that the innkeeper's name was R. Death, the scene so tickled his fancy that he made a sketch of the "Merry Undertakers" feasting at "Death's door," which he published. The picture was a huge success, and was very popular in its day.

Post-offices have rarely been attached to licensed premises in recent times, but the association is not quite unknown. There are, indeed, few public institutions for which the accommodation of the licensed inn has not in some place, and at some time or other, been drawn upon, in default of finding such public accommodation elsewhere.

There is near Dudley the Salt-wells Inn, which takes its name from the fact that a medicinal brine bath is found on the premises, and which is sometimes used for curative purposes. Not the least curious thing about the place is that the brine never ceases to bubble up from the bowels of the earth, although the spring is situated in a purely mining district, and the land all round it is completely honeycombed with pits. Here, then, is a public-house which may be designated a "cure-house." In beneficence no use could go farther than this.

The proposed municipalising of the public-house is no new idea, as some old papers recently found at Lord Verulam's mansion indubitably testify. Among these historical documents is the petition of William Mott to the Council of Colchester, in 1662. The petitioner proposes that all the inns then existing in Colchester shall be purchased by the Council and put under disinterested management; and that the profits accruing therefrom shall be devoted solely to the relief of the poor of the parish. Apparently nothing came of the petition, which was doubtless prompted by the very prevalent desire of everybody at that time to escape from the burden of the new, or comparatively new, national Poor Laws.

XXI

SOME HISTORIC INNS

Historic inns as shrines for American visitors—The Fountain Inn,
Canterbury—Used by Beckett's assassins in 1170—And com-
mended by the German Ambassador in 1299—The "Tabard,"
Southwark—And Canterbury pilgrims—Its history—Other old
Southwark hostelries—Jack Cade at the "White Hart," 1450—
The "George," Glastonbury—Visited by Henry VIII.—The
"George," Salisbury—An inventory of it made, 1473—The
"Blue Boar," Leicester—And the death of Richard III.—The
"Nag's Head," Cheapside—The legendary consecration of
Archbishop Parker there—How readily "legends" grow up
—The Bell Inn, Warwick Lane—Death of Archbishop Leigh-
ton there in 1684—The "Lygon Arms," Broadway—Charles I.'s
bedroom—The George Inn, Norton St. Philip—Monmouth's
quarters there—The Castle Inn, Marlborough—The Earl of
Chatham's stay there—The "Four Crosses," Cannock—A
reminiscence of Dean Swift.

IN bygone centuries an inn has sometimes formed the
background of a scene of historic importance; but
strangely enough, so short is the public memory, though
the episode itself has lived in history, the exact locality
of it has been forgotten, even local tradition sometimes
being at fault; for the vulgar mind often fails to realise
the significance of an event which happens under familiar
surroundings close at home. It is in such cases the
antiquarian supplements the historian.

There are still to be found in England, generally in

the remoter villages and in the quieter towns that lie off the beaten track, many of those old inns which, if not the pride of Englishmen, are always the delight of our better-read American visitors. Belonging as they do to the bygone England of history and romance, they never fail to conjure up visions of dimity-hung bedrooms, redolent of lavender-scented sheets; of tables spread with solid English fare. Some of the more hoary of these hostels, indeed, carry back the imagination to the masculine days of Elizabeth, when hospitality took the shape of fatted capons and huge venison pasties.

The Fountain Inn at Canterbury is reputed to have afforded hospitality to the wife of Earl Godwin in 1029, and to have been the destination of the four knights who arrived in such haste in 1170, with the dread and set purpose of assassinating Thomas à Becket. There is actual documentary evidence of its antiquity, dated 1299, in the shape of a testimonial from the Ambassador of the Emperor of Germany, who officially attended the marriage, in that city, of Edward I. to his second wife Margaret, sister of Philip IV. of France, in the said year.

The distinguished guest wrote :—

"The inns in England are the best in Europe, those of Canterbury are the best in England, and 'The Fountain,' wherein I am now lodged as handsomely as I were in the King's Palace, the best in Canterbury."

To Kent also belongs another very ancient hostelry in the "George and Dragon" at Speldhurst, near Tunbridge Wells, which was established in the reign of Henry III. —say before 1272.

No part of London was richer in historic hostelries than the High Street of the borough of Southwark—the thoroughfare which gave entrance to London from the

whole Continent of Europe.   Here, indeed, on the high-
road from Dover and Canterbury was to be found
accommodation in plenty "for the receipt of travellers,"
throughout the centuries of English history.

First and foremost was the Tabard Inn, from which
Chaucer's company of pilgrims, consisting of twenty-nine
"sundry folk," set forth on their famous ride to visit the
shrine of St. Thomas of Canterbury.   The house was
built in 1307 as a hostel for the Abbot of Hyde (near
Winchester), and also for an inn to accommodate the
numerous pilgrims resorting to Canterbury.   The pilgrimage sung by Chaucer is supposed to have occurred
in the year 1383.

In 1673 the sign was changed by an ignorant tenant
from "Tabard"—which was a sleeveless coat worn by
heralds—to "Talbot," a dog.   This was not the only
misfortune which befel the inn about that time, for three
years later it was partially destroyed by fire.   The building was of timber, and contained large portions of the
original structure of Chaucer's time, though with considerable additions made in the reign of Elizabeth.   It
was immediately rebuilt in facsimile of the original, with
its courtyard, galleries, pilgrims' hall, and quaint old
sleeping-rooms.   At its demolition in 1874 there was
in front of its stone-coloured wooden gallery an interesting picture of the Canterbury Pilgrims, reputed to be
from the brush of William Blake, the talented poet,
painter, and engraver, who died in 1827 ; but what
became of it is not known.

Among the other "fair inns for the receipt of
travellers," enumerated by Stow in the sixteenth century,
were the "Spurre," "Christopher," "Bull," "Queen's
Head," "George," "Hart," "King's Head," &c.   Detailed mention cannot here be made of them all ; but
it may be noted that the sign of the "George" was

originally the " St. George" (1554) ; and that the " Three
Widows" was probably a perversion of the " Three
Nuns," ignorant people after the Reformation confound-
ing the white head-dresses of the religious sisterhood
with those of disconsolate relicts.

Last, but not least, the " White Hart," famous both
in history and in fiction ; for it was here in 1450 Jack
Cade arrived, and lodged on the night of July 1st, when
he was not permitted to enter the City; and where for
a deed of violence one of his followers suffered death,
as is thus recorded : " At the Whyt Harte, in South-
warke, one Hawaydyne, of Sent Martyns, was beheddyd."
It was here, also, that the inimitable Sam Weller was
" boots," before he was " purwided" with a better situation and became body servant to Mr. Pickwick.

The " George" at Glastonbury, though probably standing on the site of an older inn, is a fine fifteenth-century,
stone-built hostelry which was put up in the reign
of Edward IV. While it is at once apparent that all the
rough-and-ready hospitality of the Middle Ages would
be forthcoming within its ample walls, nothing can
detract from the gracefulness of its panelled and traceried
Gothic stonework front, not the least beautiful feature
of which is the window-bay rising from floor to roof. It
was once called the Old Pilgrim Inn, and the bed upon
which Henry VIII. slept when he paid his visit to the
famous abbey was long preserved here.

Another ancient and interesting inn of the West
Country is the " George " at Salisbury. According to an
inventory of the house made in 1473, it contained
thirteen guest-chambers ; but no difference seems to have
been made between the living-rooms and the sleeping-
rooms, each one mentioned in the inventory containing
several truckle-beds. The massive timbers in the structure
of this house are said to have been brought from a more

ancient inn used by the pilgrims at Old Sarum; certain carvings on its woodwork indicate its erection about 1320. There is a fine Jacobean staircase reached from the garden entrance, which extends to the third storey—an unusual height for a staircase of that period. In its solar chamber is to be seen a magnificent specimen of old roof timbering. The courtyard was often used by the strolling players of the sixteenth and seventeenth centuries, and Shakespeare is said to have acted here on one occasion. Pepys, in his famous Diary, records that he slept here "in a silk bed," and had very good diet. The licence has lapsed many years, but the house is still well patronised as a private hotel.

The "Blue Boar" at Leicester was reputed to have derived its name from the cognisance of Richard III., because at Blue Boar Lane near by Crookback is said to have had his headquarters on the eve of the Battle of Bosworth. The King, mounted on a large white courser, arrived at Leicester on the evening of Saturday, August 20, 1485, surrounded by his guards, and in great pomp. He slept that night in the inn, which subsequently became known as the "Blue Boar." The massive wooden bedstead he occupied afterwards passed with the house from tenant to tenant, till late in the reign of Elizabeth. The memorable engagement took place on the Monday; and local tradition says that Richard's body, stripped of all clothing, and thrown across a horse's back "like a hog," head and arms dangling down one side, and legs down the other, was brought into Leicester after the battle, and exposed to public view in the Old Town Hall in Blue Boar Lane near the inn where the day before he had lived in regal pomp.

Mention may not be omitted of an inn associated (in repute) with one of the most important events of history. This was the Nag's Head Tavern (London) which

anciently stood in Cheapside, at the corner of Friday
Street; and the historic event was no less than the Reformation—or rather, an episode of no little import therein.
It was said, in the spitefulness and the unscrupulous
bitterness of religious prejudice at that disturbed period,
that Matthew Parker, whom Queen Elizabeth made her
first Protestant Primate in 1559, was consecrated at the
Nag's Head Inn.

Of course the ceremony used at the consecration of the
new Archbishop of Canterbury was not according to the
ancient Roman ritual ; and this scandalous fable, invented by his papistical adversaries to discredit him
in the eyes of the people (for his confirmation really
took place in the church of St. Mary-le-Bow) has had
to be refuted at some length in Strype's " Life of
Parker."

The ease with which "a legend" will sometimes grow
up around a house that is a little out of the common and
therefore likely to excite the imagination of the ignorant
and credulous, is really surprising. All that is wanted
is a little inventiveness to set it going ; and once started
it is equally surprising to note how easily confirmatory
"facts" can be found to adorn an otherwise bald and
unconvincing narrative. While examining an old inn
which possessed some rather quaint features, the landlady vouchsafed as the most striking incident in its
history, that a tiger had once escaped from a travelling
menagerie which had "pitched" in the inn field, and
had killed a little girl. As corroborative testimony she
said that there was a gravestone in the adjoining churchyard setting forth all the circumstances of the sad event.
Her interrogator, catching sight at that moment of some
remnants of old heraldic glass in one of the inn's ancient
windows, one piece displaying a lion rampant, he slily
put the question, "I suppose this is the picture of the

tiger ?" To which the ready response of the landlady was, "I believe it is, sir !"

At the beginning of the last century no finer specimens of the ancient galleried inn were to be found than the two which stood in Warwick Lane, in the heart of the City of London, namely, the "Bell," and the "Oxford Arms." For centuries these inns had been frequented by carriers, wagoners, and stage-coaches. At the "Bell" the pious Archbishop Leighton ended his earthly pilgrimage in 1684. It may appear strange to our modern ideas, but this was exactly in accordance with the good man's wishes. Bishop Burnet, in the history of his "Own Times," informs us that Leighton used to say, "if he were to choose a place to die in, it should be an inn ; it looking like a pilgrim's going home"; and in the end so it was that it came about as he had desired.

A good specimen of a Tudor-built house is the "Lygon Arms" at Broadway, in Worcestershire ; at Chipping Camden, in the same district, are two typical Stuart houses, the "Red Lion" and the "Green Dragon." At the first named of the three is shown the "Cromwell Room," perversely so called because Charles I. slept there ! It is inherently interesting, however, as is the "Nelson Room" shown at a Yarmouth inn, or the "Monmouth Room" to be seen in a West Country hostelry ; which can scarcely be said of the fine apartment which is grandiosely named "Grosvenor Room" or "Richmond Room" in some pretentious modern hotel.

A Somerset inn of much historical interest, which has recently been demolished, was the George Inn at Norton St. Philip, near Frome. It was a half-timbered, bay-windowed house, one of the most picturesque buildings of Somerset. In an upper room of the house—an astonishing stretch of space in the roof timbers—the cloth merchants held their fair at a time when the manufacture was much more important as a national industry than it is at the present time. But the chief interest in the "George" centres in the fact that the ill-fated Duke of Monmouth slept there on June 26, 1685, a few days before his defeat at Sedgemoor. As he stood at the window on that pleasant June evening, a bullet whistled past his head; for though "Zummerzet" in the main was loyal to his cause, the price set on his head was evidently too great a temptation for the man who fired that shot "at a venture."

The oldest part of the building dated from 1397, but in the whole of its long history it never saw a more stirring episode than the occurrences of that bright June day in 1685. Monmouth had planted his fieldpieces round the house in the first taste of actual warfare given him by the enemy. A small body of Royalist troops under his half-brother, the Duke of Grafton, coming upon him here, a sharp little fight had to be made of it. It was a treasured tradition of the "George" that Colonel Holmes, of Monmouth's side, finished the amputation of his own arm, which had been shattered by a shot, with the inn carving-knife.

Mr. Stanley Weyman, the eminent novelist, has called one of his most popular works of fiction after a particularly famous old English hostelry at Marlborough. His tale, entitled "The Castle Inn," introduces an actual historic incident of the year 1767, when the great Earl of Chatham, then the idol of the nation, being sufficiently recovered of his gout to leave Bath and proceed towards the capital, put up at this inn, then reputed one of the best, as it was certainly the most splendid in England, capable it is said of serving a dinner of twenty-four covers on silver, and therefore not unworthy even the distinguished patronage of this great minister who travelled with all the pomp and ceremonial, and with all that display of State, which

so pleased the popular fancy in those times. In Mr.
Weyman's entertaining narrative we may read of the
great parade of the Earl's arrival at the inn, with his
imposing procession of curricle and chariot, of coaches
and chaises, and attendant footmen ; and how when all
had descended from the carriages the whole place was
thronged with troops of his lordship's servants, till the
great house seemed peopled with the Pitt liveries.

As to the central figure in all this subdued stir and
bustle, it was but a momentary glimpse the gaping crowd
caught of his gaunt form as he was borne heavily by
his liveried servitors from the travelling carriage to the
sheltering walls of the inn, and that brief vision attracted
more by the eagle nose and piercing eyes of the pallid
invalid than by the star and ribbon which adorned his
breast.

In a trice lights flashed out from the windows of the
suite of twenty rooms required to accommodate this
princely retinue, which included secretaries and physicians, women-servants and nurses. As the minister's
company presently settled down in their respective places
and apartments, above the distant murmur from the busy
stable-yard at the rear could now be heard the rattle of
plates and the hum of voices around the hospitable
tables ; while from the open doors was emitted the
fragrant glow of warmth and welcome for which the
" Castle " at Marlborough was always renowned.

The Castle Inn, which was long the chief ornament of
the old Bath Road, stood in a snug fold of the Downs at
the point where the Salisbury road branches away south-
wards ; and in those halcyon days of inns it had its
destinies ruled by as civil, obliging, and discreet a host
as ever ushered guest into his doors. The noble proportions of the house at once impressed the visitor, who
was not perhaps particularly surprised to learn after-

wards that it had formerly been a favourite residence of
the Seymour family, that its architecture was that of a
clever pupil of Inigo Jones, and that its historic walls
had on one occasion sheltered William of Orange. It is
now a part of Marlborough College. The Bull Hotel,
which has added " Castle " to its name, dates from 1650.

The Four Crosses Inn, on the Watling Street, near to
Cannock, has been in the possession of one family for
the last three-quarters of a century. Dean Swift once
baited at this inn while on the way to his deanery in
Ireland. The landlady of his time had a raucous tongue,
her sharp play with which so exasperated the learned
dean that with a diamond he wrote on the window-pane
this distich, addressed to the landlord :—

> " Thou fool to hang Four Crosses at thy door !
> Hang up thy wife—there needs not any more."

Near by is the Shire Oak, under which Swift took
shelter from a storm, where he found a tramp and his
drab already seeking the protection of its ample branches.
While waiting for the storm to abate, conversation revealed the fact that the couple only " buttied " together,
which so scandalised the good dean he consented to
marry them, there and then. The impromptu ceremony
over, the woman asked for a marriage certificate, whereupon Swift wrote out the following :—

> " Beneath this Oak in stormy weather
> I joined this whore and rogue together ;
> And none but He who made the thunder
> Can put this whore and rogue asunder."

XXII

OTHER NOTABLE INNS

Cricketer's Inn, Hambledon—A Lancaster "beer cellar"—The
"Crooked House," Himley—The public-house next the parish
church—An inn with a "peeping" outlook—Elevated inns—
"Cat and Fiddle" at Buxton—Tan Hill Inn, both elevated and
lonely—Other inns in Cloudland—An inn in four counties—
Ancient hostelries—"Seven Stars," Manchester (1356)—"Bell,"
Finedon (1042) — "Old Green Man," Erdington (1306)—
"Saracen's Head," Newark (1341)—Mentioned in "Heart of
Midlothian"—"Saracen's Head," Southwell—and Charles I.'s
surrender—"Feathers" and the "Bull," Ludlow—"Pied Bull,"
Chester (1534)—"Blue Boar's Head," Eastcheap—"Fighting
Cocks," St. Albans—claims Saxon origin—Two Nottingham inns
of 1482—"Angel," Grantham (1213)—"New Inn," Gloucester,
temp. Edward III.—An ancient bill of the "Angel," Blyth (1274)
—Thames-side hostelries—"Star and Garter," Richmond—Its
distinguished patrons—"Lion," Hampton-on-Thames—Its long
and interesting record—The "Swan," Thames Ditton—celebrated by Theodore Hook—The "Ship" at Greenwich—
Famous Whitebait dinners—Origin of its political banquets—
Wapping old taverns—reminiscent of press-gang days—
Coaching-houses on Highgate Hill—Ancient and absurd ceremony of "Swearing on the Horns."

INNS have become notable otherwise than through
historic associations, or association with the great names
of literature. One inn will boast of its unique position,
another of its venerable antiquity ; or better still, in the
eyes of its owner, of some distinction to which no other
house of public resort can lay claim.

There are houses which rely for their distinction upon their association with sport. Take the national game of cricket, and no house can claim an earlier or more interesting connection with this than the Bat and Ball Inn at Hambledon, in Hampshire. As exponents of the game the " Hambledon men " had no equals for nearly half a century, led from 1750 to 1791 by that famous old cricketer, Richard Nyren.

A curious licensed house is (or was) Wilton Wood's Vaults in the ancient town of Lancaster. The premises consisted partly of a cellar and partly of an adaptation of a cottage. A yard had been roofed over with glass, and this was one of the special rooms. The beer cellar itself was part of the licensed premises, and beer was served there, and also at " the cellar head." The peculiar features of the house were its chief attraction for many years.

More curious still is a little tavern known as the " Crooked House" at Himley, on the Earl of Dudley's estate. It is a red brick building, with a wide passage through to the back premises ; but as a result of mining operations—the whole district is honeycombed with coal-pits—it has fallen out of the perpendicular to an alarming extent. It is as difficult to walk through the doorway as to pace the deck of a vessel in a rolling sea ; the warped floor and the leaning walls make it difficult to maintain a vertical position, the more so as all the rooms are out of joint and present a remarkable optical illusion. The clocks on the walls, although absolutely perpendicular, as their pendulums testify, appear to be hanging sideways at a very pronounced angle. A shelf which is really level, appears to be a foot higher at one end than at the other. If marbles be placed on what appears to be the lower end of the tap-room table, they apparently roll uphill and fall over with a bump !

With regard to the situation of inns, it has often

THE " LEATHER BOTTLE," COBHAM.

[*Page* 249.

THE "FOX-UNDER-THE-HILL," ADELPHI.

[Page 250.

been remarked that there is almost sure to be a public-
house near to the church ; or, as it is sometimes put, the
Devil's house is generally next-door to the house of God.
Apropos of this, did not Defoe pen the lines—

> "Wherever God erects a House of Prayer,
> The Devil's sure to build a chapel there,
> And 'twill be found upon examination,
> The latter has the larger congregation" ?

It would not be difficult to find an inn standing, if not
within the sacred precincts of a churchyard, certainly
looking into it. The Bell Inn at Harborne is actually
within the churchyard.

In some slow-going villages and old-fashioned towns
it has been known, not a century back from the present
year of grace, for the members of the choir, and sometimes even the churchwardens to slip into the nearest inn
during sermon-time for a pipe of tobacco, and, maybe,
something with which to wet it.

Situation, as everybody knows, is the most important
factor in determining the value of a licensed establishment. But at St. Leonards-on-Sea one important hotel
seems to have derived both its sign and its importance
from its peculiar location. It is at the end of the sea-
front, and therefore convenient as a tramway terminus ;
but as it stands back, squeezed as it were into a corner
from which it can only peep out on to the front, it is
with a spice of humour called the " Bo-peep."

The claim to be the highest situated licensed house in
England is generally preferred on behalf of the Cat and
Fiddle Inn, on the Cheshire boundary of the moorlands,
five miles out of Buxton. The altitude of this house above
sea-level is 1,690 feet. But the Tan Hill Inn, on the
summit of Stainmoor, in the North Riding of Yorkshire,
is stated to be 1,727 feet above the sea. Like the former,

which is mentioned by Sir Walter Scott in " Peveril of
the Peak," it is in a lonely situation, being situated on a
little-frequented road from Brough in Westmoreland to
Reeth in Swaledale, Yorkshire, and gets few patrons in
the year except at Brough annual horse fair. The next
in altitude after the " Cat and Fiddle " is its comparatively
near neighbour, the " Traveller's Rest " at Flash, on the
Leek and Buxton road, which ranks third at 1,535 feet.
The next three inns of the Cloudland series are further
afield. There is Isle of Skye Inn, near Holmfirth,
1,500 feet above sea-level ; the " Traveller's Rest " at the
top of Kirkstone Pass, between Windermere and Patter-
dale, 1,476 feet ; and the " Newby Head " between Black
Hawes and Ingleton, 1,420 feet. In a Sunday Closing
Bill recently before Parliament, it was proposed to exempt
from its operation all public-houses over 1,450 feet
above sea-level ; and it was then declared there were only
three hostelries in the country which would be benefited
by the clause.

An inn which is neither ancient nor elevated, but is
perhaps remarkable for its situation, is that known as
The " Four Counties Inn," on No Man's Heath, where
the four counties of Warwick, Stafford, Leicester, and
Derby come together.

Claims to the distinction of being the oldest inn in
England have been put forward on behalf of many old
houses in many different parts of the country. A recent
authority states that there are documents in existence
which show that the " Seven Stars," in Withy Grove,
Manchester, was in existence as a hostelry prior to 1356.
But this date is completely eclipsed by the supporters of
the claim of the " Bell " at Finedon, in Northampton-
shire, which, say they, was used as an inn in 1042 ! That
an inn may stand on the site of an ancient hostel to some
religious house of Saxon foundation is not impossible.

The point is one which can never be settled satisfactorily; but this fact cannot divest of their interest numbers of venerable old establishments which, century after century, have sheltered a long succession of guests, and witnessed many striking episodes, thus constituting a background in the pageantry of the nation's social history.

The "Old Green Man" at Erdington, on the confines of Sutton Chase, advances 1306 as the date of its establishment: its alternative name, "The Lad in the Lane," seems to indicate its origin as an illicit drinking-house for the use of the Earl of Warwick's foresters. The "Saracen's Head," at Newark, can be traced by actual title-deeds to 1341. In his history of that town, published in 1805, Dr. William Dickenson, an eminent lawyer of his time, reproduced the deeds of repeated transfers of this inn, from which it is traced to the remote reign of Edward III. The first quotation reads : "A release from Wm. Burnach, of the 'Saracen's Head' Inn ; fourteenth of Edward III." The second document is : "A deed of feoffment of the part of the said inn," dated "twenty-second of Richard II." Fifteen irrefutable deeds of transfer bring the history of this hostelry to the date of the issue of Dr. Dickenson's work, when its owner was the Duke of Newcastle.

It is at the "Saracen's Head," Newark, that Scott represents Jennie Deans, the heroine of "The Heart of Midlothian," as being hospitably entertained by the landlord, and set again on her perilous road towards London—to the credit of the innkeepers' calling it is also recorded that previously at York the forlorn damsel had been similarly entreated by the kind-hearted hostess of the "Seven Stars" in Castlegate.

The White Hart Inn at Newark, however, is the architectural treasure—along its top storey has run a continuous open gallery, now glazed in ; while on the front of the first floor is a series of rich canopied niches of plaster-work, those over the cart-way still retaining their figures, holding emblems, and their feet supported upon hogs' masks—work which has come down from the middle of the fourteenth century.

At Southwell there is another "Saracen's Head," equally interesting. It is an old house, with its ancient massive gates of oak still hanging on their original hinges ; and on the other side of the yard from the coffee-room the stairs are of solid oak blocks. But the interest of the house lies in the fact that it was here Charles I. slept his last sleep and ate his last meal as a free man. Out of its historic gateway he rode in the morning of the fatal day that he surrendered himself to the Scottish army encamped in the neighbourhood.

The county of Salop is peculiarly rich in its old domestic architecture, particularly in that picturesque variety which is sometimes tersely described as of the magpie order. The "Feathers," at Ludlow, is a fine old specimen, with a grandly decorated Tudor front. Opposite is the "Bull," a comfortable hostelry in which one may dine in a room very ornately oak-panelled, every panel richly carved in heraldic devices, the spoils of Ludlow's ruined castle in which Milton's "Comus" was first performed.

At Chester, the "Pied Bull," in Northgate Street, is a quaint old house, now modernised for comfort, which was first erected in 1534. In 1829 the "White Hart," Bishopsgate, a famous old London tavern, was entirely rebuilt. The "Boar's Head" in Eastcheap, which Shakespeare makes the rendezvous of Prince Hal and his dissolute companions, is known to have really existed in the time of Henry IV., though its full title seems to have been the "Blue Boar's Head." The tradition of the merry carousings there of Prince Hal, Falstaff, and the

rest of them, seems to have been well founded. Goldsmith
has a whole essay on the subject, and Hutton, on his
visit a century ago, speaks of the very seats where the
Prince and Old Jack got drunk together, and says he
wished only for a cup of sack to drink to the happy
memory of the bulky knight.

The Fighting Cocks Inn, an old "round house,"
standing on the little River Ver at St. Albans, claims to
be the oldest inhabited house in England. It is a curious
structure—of octagonal shape—of early Saxon origin,
having been built as a boat-house to the ancient
monastery founded at St. Albans by King Offa about
the year 795, and is thus over 1,100 years old. A sub-
terranean passage, now blocked up, runs from the base-
ment to the ruins of the monastery, a distance of about
200 yards. It was used also as a storage for the fishing
tackle of the monks. There is a shed at the back of the
house where, it is said, Oliver Cromwell stabled his horse,
himself once sleeping under its roof during the Civil
War.

The Nottingham borough records mention, under date
January 28, 1482–3, the name of two old inns in that
town, namely, the "Crown" and the "Ram." But it
has been sought by an old rhymster ("Notes about
Nottingham") to show that the latter dates back upwards
of three centuries earlier :—

> "In good King Stephen's days, the Ram,
> An ancient inn in Nottingham,
> Was kept as all good people knows
> By a buxom wife yclept old Rose."

There are other claimants for the coveted honour
of greatest antiquity, and in the absence of authentic
records, particularly as to continuity of use or licence
and identity of situation, it must always be impossible
to decide between them authoritatively.

The *Academy* says that the " Angel " at Grantham bore
that name as early as 1213. The New Inn at Gloucester
is no mean competitor. Of this picturesque establishment, which is to-day the resort of motorists and the
delight of visitors with antiquarian tastes, the *Gloucestershire Chronicle* gives the following account :—

" The assassination of Edward II. at Berkeley Castle, his burial at
Gloucester, and the excitement consequent thereon in religious
bodies, combined to attract large numbers of pilgrims to the shrine
in the Cathedral. To accommodate these, large hostelries were
built. Edward II. was murdered in 1327. The ' New ' Inn must,
therefore, have been built on the site of the ' Old ' Inn. Rudge says
that in the time of Abbot Seabrook, who presided over the monastery
from 1400 to 1457, the New Inn, in Northgate Street, was built by
John Twyning, a monk, who caused an underground passage to be
made from it to the Abbey. The New Inn was spacious, and was
constructed of ponderous materials. The buildings surrounded two
square courts, and, so far as can be seen, were provided with stairs
leading to two tier galleries. These led to numerous large and
small rooms. It was commonly said to be built of chestnut—large
beams, the spaces filled with brick nogging and plaster."

In the same city, that portion of the Fleece Hotel
known as the Monks' Retreat, is part of some old
monastic cellaring, and therefore doubtless of mediæval
origin. The New Inn was erected on the site of an
older and smaller hotel ; at the Dissolution it became the
property of the Dean and Chapter.

Perhaps the inn of which the most ancient bill can
be produced is the " Angel," at Blyth, in Notting-
hamshire. Richard de Insula, upon his appointment to
the bishopric of Durham, in 1274, journeyed to London,
in company with the Prior of Durham, to seek an inter-
view with the King. Returning in the October of that
year, the two distinguished churchmen, travelling with a
retinue befitting their rank, found hospitality at various
monasteries along the route ; but it is on record that one

of the stopping-places was the Angel Inn, at Blyth.
The bill they ran up at this hostelry on the occasion, still
preserved, is set out in this wise :—

						s.	d.
In pane	...	...	...	...	...	10	0
In cervisia et vino...	...	...	...	...	...	33	5
In coquina ...	...	...	...	...	...	27	5½
In prebenda feno et litera		...	...	...	...	18	9

The charges for bread, for the venison and the wine,
for the provender, hay, and litter for the horses, would
all appear to be reasonable ; but bearing in mind the
relative value of money in the thirteenth century, and
multiplying 27s. 5d. by 20, the item set down for
cooking would appear to be somewhat excessive.

There is scarcely an old town throughout the length
and breadth of the country which cannot boast some
hostelry whose traditions stretch back at least a century or two. In such works as the "Inns of Eastern
England" have been enshrined the inn lore, and much of
the social history which always accompanies it, of various
localities and sections of the country. Volumes dealing
with subjects like "Coaching Days and Coaching Ways"
are full of interesting allusions to the old calling inns
and posting-houses which were once dotted along the
highways and turnpike roads.

Some houses have attained the dignity of a separate
published history, as for instance, "The Book of the
Cheese," written by S. W. Reid, which gives the history
of that famous resort of Dr. Johnson and his illustrious associates, The Cheshire Cheese Tavern, in Wine
Office Court, Fleet Street. To attempt the history of
London's famous inns would require volumes ; a brief
notice, however, may be given of some of the better-
known river-side houses.

Royalties, foreign potentates, and other eminent personages have, of course, been entertained, time after time, in a number of the high-class hotels of the capital. But passing mention, at least, may be made to the well-known Star and Garter Hotel at Richmond. In 1809 this famous riverside hostelry passed into the hands of Mr. Crean, at whose death it was sold to Mr. Joseph Ellis (father of a much-esteemed alderman and ex-mayor of London, Sir J. Whittaker Ellis, Bart.), who, by making various improvements and considerable extensions, brought the establishment to the height of its greatest reputation ; and under his management it enjoyed un-exampled prosperity. After his death it was acquired from his son, in 1864, by a limited liability company, when the present imposing buildings were erected from the designs of Mr. Barry, the architect, at a cost of £140,000. This hotel boasts the "finest view in England" ; did not the poet Thompson write :—

> "Say, shall we ascend
> Thy hill, delightful Sheen ? Here let us sweep
> The boundless landscape " ?

Among the many distinguished persons who at one time or another have visited the hotel may be mentioned Marshal Soult (when he came to England as Ambassador from France in 1838 on the occasion of the Queen's Coronation) ; Queen Marie Emelie and Louis Phillipe, when they were visited here by her Majesty the Queen in 1848, as well as by M. Guizot (the French historian) ; Napoleon III. ; Emanuel, King of Sardinia ; the Emperor Maximilian of Mexico ; the Duc d'Aumale ; the Empress of Austria, and the Prince Imperial.

The Lion Hotel at Hampton-on-Thames has a long and extremely interesting record. This inn has existed

in one form or another from the time of Cardinal
Wolsey at least, for it is recorded that the superior
artisans engaged in the erection of Hampton Court
Palace lodged here. It was the favourite place of
call for the gay hunting parties of Henry VIII., after
the formation of the Royal Chase.

During the reign of Charles I. the landlord was one
of the King's post-masters, and as such had during the
King's sojourn in the neighbourhood to provide horses
every half-hour for the messengers travelling between
Whitehall and the Palace. It is also recorded that
Charles II. frequented the house and took part in some
of his "exclusive" orgies there.

In the reign of Queen Anne, Hampton was the summer
resort of most of the literary and dramatic celebrities
of the day, and Dryden, Pope, Swift, Bolingbroke,
Colley Cibber, Quin, Peg Woffington, Kitty Clive, and
others are known to have frequently patronised this
riverside hostelry and dined there on their boating
excursions.

The "Lion" is reputed to have been the scene of the
celebrated drinking bout between Addison and Pope,
"which gave the crooked, ugly little thing that asks
questions" so bad a headache that he went about for
months denouncing the great essayist as a terrible and
confirmed drunkard.

When George III. took up his abode at Windsor,
the "Lion" became celebrated as a posting-house, and
on the Hurst becoming famous for its prize-fights, it
flourished more vigorously than ever. In more recent
times the Duke of Clarence dined here, whilst Michael
Balfe, Alfred Bunn, Charles Mathews, and Madame
Vestris were among the regular patrons of this noted
old establishment.

Another notable riverside house is the "Swan" at

Thames Ditton, which the famous practical joker and
humorist, Theodore Hook, thus celebrated in song :—

"The Swan, snug inn, good fare affords,
　　As table e'er was put on,
And worthier quite of loftier boards,
　　Its poultry, fish, and mutton ;
And while sound wine mine host supplies
　　With beer of Meux or Tritton,
Mine hostess with her bright blue eyes,
　　Invites to stay at Ditton."

These lines, which constitute a seventh part of the
original ditty, were written by Hook in a punt, when
he was fishing in the neighbourhood of Thames Ditton.
It seems, says Mr. J. Ashby-Sterry, the irrepressible
humorist had occasionally his placid moments when
he devoted himself to the gentle and contemplative
art.

Some of the riverside inns of the Thames are well-
known landmarks. Two at least constitute starting-place
and winning-post. The old Swan Pier, for instance, near
London Bridge, began the course which the Swan
Tavern at Chelsea, four miles away, terminated, in the
annual rowing races for the Dogget Coat and Badge.
This much-coveted prize for Thames watermen was
founded in 1722, and is contended for every 1st of
August.

The "Ship" at Greenwich, which recently (1908) had
to close its doors owing to dwindling trade, had long
been famous for its fish, especially its whitebait, dinners.

John Timbs, in his "Club Life of London," states
concerning these riverside fish dinners : "During June,
July, and August immense quantities are consumed by
visitors to the different taverns at Greenwich and
Blackwall."

The old "Ship," like the "Crown and Sceptre," and

the "Trafalgar," well-known inns, was built with a weather-board front and old-fashioned bay-windows, where the guests might sit and watch the shipping passing up and down the Thames. The original "Ship" stood in the vicinity of the Royal Naval Hospital, but in 1846 it was pulled down and a more pretentious building was erected on the existing site.

Of the origin of the famous political dinners at the "Ship," Mr. Edward Walford states, in his "Old and New London," that Sir Robert Preston had a fishing cottage on the banks of Dagenham Reach. His most frequent visitor was the Right Hon. George Rose, Secretary to the Treasury, who later introduced Pitt. As Pitt found Dagenham inconvenient, the venue was changed to Greenwich, where he brought Lord Aberdeen later. Soon afterwards Mr. Charles Long (who became Lord Farnborough) was invited. More famous men appeared at these gatherings, and it was at last arranged that Sir Robert Preston, at whose invitation the dinner was held, should only contribute the buck and the champagne, and that the other charges should be shared by the guests. Most of the Cabinet Ministers eventually attended these festive meetings.

By degrees the dinner took a political or semi-political character, and when Sir Robert Preston died the invitations were issued by Lord Farnborough. Then the Conservative Ministerial dinners regularly took place at the "Ship," and those of the Liberals at the "Trafalgar," till they at last died out under Gladstonian neglect.

At Wapping stands an old tavern with a straggling banqueting-hall in the rear, where the press-gangs of a century ago startled many a jovial company and caught the nucleus of many a sturdy crew. Close by is the neighbouring dockside tavern boasting the unique name of " Paddy's Goose," where they learnt to outwit the press-gang. By an arrangement of secret stairs to the roof and loose planks for crossing in mid-air from one building to another, the frequenters of this house invariably made their escape to adjoining streets before the press-gangs had completed their investigation of the tavern. The secret stairs were useful in later years as a means of escape from the police when the *habitués* of the " Goose " were known to be given to the practice of drugging and robbing the seamen who had just been paid off in the docks. The stairs to the roof are still to be seen to-day, though the " Goose " itself has forsaken its former ways and shaken itself free from both land shrimps and publicans. It now offers help and advice to the seaman where of old he used to be notoriously robbed.

No place has more interesting reminiscences of the old coaching days than Highgate, just outside London. A century ago upwards of eighty stage-coaches a day passed through Highgate, travelling between the Metropolis and the North ; and although nothing more than a quiet and sleepy old village, it was remarkable for the number of inns to be found there. In 1826 there were no less than nineteen, of which Hone, in his " Every-day Book," gives the signs.

At these public-houses a quaint and curious custom prevailed. As soon as a coach drew up at the door of the inn which happened to be its calling-place, pressing invitations were given to the company to alight ; and after as many of the travellers as possible could be collected in the parlour, the ceremony known as " Swearing on the Horns " was introduced. A little artifice at once detected the uninitiated, and as soon as this discovery was made the horns were introduced. A pair of horns were fixed on the top of a pole or stick, about 5 feet high ; at the "Gate House" and ten others they were stag-horns ; at the "Red Lion" and several other inns they were rams' horns, while a few had bullocks' horns ; some of them were silver-tipped and handsomely mounted.

Into the parlour would march the host as swearer-in, solemnly clad in a black gown with white bands, and wearing a mask and wig ; followed by his clerk, also gowned, and carrying the horns, and a large book from which the oath was read. There were several versions of the ritual, some in verse, some in prose ; but the gist of it was that the landlord "made" the neophyte his "son" and a "freeman" of Highgate. Of course the whole thing was a burlesque. The newly-made member was sworn "upstanding and uncovered," kissing the horns at each separate oath ; he vowed not to cozen the host, but to acknowledge him as his "father," and manfully pay for a bottle of wine after his initiation ; never to drink small beer when he can get strong, eat brown bread when he can obtain white, nor kiss the maid when he can salute the lips of the mistress ; and with hearty good wishes for his safe journey through Highgate, and also through life, the ceremony terminated with—"God save the King and the Lord of the Manor."

The origin of this ancient but absurd custom is veiled in obscurity. One account says it dates from the Reformation, and was originally intended as a parody on the admission of neophytes into the religious confraternities of the Catholic Church ; another alleges it was devised by a landlord who had lost his licence, and used this form of tomfoolery to cover the sale of his liquors. Anyway it was a practice which was certainly kept up "for the good of the house." It is to be regretted that the registers of the members sworn at every one of these houses have been lost ; for they would have disclosed

some notable names among those who have kissed the
mystic horns, among them Lord Byron, who has left on
record the fact that at one time both sexes were eligible,
and that dancing accompanied the celebration of the
whimsical ceremony ; he says :—

"Many to the steep of Highgate hie ;
Ask, ye Bœotian shades, the reason why ?
'Tis to the worship of the solemn Horn
Grasped in the holy hand of Mystery,
In whose dread names both men and maids are sworn
And consecrate the oath with draught and dance till morn."

At any time the "swearing" occasioned much merriment, and all over the kingdom would be heard the catch
question, "Have you been sworn at Highgate ?"—and,
indeed, there was a way of finding out the uninitiated,
by noting the absence of emphasis placed on the word
"that" in his reply to a certain test query.

With the decline of the coaches the custom gradually
died out, "The Fox under the Hill" being the last
to celebrate this droll rite. The three inns which
kept up the custom longest did so with much rivalry,
and labelled themselves respectively, "The Original
House," "The Old Original House," and "The Real
Original House." The most dignified of the houses was
the Old Gate House Hotel, an inn dating back five
hundred years, and so called from the original building
which crossed the road, and from which the hamlet took
its name. This house of entertainment was rebuilt less
than twenty years ago, carefully preserving some of its
old-fashioned features, as all historic inns should do.

XXIII

THE INNS OF FICTION

Shakespeare's inns—The "Boar's Head"—The inn-yard at Rochester
—Washington Irving's pilgrimage to the "Boar's Head"—and
the "Mason's Arms"—Falstaff's goblet—The legend of Robert
the Waiter—Farquhar's Lichfield inn—as described in the
"Beaux' Stratagem" (humorous extract)—Fielding's inns—The
pious Parson Adams—and the reverend punch-maker—frater-
nise in an inn—The passing of the humble wayside inns of
Smollet and Crabbe—Inns becoming more exclusive with the
advent of the fast mail-coach—Goldsmith's inns—Dramatic
episode in "The Vicar of Wakefield"—A Dickens inn—The
"Maypole" at Epping—Its looting by the rioters described—
The "Mitre" at Chatham—Marryat's inns—The Silent Inn of
Halliwell Sutcliffe.

SOMEWHERE in his "Obiter Dicta" Mr. Augustine
Birrell has said, speaking of Fielding, that "his novels,
like most good ones, are full of inns."

The traditional homeliness and freedom of the inn
have passed into the figurative language of the nation ;
thus a recent writer, describing the literary sentiments
and idiosyncracies of Mr. G. K. Chesterton, says of him :
" He is not a rebel. He is a wayfarer from the ages,
stopping at the inn of life, warming himself at the fire,
and making the rafters ring with his jolly laughter."
That was the proper behaviour for the frequenter of
inns.

A considerable change has taken place in the manners of the people in regard to taverns. Formerly they were the general place of resort for men of genius, rank, and fortune ; and even princes did not disdain to visit them. The "Boar's Head" was celebrated for having been the place where our fifth Harry, when Prince of Wales, revelled with Falstaff, and all "the merry men of Eastcheap." It was at this tavern also that Henry's brothers, the Princes Thomas and John, revelled a whole night in 1410, when their attendants got into an affray, which could not be appeased without the interference of the mayor, sheriff, and principal citizens.

Shakespeare's comedy scenes in 1 *King Henry IV.*, the best of which are laid in taverns, display the dramatist as a humorist of the first water. The fun is so rich, the comedy so humorous, and the action so laughter-provoking that no extract for which there is space here could do justice to it. Of all hostesses who ever presided over an inn, where is there one like the garrulous Dame Quickly of Eastcheap, so comely, so comfortable, and so confiding ? Well might the tavern-haunting Falstaff feel at home in her house, and settle himself down contentedly in it, with the self-satisfying query—

"Shall I not take mine ease in mine inn ? "

But brilliant as the scenes at the "Boar's Head" are, they rightly leave an unsatisfactory impression on the moral sense, as they are no doubt intended to do.

Then the earlier scene in the inn-yard at Rochester is one of those little pictures which live for ever in the memory, because they are so thoroughly true to nature. Who that has read that scene, and has looked out upon the darkness of a winter morning, has not thought of "Charles' wain over the new chimney ? " Who has

THE ANGEL HOTEL, ST. CLEMENT DANES. 1854.

[*Page* 278.

Photo] [Pictorial Agency.

SIGN OF THE "BULL AND MOUTH."

[Page 289.

INTERIOR OF THE OLD COCK TAVERN.

[Page 278.

not speculated upon the grief of the man with one idea, like Robin Ostler, who "never joyed since the price of oats rose ? " Though we see not "the franklin from the wild of Kent, who hath brought three hundred marks with him in gold," we can readily conjure up a mental picture of that sturdy English yeoman. Even the "eggs and butter" which the travellers have for breakfast interest us. And it is by art like this that fiction becomes a reality to us.

When Washington Irving, with the devotion of a true American, was worshipping at English shrines, he went on a quest in search of the Boar's Head Tavern in Eastcheap. But he sought in vain for the ancient abode of Dame Quickly, and the only relic of it was a boar's head carved in stone, which formerly served as the sign, but now built into the parting line of the two houses which stand on the site of the renowned old tavern.

The original building, alas ! had disappeared in the Great Fire of London, but it was soon rebuilt, and continued to flourish under the old name and sign, until a dying landlord, struck with remorse for double scores, bad measures, and other iniquities, which are incidental to the sinful race of publicans (according to Irving, whom we are here quoting), endeavoured to make his peace with heaven by bequeathing the tavern to St. Michael's Church, Crooked Lane, towards the supporting of a chaplain.

For some time the vestry meetings were regularly held at this church-owned tavern ; yet it was observed that the old Boar never held his head up under ecclesiastical government, and, gradually declining, he gave his last expiring gasp about the year 1790, when the premises were converted into shops.

Unsuccessful in this part of his pilgrimage, Washington Irving, as related in his charming "Sketch Book," pursued

his researches in an endeavour to trace certain relics of
the old tavern. Following up information vouchsafed
him by the sexton, he transferred his inquiries to a small
tavern in the neighbourhood, known as the "Mason's
Arms," in Miles Lane, to which establishment the choice
vessels of the vestry had been removed on the demolition
of the old "Boar's Head," and in the club-room of
which the vestry meetings had continued to be held.
Dame Honeyball, of the "Mason's Arms," a plump,
bustling little woman, and no unworthy successor to that
paragon of hostesses, Dame Quickly, was delighted with
the opportunity to oblige the American antiquary. Not
only did she produce for his enraptured inspection all the
precious vessels of the parish club, which included an
antique drinking-goblet from the old "Boar's Head,"
bearing an inscription to the effect that it was the gift
of Francis Wythers, Knight, but also a japanned iron
tobacco-box of almost equal interest. The box was of
gigantic size, and out of its capacious recesses the vestry
had smoked at their stated meetings almost from time
immemorial, vulgar hands not being permitted to profane
it on common occasions. On the outside of this venerable relic was a painting of the Boar's Head Tavern,
with a convivial group at table in full revel, all delineated
with wonderful force and fidelity ; and that there should
be no mistake in understanding the picture, the names of
Prince Hal and old Jack Falstaff had been inscribed on
their respective chairs by the cunning limner. On the
inside of the lid was an inscription recording that the
box was the gift of Richard Gore, for the use of vestry
meetings at the Boar's Head Tavern, and that it had
been repaired and beautified by his successor, Mr. John
Packard, in 1767.

As to the drinking cup aforementioned, we are asked
to believe that it was the identical vessel to which

allusion is made in Part 2 of *Henry IV.*, in the passage beginning—

"Thou didst swear to me upon a parcel-gilt goblet, sitting in my Dolphin chamber at the round table, by a sea-coal fire, on Wednesday, in Whitsun week . . ."

For, of course, everybody believes that Falstaff and his merry crew did actually live and revel here in Eastcheap—a hero of fiction, as limned by a master-hand, is often far more real to us than numbers of the vague heroes which flit across the pages of history.

Adjoining the church, in a small graveyard immediately under the back window of what was once the "Boar's Head," was found the tombstone of Robert Preston, whilom drawer at the tavern. Of this honest servitor a legend ran to the effect that his ghost, while one night taking an airing in the churchyard, was attracted by the familiar call of "Waiter!" from the interior of the old inn; and in response thereto suddenly made his appearance in the midst of a roaring club, just as the parish clerk was singing a stave from the "Mirre Garland of Captain Death," to the terror of the company, which included several bold train-band captains, and to the conversion of an infidel attorney, who became a zealous Christian on the spot, and was never known to twist the truth afterwards, except in the way of business.

Be this as it may, the said Robert Preston seems to have been a worthy successor to the nimble-tongued Francis, who attended upon the revels of Prince Hal, with his ever prompt response, "Anon, anon, Sir"; indeed he was far honester than his predecessor. For while Falstaff flatly accused Francis of putting lime in his sack, the epitaph on honest Robert lauds him for the sobriety of his conduct, the soundness of his wine, and the fairness of his measure.

The lines on the gravestone were no doubt the production of some choice spirit who frequented the tavern in the early part of the eighteenth century, when Preston flourished there ; they are worth transcribing—

> "Bacchus, to give the toping world surprise,
> Produced one sober son, and here he lies.
> Though reared among full hogsheads, he defy'd
> The charms of wine and every one beside.
> O reader, if to justice thou 'rt inclined,
> Keep honest Preston daily in thy mind.
> He drew good wine, took care to fill his pots,
> Had sundry virtues that excused his faults.
> You that on Bacchus have the like dependance
> Pray copy Bob in measure and attendance."

A humorous scene at an inn occurs in Farquhar's well-known comedy, "The Beaux' Stratagem," written in 1707. The two characters represented in this amusing episode are the Host of the inn, and Viscount Aimwell, one of the " Beaux," who, in disguise, is seeking to gain the hand of Dorinda, daughter of Lady Bountiful.

SCENE—An Inn at Lichfield.

Enter BONIFACE and AIMWELL.

Boniface. This way, this way, sir.

Aimwell. You're my landlord, I suppose ?

Bon. Yes, sir, I'm old Will Boniface ; pretty well known upon this road, as the saying is.

Aim. Oh, Mr. Boniface, your servant.

Bon. Oh, sir, what wilt your honour please to drink, as the saying is ?

Aim. I have heard your town of Lichfield much famed for ale ; I think I'll taste that.

Bon. Sir, I have now in my cellar ten tun of the best ale in Staffordshire : 'tis smooth as oil, sweet as milk, clear as amber, and strong as brandy, and will be just fourteen years old the fifth day of next March, old style.

Aim. You're very exact, I find, in the age of your ale.

Bon. As punctual, sir, as I am in the age of my children. I'll show you such ale. Here, tapster, broach number 1706, as the saying is. Sir, you shall taste my "anno domini." I have lived in Lichfield, man and boy, above eight-and-fifty years, and I believe have not consumed eight-and-fifty ounces of meat.

Aim. At a meal, you mean, if one may guess by your bulk?

Bon. Not in my life, sir; I have fed purely upon ale. I have ate my ale, drank my ale, and I always sleep upon my ale.

Enter TAPSTER *with a Tankard.*

Now, sir, you shall see. . . . Your worship's health. (*Drinks*). Ha! delicious, delicious: fancy it Burgandy, only fancy it—and 'tis worth ten shillings a quart.

Aim. (*Drinks.*) 'Tis confounded strong.

Bon. Strong! it must be so, or how would we be strong that drink it?

Aim. And have you lived so long upon this ale, landlord?

Bon. Eight-and-fifty years, upon my credit, sir; but it killed my wife, poor woman, as the saying is.

Aim. How came that to pass?

Bon. I don't know how, sir; she would not let the ale take its natural course, sir; she was for qualifying it every now and then with a dram, as the saying is; and an honest gentleman, that came this way from Ireland, made her a present of a dozen bottles of usquebaugh—but the poor woman was never well after; but, however, I was obliged to the gentleman, you know.

Aim. Why, was it the usquebaugh that killed her?

Bon. My Lady Bountiful said so. She, good lady, did what could be done: she cured her of three tympanies: but the fourth carried her off; but she's happy, and I'm contented, as the saying is.

Aim. Who's that Lady Bountiful you mentioned?

Bon. Odds my life, sir, we'll drink her health. (*Drinks.*) My Lady Bountiful is one of the best of women. Her last husband, Sir Charles Bountiful, left her worth a thousand pounds a year; and I believe she lays out one-half on't in charitable uses for the good of her neighbours.

Aim. Has the lady any children?

Bon. Yes, sir, she has a daughter by Sir Charles; the finest woman in all our county, and the greatest fortune. She has a son, too, by her first husband, 'Squire Sullen, who married a fine lady from London t'other day; if you please, sir, we'll drink his health. *Drinks.*)

Aim. What sort of a man is he?

Bon. Why, sir, the man's well enough; says little, thinks less, and does nothing at all, faith; but he's a man of great estate, and values nobody.

Aim. A sportsman, I suppose?

Bon. Yes, he's a man of pleasure; he plays at whist, and smokes his pipe eight-and-forty hours together sometimes.

Aim. A fine sportsman truly!—and married, you say?

Bon. Ay; and to a curious woman, sir. But he's my landlord, and so a man, you know, would not—— Sir, my humble service. (*Drinks.*) Though I value not a farthing what he can do to me; I pay him his rent at quarter-day; I have a good running trade; I have but one daughter, and I can give her—— But no matter for that.

Aim. You're very happy, Mr. Boniface. Pray, what other company have you in town?

Bon. A power of fine ladies; and then we have the French officers.

Aim. Oh, that's all right; you have a good many of those gentlemen. Pray how do you like their company?

Bon. So well, as the saying is, that I could wish we had as many more of 'em. They're full of money, and pay double for everything they have. They know, sir, that we paid good round taxes for the making of 'em; and so they are willing to reimburse us a little; one of 'em lodges in my house. (*Bell rings.*) I beg your Worship's pardon; I'll wait on you in half a minute.

Good as is this scene of the sprightly Farquhar, it is not so good as the tavern scenes in which Mrs. Quickly figures, nor so poetical as the Host in Fletcher's *Lover's Progress*.

Fielding, of all our novelists, holds up the mirror most truly to the life of his times; he shows us, as with photographic exactitude, how inns were used in the middle of the eighteenth century. In his novel, "Joseph Andrews," we see men like that immortal character, the pious and learned Parson Adams, showing no hesitation, evincing not the slightest qualms, about indulging to the fullest in the hospitalities of the ordinary inn of the time. (We see exactly the same thing, too, in Goldsmith's "Vicar of

Wakefield.")   He makes that good man avail himself of
every accommodation offered by the public inn :—

> " It was the dusk of the evening," writes Fielding, "when a grave
> person rode into an inn, and, committing his horse to the ostler,
> went directly into the kitchen, and, calling for a pipe of tobacco,
> took his place by the fireside, where several other persons were
> likewise assembled."

The grave person was Parson Adams, a clergyman of
much learning but humble means, who had been
accustomed to take his cup of ale in the kitchen of
the squire who had given him his curacy of twenty-
five pounds a year, and whose lady did not think the
parson's dress good enough for him to sit with the
gentry at her table.   In a finer apartment of this same
inn there was another clergyman named Barnabas, who
had condescended to administer ghostly consolation to
a poor man supposed to be dying, but "proceeded to
prayer with all the expedition he was master of, some
company then waiting for him below in the parlour,
where ingredients of punch were all in readiness, but
no one would squeeze the oranges till he came."
Select as the company in the parlour might be, there
was no distinction in the kitchen.   The next day, in
that general temple of good cheer, the reverend punch-
maker, the surgeon, and the exciseman "were smoking
their pipes over some cider-ale"; and Parson Barnabas
having learnt the profession of Parson Adams (for his
cassock had been tied up when he arrived) invited him
to adjourn, with the doctor and the exciseman, to
another room, and partake of a bowl of punch.   This
libation finished, Barnabas takes his seat upon a bench
in the inn-yard to smoke his pipe ! In this diverting
picture of two clergymen fraternising with the doctor
and the exciseman, and drinking together in the kitchen

of an inn, we have a reflection of the actual everyday life of the period.

This inn, however, is a very different place from the inn described by Smollett in " Sir Launcelot Greaves." It is a large coach inn—not of the fast mail-coach, however, but the earlier class of inn associated with the slow coach such as Parson Adams was able to outstrip as he strode along the high-road, brandishing his crab-stick.

Smollett's inn was but a little wayside public-house, in which the kitchen was the only room for entertainment in the house, paved with red bricks, furnished with a few Windsor chairs, the whole place scrupulously clean, perhaps with its "floor neatly sanded" (as Goldsmith has told us in his description of another village inn of this humble type) and "adorned with shining plates of pewter and copper saucepans, nicely scoured, that even dazzled the eyes of the beholder."

The inns of Fielding and Smollett's time have passed, as have also those described a little later by Crabbe, as flourishing in the small English "borough" during the first decade of the nineteenth century. All these old hostelries are as obsolete as the old signs over the London shops. We now fail to find the Head Inn, of the time when the world travelled in carriages with post-horses ; when the ready chaise and smart driver were to be had at five minutes' notice ; when the ample inn-yard was surrounded by well-filled stabling and well-appointed travelling carriages awaiting the public call ; when the accomplished host bowed in his pride to the parting guest, as graciously as he welcomed the newly-arrived visitor ; when the lady hostess governed the bar and schooled the kitchen ; and all was most admirably managed for the traveller who could pay for so much solicitude.

It must be confessed that the inns described by
Fielding and Smollett had passed away even in Crabbe's
time. With the advent of fast coaches landlords and
landladies had become more exclusive, and despised
vulgar company. The traveller on foot was ever received
but coldly ; if a bedroom were found for him it was one
little better than a prison cell, and if he were supplied
with refreshments he was set down to take them at the
same table as soldiers and the servants. But when, the
next day being Sunday, the pedestrian who relates these
experiences, put on his clean linen, we read that he was
shown into the parlour, and addressed in more respectful
terms—and, as he humorously records, he was suffered
to pay like a gentleman.

In that reliable mirror of eighteenth-century life, Goldsmith's " Vicar of Wakefield," we find all the characters
who have occasion to travel abroad, resorting to inns
for rest and refreshment as a matter of course. On one
occasion the good vicar does not hesitate to enter an
alehouse in the company of a troupe of strolling players ;
while on another, he and a brother of the cloth adjourn
to an inn, as the most natural thing in the world, to
discuss orthodoxy and other high matters, over a social
drink.

But the most dramatic situation in the book occurs
when two guests are found staying unknown to each
other in the same inn, the one the good clergyman
himself, and the other no less than the long-lost innocent
daughter of whom he is in search. While the kindly
disposed vicar sits at the kitchen fire sharing his pint of
wine with the landlord, he becomes aware of a fierce
tirade going on in another part of the house, and hears
the irate landlady's voice raised in heaping insult and
calumny upon a poor woman whom she is turning out
for being unable to pay the lodging bill she has incurred.

Going to see the cause of all the disturbance, his astonishment may be imagined when he discovers in the unfortunate creature his own beloved daughter Olivia, who at once finds shelter from the landlady's fury in the protecting arms of her father. Surely no inn ever formed the background to a more melodramatic scene than the one here depicted by the novelist.

No finer ideal of an old roadside inn was ever created than the drawing of the "Maypole" at Epping Forest with which George Cattermole illustrated "Barnaby Rudge." So talented an artist, however, could not fail to be influenced by, and draw the right inspiration from, Dickens's vivid description of this "old building with its huge zigzag chimneys and more gable-ends than a lazy man would care to count on a sunny day"—with its diamond-pane lattices, massive beams, and its quaintly and grotesquely-carved porch, in which two grim-looking, high-backed settles guarded the entrance to the mansion. With its vast stables, now empty, gloomy, and ruinous, it had once been the private residence of a family of position and affluence; it was said to have been built in the reign of Henry VIII., and there was a legend (says the novelist, than whom no one knew better all the concomitants necessary to make up a typical establishment of this kind) that not only had Queen Elizabeth, while on a hunting excursion, slept there one night, to wit in a certain oak-panelled room with a deep bay window; but that next morning, while standing on the mounting-block before the door, with one foot in the stirrup, the virgin monarch had then and there boxed and cuffed an unlucky page for some neglect of duty. With touches like this is a verisimilitude given to any legendary episode, as Dickens well knew.

Then later in the work is the great master's equally powerful and realistic description of the looting of the

"Maypole" by the "No Popery" rioters of 1780, when
old John Willett, the landlord, seated deep in his armchair, stupefied and overwhelmed by the strangeness
of the scene around him, watches the destruction of
his own property in a dazed sort of way, as if all the
proceedings had no reference to himself whatever.

"Yes. Here was the bar—the bar that the boldest never entered
without special invitation—the sanctuary, the mystery, the hallowed
ground; here it was, crammed with men, clubs, sticks, torches,
pistols; filled with a deafening noise, oaths, shouts, screams, hoot-
ings; changed all at once into a bear-garden, a mad-house, an
infernal temple; men darting in and out by door and window,
smashing the glass, turning the taps, drinking liquor out of china
punchbowls, sitting astride casks, smoking private and personal
pipes, cutting down the sacred grove of lemons, hacking and
hewing at the celebrated cheese, breaking open inviolable drawers,
putting things in their pockets which didn't belong to them,
dividing his own money before his own eyes, wantonly wasting,
breaking, pulling down, and tearing up."

And so proceeds this fantastic and picturesque description of a scene in which riot, plunder, and wanton
destruction overtake a house hitherto sacred to all the
kindly social laws of orderliness, hospitality, and good
fellowship.

There are many "Leather Bottles," but surely none
better or more to be desired than "the clean and
comfortable village ale-house" to which Mr. Pickwick,
Mr. Winkle, and Mr. Snodgrass found their way in
their search for the truant Tupman, whom they discovered in the parlour of that establishment; a long,
low-roofed room furnished with a large number of high-
backed, leather-cushioned chairs, of fantastic shapes,
and embellished with a great variety of old portraits
and roughly coloured prints of some antiquity:
but the home-like comfort of which was most truly
evidenced by a table at the top end, with a white cloth

upon it, and well covered with a roast fowl, bacon, ale, and all the etceteras.

What Charles Dickens did not know of inns—those of the good old-fashioned sort, of course—was not worth knowing. He knew that the first desideratum of an inn was snugness and comfort. And so when he gives us a description of the "Mitre" at Chatham, a capital old inn at which Nelson and William IV., when he was Duke of Clarence, had frequently stopped, he conveys the right impression to our minds in a pregnant sentence like this : "It had an ecclesiastical sign—the Mitre—and a bar that seemed the next best thing to a bishopric, it was so snug." Every Dickensian inn is said to have been drawn from reality.

Near the "dark arches" of the Adelphi, which made such an impression on the youthful mind of Charles Dickens, and standing at the bottom of Ivy Lane, was the "Fox-under-the-Hill," described in David Copperfield as "a little, dirty, tumble-down public-house." Mr. Austin Brereton, in his "Literary History of the Adelphi" informs us that this ramshackle building disappeared at the making of the Victoria Embankment ; after remarking that Ivy Lane remains one of the most interesting bits of old London, our authority proceeds to tell us that the Ivy Pier "was the landing-place for the halfpenny steamboats which plied between London Bridge and the Strand. Here a lamentable explosion, by which many people were killed, occurred in August, 1847, and soon afterwards the 'Fox' landing-stage was disused."

Captain Marryat, whose novels are so largely devoted to seafaring life, naturally affects those inns patronised by sea-going folk. Those named most prominently in his works are the "Fountain," the "George," and the "Blue Posts," at Portsmouth. The "Fountain" has been converted into a Sailors' Institute, and the original building of the " Blue Posts" was burnt down in 1870.

The last named, to which midshipmen very largely resorted, was marked by two large blue posts fixed at the door next the coach-office; and when Peter Simple was first driven to this inn, his coachman was good enough to inform him, with a sly look in his eye, that it was "the Blue Postesses where the midshipmen leave their chestesses, call for tea and toastesses, and sometimes forgets to pay for their breakfastesses."

The inn which figures as the scene of that exciting fight described by Halliwell Sutcliffe, in his stirring north-country romance, " Ricroft of Withens," was recently (1907) scheduled by the Justices of Bingley for closing under the compensation clauses of the most recent Licensing Act. The novelist calls it the Silent Inn; really it was the Eagle Inn, at Stanbury, in the West Riding.

The inns most successfully described by the fictionist, it will be observed, are those found to have had an actual existence.

XXIV

INNKEEPERS AND INNKEEPING

Temperamental qualifications of a good innkeeper—The homely welcome of the old-time inn—A guest only a "number" in the huge modern hotel—The modern hotel—Where innkeeping is no longer "a fine art"—Business, not hospitality, in the palatial hotel—The cosy inn as described by Dickens—Tom Smart and the buxom landlady—Women as innkeepers—The term "brewster" considered—A "brew-house" once a common domestic office—Dishonest tricks of the old Ale-wives—Relationship of host and guest—No personal solicitude now—The new serve-to-order style—Boniface—The typical English host—Who *is* the patron saint of innkeepers?—Some famous English hosts—Earliest landlord known by name—The eminent hosteller of the "Tabard," *temp.* Henry III.—An accommodating host—who gave the tasting guarantee to Prince Rupert—Tom Pierce—An accomplished restaurateur—Amusing anecdote of two West of England rival publicans—A parson publican—A tavern-keeper with an unfavourable reputation—The legend of Dirty Dick—One of the last of the race of typical landlords—The overcharges of innkeepers—The running-up of drink scores—and the killing of "Poor Trust"—Public-house rhymes and precepts—Innkeeping an honourable calling—A businesslike epitaph—Successive generations in inn proprietorship.

IN the pre-railway era innkeeping was a calling of no little importance to the travelling public. It was one which called for a combination of temperamental qualifications not too frequently met with, not the least of which were a genial presence, a capacity for handling a staff of dependents so as to ensure a service enhanced as much by its promptitude as by its willingness, a sound knowledge of all the mysteries of the *cuisine*, a nice taste in wines, and, above all, a scrupulous regard for cleanliness.

It may be asserted that with the advent of railways, innkeeping began steadily to decline, and, so far as real inns or roadside hostels are concerned, has never fully recovered. With the rush of railway travelling came that class of people who live to make things pay, rather than to make them worth paying for. There was a time, before that multiplication of travellers which was brought about by the iron horse, when the ideal English inn offered a welcome that never failed to make glad the stranger's heart, and was not merely a place to sell him, on strictly commercial terms, a certain amount of the indispensable conveniences of life. But perhaps the modern host must always fail in the discharge of those old-time duties of the profession, because it is humanly impossible for any one to abound in cordiality towards the crowds of travellers which have been launched upon the public accommodation of the country by railways. The hospitable state of mind, cultivated by the most painstaking of innkeepers, would in these times find itself too soon exhausted at a prosperous inn by the endless succession of guests who entered its doors between the earliest arrival in the morning and the last omnibus to the station at night, with persistent and peremptory cries for breakfast, lunch, dinner, or supper; for chops or steaks, wine or beer; for bacon and eggs or tea and toast; for beds or baths, towels or hot water; all and everything wanted expeditiously, because the trains wait for no man. All these things and much more, may be provided by crack hotels, highly organised and replete with every modern luxury; but they are manifestly beyond the resources of the average old-fashioned country inn. But the individuality of the inn, and the personality of the landlord, are missing from the huge caravansary hotels where the host is but a salaried manager and the guest is only known as a "number."

The modern hotel is a shop at which may be obtained, at a price, all that one has the mind and the means to exact. But as to being homelike, or presenting any aspect that can make the visitor feel at home, nothing could be more hopelessly lacking. There is always a sense of gratification, as of something achieved when, any part of the day's travelling being over, a stopping-place in the journey for rest and refreshment is reached; but there is a certain sense of disappointment when one is received in a mechanical and perfunctory manner by a whole retinue of clerks and porters, waiters and chambermaids, instead of being personally welcomed by the more interesting presence of a host or hostess. The first element of the old-time innkeeping, cordiality of welcome, is now missing, or at least is becoming rare in England. That alone, says a writer discussing "Inn-keeping as a Fine Art" is—

"a damper to the gentle expression of heart with which you draw up at the door of an inn. The idyllic feeling is at once checked, and you pass from any hope of a realised ideal of art into the state of mind of the mere customer. And, of course, what is true of the deficiency in the feeling with which you are received, is apt to be equally true of the deficiency in the external amenities with which that feeling is expressed. Abroad there is still a preference for decorated entrances, for bright oleanders or other flowers to flank the steps of the entrance. In England even the great tree opposite the inn-door, or the old-fashioned inn-gardens at the back which used sometimes to make up for a homely entrance, are fast disappearing without anything to take their place. There is no external grace or charm presented to the appearing or the disappearing stranger. You feel at once that you are looked upon by the eye of strict business, not by the eye of hospitality."

SHOP SIGNS AT OLD TEMPLE BAR. 1620.

[*Page* 283.

OLD "LA BELLE SAUVAGE." THE INNER COURT.

[Page 107 295

The distinction between the inn and the hotel seems to be determined by age and position. The latter establishments are generally the modern hostels of the town or much-frequented place of resort; the former are the older houses of rest and entertainment found along the roadside, and marking welcome intervals along every arterial thoroughfare of the country. The traditions of such inns as the "Tabard" in Southwark, the "Bell" at Stilton, and the "Chequers" at Canterbury, involve the social history of all the bygone centuries. The comfortable inn is indigenous to the soil of old England; the palatial hotel is but an exotic introduced by the quicker methods of locomotion and the greater concentration of population in particular centres.

What writer has feasted the imagination on the cosy comforts of an old wayside inn with more zest than Charles Dickens? His description, for instance, of Tom Smart's adventure, is thoroughly enjoyable. We learn how the bagman, driving his vixenish mare in the clay-coloured gig with red wheels, across the dreary expanse of Marlborough Downs, on a tempestuous winter evening, at last drew up at the hospitable doors of the last roadside inn, "on the right-hand side of the way, about half-a-quarter of a mile from the end of the downs."

The inn, like many more of its kind in those days, was a strange old place, with a deep porch and gable-topped windows that projected completely over the pathway, but comfortable-looking, with a strong, cheerful light in the bar-window that shed a bright ray across the road, and even lighted up the hedge on the other side. But more to the purpose of a cold and hungry traveller was the red, flickering light of the opposite window, one moment but faintly discernible, and the next gleaming strongly through the drawn curtains, which intimated that a rousing fire was blazing within; all of which was taken in by the experienced eye of the traveller, and within five minutes Tom was snugly ensconced within that room with his slippered feet on the fender. When the neat and smart waiting-maid presently came in and commenced to lay a particularly clean, white cloth on the table for his supper, Tom, having his back to the open door, saw reflected in the glass over the chimney-piece a charming prospect of the bar, with delightful rows of green bottles and gold labels, together with jars of pickles and preserves, and cheeses and boiled hams, and rounds of beef arranged on shelves in the most tempting and delightful array. All of which presents to the mind's eye, in the characteristic Dickensian style, the comforts and resources of an old-fashioned roadside inn of the early nineteenth century.

Of course the proprietor of the inn and all its delectable contents was a "buxom widow"—did not the gallant Tom afterwards marry the supreme ruler of all these agreeable possessions ?—which fact forces upon our consideration the long and intimate association of women with the brewing and selling of ale, and all that pertains to the keeping of inns and such-like houses of entertainment. In this connection etymology offers us evidence which is as interesting as it is valuable.

A brewer is one who brews, who concocts, who prepares a beverage by steeping, boiling, and fermentation. One is said to brew tea; and the word "broth" is connected with the term "to brew." Brewster is the feminine form of brewer; and it is significant of brewing being anciently a woman's occupation that we still speak of a licensing sessions as "brewster sessions."

Brewster, and all words of similar ending, as baxter, and spinster, come from the times when brewing, baking, weaving, and spinning were purely female industries. The word tapster, again, contains the same termination, said also to be indicative of the feminine, making its signification—and it was literally so till the thirteenth century—almost equivalent to our modern word barmaid. One learned authority, however, contradicts this, and says the "ster" in tapster is no more a sign of the feminine than it is in barrister or in master, being here the Saxon word *steor*, meaning "mastery." Certainly, the masculine form of tapster was tapper.

And while examining the terminology of the subject, it may be pointed out as a relic of the time when brewing was a universal domestic industry in this country, that the place in which it was done was called a brew-house—in fact the name brew-house till very recent years was given in the Midland counties to the outhouse commonly known elsewhere as the wash-house—whereas, when brewing became an organised industry employing a number of workmen, the old Saxon name was discarded for the more Frenchified word "brewery."

Nor were these women traders of old exempt from the ordinary failings of the opposite sex engaged in business. Mediæval Ale-wives were not above putting pitch in the beer measure, thereby lessening the quantity of the vended quart; and in the play of *Henry IV.* is mentioned another ingenious device of the unscrupulous beer-seller—that of putting soap into the tankard to bring a head on to the ale.

On the other hand, there is much which might be said in favour of the more modern female innkeeper. A cheery hostess can make an inn very homelike.

Dr. Andrew Carnegie holds a high opinion of the catering capabilities of women. Speaking of hostelries some time ago, he remarked : " In an hotel I look once at a man who is presumed to be the master and three times at the woman, for the success of an hotel depends upon the landlady."

By Scot's law women were forbidden to go drinking in beer-houses unless accompanied by their husbands, a statute to that effect dating back to 1454. The Scottish authorities seem to have looked sharply after women in public-houses long before the present agitation in that country for the abolition of barmaids, a bylaw of the city of Edinburgh, made in 1695, strictly prohibiting their employment in such capacity. But in England the "hostess of the inn" may almost be reckoned among our national institutions.

The previously quoted authority on the ancient art of innkeeping, laments that the old relationship of guest and host, which he says was not unlike that of patient and physician, has given way to a mere commercial and totally impersonal relationship, in which the supply often falls short of the demand. No longer does the genius of innkeeping anticipate the traveller's wants, and surround him with a genial care that does not throw him entirely upon his own resources when out of his accustomed environment. He is not seized upon as soon as he arrives and asked with anxious solicitude what he would like ; he is told what he can have, and the manifest indifference to his personal preferences seems to leave his choice more limited than the actual resources of the establishment really are. And all this because innkeeping is now conducted as a trade, rather than as the fine art it was in our grandfathers' days.

"Nothing," says our authority, "can be less like the generous pleasure in making much of a stranger than the unimaginative and strictly served-to-order meals of the modern hotel. There is no effort to tempt the appetite of a guest, nothing but at best a strict compliance with orders issued. There is no delight taken in the appearance of the table—no rolls and toast and oat-cakes, pikelets and tea-cake at tea or breakfast; no fruit, no generous supply of milk cream; only the bare allowance of bread and butter or leathery toast positively ordered, and as much skim-milk as will be barely sufficient to render the tea drinkable. In a word, the table is never laid out as it would be for a little private feast, but only just up to order, even if the resources of the inn will admit of that.

" Now the imagination of the host used to be thought far more active and efficient in making these sort of meals tempting, than the imagination of the guest—for the host had made a study of it, while the guest had not—and it was once part of the fine art of innkeeping to exceed the guest's anticipation, and make him marvel at the resources of hospitality."

An inn at best is not a home, but for a short time at least it may be made an agreeable variation, a pleasant change, even on a home. The more homelike the inn, the greater the assurance for its patronage, popularity, and prosperity.

The term " Boniface " applied to the English innkeeper in general, seems to have been adopted through an erroneous interpretation of its literal form. The name in its pure Latin form signified "the well-doer," and was conferred on St. Winifrith, an Anglo-Saxon born at Crediton, in honourable recognition of his life-work of converting the Germanic peoples to Christianity. St. Boniface, though libellously described by one bio-grapher as being, before his conversion, " a stout man, addicted to drink," had no association whatever with innkeeping; but the name presenting itself in its English form and pronunciation seems to have been accepted as " Bonny face "; and adopted in this sense it became peculiarly applicable to the typical English landlord, who is traditionally supposed to be a sleek, good-tempered, jolly sort of fellow. Used in this way, as the generic name for an innkeeper, Boniface makes its first appearance in literature in Farquhar's comedy, *The Beaux' Stratagem*, quoted in the previous chapter.

In the New Testament we find St. Matthew described as a "publican"—a word which would have been better translated "tax-gatherer." That the term "publican" should have caused confusion in the lay mind is not surprising; but it is amusing to learn, on good authority too, that a dignitary of the Church once laboured under the misapprehension that St. Matthew, being a publican, must have sold beer; and he therefore, as an appropriate tribute, regularly decorated his church every St. Matthew's Day, with hops.

It is neither St. Boniface nor St. Matthew who has been chosen patron saint of innkeepers, but (according to one authority) St. Theodotus, whose name appears in the Calender on May 18th. St. Theodotus was himself an innkeeper and a citizen of Ancyra, the capital of Galatia, where he suffered martyrdom in the year 303 A.D.

Another authority names St. Martin as the guardian and protector of the publican interest. There seems no doubt that the autumnal wine-feast of the pagan world became confused with the mediæval Feast of St. Martin. Hence he was made the "patron" of tavern-keepers, wine merchants, and other dispensers of good cheer. One ludicrous result of this is that the good old French Bishop figures beside the god Bacchus among the paintings and statues in the hall of the Vintners' Company, near London Bridge.

There was a Saint Bacchus, a fourth-century martyr, but he has not found sufficient favour to be made the patron of publican, brewer, or wine merchant. The hagiology of the trade seems rather mixed.

Perhaps the earliest English host of whom we have knowledge was that "seemly man" Harry Bailey, landlord of the "gentil hostelrie, highte the Tabard," at Southwark. From the immortal poem of Sir Geoffrey Chaucer, we learn how some five hundred years ago, whilst a troop of pilgrims were assembled in the guesten-room there, and the best wine the " Tabard " could supply was passing round among them, the host, with a boldness sometimes to be seen in men of his craft, proposed to join them on the morrow in their pilgrimage. Nay, he goes further. He takes the liberty of suggesting that it would be a good means of shortening the tedium of the journey between London and Canterbury if each pilgrim were to tell one tale going, and a second while returning ; and (with an eye to business, characteristic of his calling) that the one who tells the best story should, on their safe return, have a supper at his inn at the expense of the rest. And that the thing should not fall through for lack of initiative, without more ado, he offers his own services as judge of the performances. Needless to say the approval of every one present was won by this energetic landlord ; the company retired to rest in good spirits, and next morning, when sun was up, they mounted their horses at the door of the "Tabard," gladly allowing him to ride with them, at his own cost, and to be their guide.

Commenting on this personality, Timbs, the antiquary, says :—

"Henry Bailly, the host of the Tabard, was not improbably a descendant of Henry Tite or Martin, of the borough of Southwark, to whom King Henry III., in the fifteenth year of his reign, at the instance of William de la Zouch, granted the customs of the town of Southwark during the King's pleasure, he paying to the exchequer the annual fee and farm rent of £10 for the same. By that grant Henry Tite or Martin was constituted Bailiff of Southwark, and he would therefore acquire the name of Henry the Bailiff, or Le Bailly. Be this as it may, it is a fact on record, that Henry Bailly, the hosteller of the Tabard was one of the burgesses who represented the borough of Southwark in the Parliament held at Westminster 1376, and was again returned to the parliament held at Gloucester, 1378."

It is evident that Henry Bailey was a man of substance, and popular amongst his fellow-townsmen, as well as an "ostyler"—as he is described in a Subsidy Roll of Richard II.

The accomplished host is the one who is ever ready to accommodate himself to the whims of his guests. At the outbreak of the Civil War the fiery Prince Rupert found himself on one occasion at the Castle Inn, Nottingham, where he called for a bottle of wine, bidding the attendant open it and drink the first glass. The latter order was apparently a relic of the old tasting guarantee once demanded by potentates and tyrants living in constant fear of the poisoner; but however it might have been in consonance with German habits, to the honest, simple-minded Englishman it sounded like a madman's freak. Or it may have been the peremptory and hectoring tone in which the "Mad Cavalier" gave the order. Anyway the waiter was so frightened he bolted from the room, and jumped right over the gallery into the yard below. The host, apprised of the strange request, promptly presented himself before his distinguished guest; bowing and smiling, he said, "Your Highness will forgive the fellow because he never drinks anything strong. But if you will graciously permit me to attend upon you, it will honour me to drink the first glass of every bottle, let your Highness call for as many as you may." This was spoken as should be.

A famous restaurateur of the period when the exquisites of fashion were just as remote from the "simple life" as are the millionaires of modern times, was Tom Pierce, of the "Castle," near Covent Garden. It is related that on one occasion the gallants present at a fashionable assembly

held in his house took off the shoe of a noted belle, and
filled it with wine, which they drank off to her health.
Having toasted the lady in this extraordinary manner,
they then handed the shoe to Pierce to dress for them ;
and surely enough this accomplished culinary artist
failed not to produce it for them at supper exquisitely
ragooed.   It cannot truthfully be said of manners characterised by insane indulgences such as these, that—

"No cook with art increased physicians' fees
Nor served up death with soup and fricassees."

An amusing tale is told of two West of England
publicans, one named Sam Henry, a very civil, obliging
fellow, and the other, Tom Irwin, a man of envious
disposition.   Sam set up a little ale-house, the sign of
which was the "Goose," painted by Sam himself.   When
the neighbours dubbed the landlord Sam Goose, he was
rather pleased than offended with the nickname, wittily
observing, "There is one difference between us : the
goose is plucked himself, but it is my business to pluck
others."   Sam's good-humour brought him plenty of
custom, poorly as his house was furnished ; he was
patronised by the parson of the parish, for whom the
only chair in the establishment was specially reserved on
the occasions when he honoured Sam with a visit.

All this success was resented by his rival, Irwin, who,
having scraped a little money together, rebuilt his house
on a larger scale.   The new establishment had three
rooms, and half a dozen glass windows ; it was provided
with suitable furniture, including a large polished oak
table ; drinking glasses took the place of horns, and,
more wonderful than all, the chief room was provided
with a bell, the first ever known in that countryside.
When it came to selecting a sign, Tom at length fixed

on a Fox running away with a Goose; which he had painted so skilfully as to introduce the features of Sam in the head of the Goose. The new house, together with its humorous sign, had the effect of attracting most of the custom from the old favourite resort. But Sam was not to be outdone; and after much pondering he devised a new sign for himself—he had cleverly painted over the door the Goose running away with the Fox! The thing took, and the genial Sam once more enjoyed the lion's share of the village custom.

A curious little book published at York in 1806, with the title "Anecdotes and Manners of a few Ancient and Modern Oddities," contained a chapter on a certain Parson Publican. It is therein recounted that a Rev. Mr. Carter was curate of Lastingham; and as he had to support a family of thirteen children on a stipend of £20 per annum, his wife had kept a tavern to eke out the miserable pittance with which a wealthy Church pretended to reward her husband's services. When, at the visitation of the Archdeacon, an attempt was made to bring this outrageous parson to book, he did not shrink from the ordeal, but had the boldness to defend his anomalous position. His address to the Archdeacon is too long to quote in its entirety, but a few extracts from it will serve for our present purpose. After alluding to the insufficiency of his stipend with which to meet the calls of his large family, he said :—

"My wife keeps a public-house, and as my parish is so wide that some of my parishioners have to come from ten to fifteen miles to church, you will readily allow that some refreshment before they return must occasionally be necessary; and when can they have it more properly than when their journey is half performed?

". . . To divert their attention from foibles over their cups, I take down my violin and play them a few tunes, which gives me an opportunity of seeing that they get no more liquor than is necessary for refreshment ; and if the young people propose a dance I seldom answer in the negative. . . .

"Thus my parishioners enjoy a triple advantage of being instructed, fed, and amused at the same time."

And so through a long and eloquent address, the peroration of which touches on the duty of cheerfulness, this unconventional clergyman justifies his conduct so admirably that the Archdeacon has to acknowledge the soundness of his arguments, and acquit him of any clerical impropriety.

One London tavern-keeper left behind him a reputation so queer that, though it was uncomplimentary to himself personally, it yet had the effect of establishing his business firmly in the public favour ; so firmly, indeed, that the only inference is that this popularity was gained, in spite of adverse surroundings, by the high quality of the liquors he vended. In Bishopsgate, in the heart of the City, will be found the still flourishing wine-cellars of "Dirty Dick," whose name has been celebrated in the once popular song, "The King of the Cannibal Islands" :—

> "His palace was like Dirty Dick's—
> 'Twas built of mud for the want of bricks."

The central episode in the history of this eccentric individual—his name, by the way, was not Dick at all, but Nathaniel Bentley—was of a somewhat romantic nature. The business was established in 1745 by his father, who quickly amassed a fortune in it, and gave his son a most excellent education. Dying in 1761, he left the whole of his property to his son, who on his succession to the business was quite a dandy, always appearing in public in the most fashionable attire, and with his hair arranged by a Court perruquier. The character of young Bentley was, in fact, at that time

exactly the reverse of what it subsequently became, after
he had acquired those untidy and neglectful habits which
obtained for him the nickname of Dirty Dick.   He
became not only negligent in appearance and morose
in habit, but extremely parsimonious, dispensing with
all service, even mending and washing his own clothes.
When remonstrated with upon his want of personal
cleanliness, he would answer, " It's no use ; if I wash
my hands to-day, they will be dirty again to-morrow."

The event which brought about this extraordinary
change in his manners and habits was a "love affair."
He was engaged to be married to a beautiful girl to
whom he was devotedly attached.   The wedding was
arranged ; but on the day appointed for a splendid
entertainment, to which he had invited a number of
his closest friends in celebration of the engagement, he
received the news of the lady's sudden death.   The
shock not merely distressed the expectant bridegroom,
it changed him forthwith from a polite and polished
beau to a dirty, slovenly miser.

For fifty years he admitted no one to the upper portion
of the premises; and when, at his death, an entrance was
forced, ruin and dilapidation, dust and cobwebs everywhere met the eye; while in the chief room of the house,
where the furniture had once been of an elegant and
costly character, the decay was even more apparent—
wood worm-eaten and hangings moth-eaten, steel heavy
coated with rust, and gildings tarnished black, colours
faded, brightness and polish swallowed up for ever in
stains, mould, dampness, and accumulated dirt.

It is by no means improbable that the idea of the
abandoned wedding-feast in a locked-up room, which
appears in "Great Expectations," was inspired by the
life-story of Dirty Dick; this story was certainly familiar
to Charles Dickens, because a rhymed version of the

"legend of Bishopsgate" appeared in *Household Words*, the journal conducted by the great novelist. It is entitled "The Dirty Old Man," and commences :—

> "In a dirty old house lived a dirty old man,
> Soap, towels, or brushes were not in his plan."

Quite a number of verses are devoted to a full description of the exterior of the house. Then we read :—

> "Within these there were carpets and cushions of dust,
> The wood was half rot, and the metal half rust ;
> Old curtains, half cobwebs, hung grimly aloof,
> 'Twas a spider's elysium from cellar to roof."

Of the mysterious banqueting-room we learn that—

> "Full fifty years since, turned the key in that door,
> 'Tis a room deaf and dumb 'mid the city's uproar ;
> The guests for whose joyance that table was spread
> May now enter as ghosts, for they are everyone dead."

The race of innkeepers is not quite extinct—the man who is proud of his calling and lives up to all its worthiest traditions still finds one bright exemplar in Mr. Harry Jones, the landlord of the King's Arms Hotel, Malmesbury, Wiltshire. In outward appearance mine host Jones suits the part he has to play in life most admirably ; his portly figure and jolly red face of the Tony Weller type are set off to perfection in the old-world habiliments it is his delight to affect—trousers turned up at the ankles, a long, loose-fitting coat of a cut of other days, a white, or else a highly coloured, waistcoat of the Dick Swiveller pattern, and on his head a tall, straight-brimmed hat of a style which was popular fifty years ago—such is the outward semblance embodying the spirit of genial hospitality with which wayfarers are welcomed into the chief inn at Malmesbury. Inside, the comforts provided are of the true Dickensian order—that old British fare which needs nothing but its prime quality and honest substantiality to recommend it. As there is good cheer for the man, so is there warm stabling for his beast in this typical old West of England establishment.

> "Good horse and fly, with safe linch-pin,
> Always to be hired at Jones's Inn.
> For never a bone nor never a skin
> Was ever broken from Jones's Inn ;
> Stable warm and good corn bin
> Are always open at Jones's Inn."

The "King's Arms" is not identical with the ancient Malmesbury inn, though no doubt it was originally part of the abbey buildings.

That over-charging by landlords is no new grievance against them is gathered from the following, written early in the eighteenth century :—

"The change that has taken place in respect to the company frequenting taverns is supposed to be owing to the increased expense ; but extravagant charges in Queen Anne's time were not less deserving of complaint then than they are now. The Duke of Ormond, who gave a dinner to a few friends at the 'Star and Garter,' in Pall Mall, was charged twenty-one pounds, six shillings, and eight pence for four dishes and four, that is, first and second courses, without wine or desert."

The pernicious practice of "running up a score" for drink obtained on credit is possibly as old as public ale-houses themselves. Does not Christopher Sly, the drunken tinker of Burton Heath, seek to prove his identity by the effective proof that he is known to Mistress Marian Hacket, "the fat ale-wife of Wincot," to whom he owes "fourteen pence on the score for sheer ale" ?

The running up of public-house scores, the contracting of debt for intoxicating liquor supplied till the customer is able to pay at the week-end when he receives his wages, is sometimes encouraged nowadays by innkeepers of the baser sort. But in many respectable old-fashioned inns the practice of "giving trust" is severely frowned down by the posting up of "Public Notices" on the walls of bars and tap-rooms.

This notice sometimes takes a pictorial form, the favourite one representing a dead dog lying near a barrel of beer in a cellar, and just discovered by the cellarman, who stands at the foot of the steps holding a lighted candle in his hand. Round the collar of the dog appears his name, "Trust," and beneath the picture appears the significant label, "Poor Trust is dead I Bad pay killed him!"

Even a drink-sodden brain could scarcely fail to interpret this allegorical picture ; however, in most places the message is conveyed more directly in words.

An epigrammatic style of putting the rules of the house before the customer was the printing of a bold notice :—

"To-morrow we give credit, but not to-day."

Or the same may be conveyed in this fashion :—

"Call frequently
Drink moderately
Part friendly
Pay to-day—Trust to-morrow."

Or in rhyme thus :—

"Since man to man is so unjust
In word or deed you scarce can trust.
I've trusted many, to my sorrow.
So pay to-day—I'll trust to-morrow."

Over the fireplace of a famous inn, immortalised by Charles Dickens, are these lines :—

"All you, who stand before the fire,
I pray sit down—it's my desire
That other folks, as well as you,
May see the fire and feel it too.

N.B.—My liquor's good
My measure's just
Excuse me, Sirs,
I cannot trust."

The foregoing notice, in its entirety, or in parts, is a somewhat stereotyped form.   Sometimes it is commenced with the couplet—

"All you who bring tobacco here,
Must pay for pipes as well as beer."

It then proceeds, "And you that stand before the fire," and so on as before.   A similar notification about the purchasing of pipes will be found in the chapter on " Smoking."

Some old-established houses, particularly those of the type known as " liquor vaults," or sometimes as " wine cellars," which have descended from father to son for a generation or two, and acquired a high reputation for the quality of the liquors supplied, post up a code of rules for the conduct of the business, which are positively austere.   These rules vary in form, in number, and in modes of expression ; but besides prohibiting smoking, forbidding bad language, and containing other commonplace features, are to this effect :—

" NO PERSON WILL BE SERVED TWICE."
" NO PERSON WHO IS IN THE LEAST INTOXICATED WILL BE SERVED."

THE FAMOUS SIGN OF "THE FIVE ALLS," AT MARLBOROUGH.

[*Page* 293.

THE "GOOD OR QUIET WOMAN" AT WIDFORD,
IN ESSEX.

[*Page* 293.

THE "MERRY MAIDENS," AT SHINFIELD, NEAR READING.

[*Page* 297.

THE "NOW THUS," A SIGN
WITH A CURIOUS
HISTORY.

[*Page* 297.

THE SIGN OF THE "THREE LOGGERHEADS."
WHO IS THE THIRD?

[*Page* 301.

And sometimes even go to the length—

"DRINK UP QUICKLY AND DEPART QUIETLY."

In one well-known London house the last-named rule is expressed in this form :—

"WHEN YOU ARE IN A PLACE OF BUSINESS, TRANSACT YOUR BUSINESS AND GO ABOUT YOUR BUSINESS."

Is there any other trade in which such " self-denying ordinances " have prevailed ?

Innkeeping in the past has always been regarded as an honourable calling, being one which called for the exercise of not a few of the best characteristics developed by human intercourse—hospitality brightened by an all-pervading geniality ; a considerateness and solicitude for the welfare of guests that leaves the performance of no service unsupervised, the rendering of no obligation undischarged ; and withal that honesty and straight-forwardness of dealing which is best calculated to convert the casual customer into a regular one, and perchance presently into something approaching a personal friend. The faculty for innkeeping, which embraces so many of these qualifications, has not been unknown to descend from father to son for several generations.   Only recently there was an example of an inn at Kingsclere which had been kept by members of the same family for more than a century.

Apropos succession of proprietorship in inns, there is that amusing epitaph in Upton churchyard—

"Here lies the landlord of the Lion
His soul is on the way to Zion ;
His widow carries on the business still
Resigned unto the Master's will."

Whether this amiable landlady was the one who palmed off her Worcestershire perry as the sparkling vintage of champagne on the complacent Tom Jones and his flighty companion, Mrs. Waters, history is not explicit enough to determine. But as is well remembered by all lovers of English literature, the name of the " Lion " at Upton-on-Severn is immortally associated with the most scandalous scenes in the extraordinary career of Fielding's " Tom Jones." It was in this house the truant hero was overtaken by one love-sick woman, at the very moment he was philandering with another lady, and where some of the most lively and humorous situations naturally arose as a consequence. In fact, in the delineation of the various scenes of comedy-romance supposed to be enacted at this inn, the great novelist excels himself; and bearing in mind that in Fielding's great masterpiece we have a true reflection of the life and manners of the eighteenth century, no better conception of the daily routine of a country inn at that period can be obtained elsewhere, either in the domain of fiction or in the serious pages of history. The " Lion " at Upton remains practically as it was a century and a half ago.

One more example of the heredity of the innkeeping temperament and our causerie on this interesting subject must be brought to a close. The licence of the Boot Tavern, Cromer Street, Gray's Inn Road, described in " Barnaby Rudge" as the resort of the Lord George Gordon rioters—the old premises were pulled down in 1801 and the present building erected on its site—has been in the hands of one family for 150 years. In such instances the poet is not justified of his judgment—

> " Oh me ! how seldom see we sons succeed
> Their father's praise."—HALL.

XXV

INNKEEPERS' TOKENS

The Guildhall collection of tokens—Tradesmen's tokens plentiful—
Necessitated by shortage in the currency—"Brass farthings"—
Queen Bess's contempt for coins other than of precious metal
—Circulation of traders' tokens steadily increases from her
reign—Some specimens named—Ship Tavern, Greenwich, 1640
—Another "Boar's Head" and a "Sir John Fastolf"—A curious
sign—A number of Southwark tokens—The Pageant Tavern,
Charing Cross—"The Bear-at-the-Bridge-Foot"—Exempted
from closure in 1633 because of its convenience to Greenwich
passengers—"Boar's Head," Eastcheap—Its sign preserved at
Guildhall—Tokens of other famous old inns—"Gone to the
Devil"—Ben Jonson's Apollo Club—And its "social rules"—
Sign of the Devil Tavern preserved at Child's Bank—"Cock
Tavern," Temple Bar—Its tokens called in at the Fire—House
immortalised by Tennyson in "Will Waterproof's Lyrical
Monologue"—The Angel Inn—Country tokens—An interesting
specimen of Stratford-on-Avon—All private issues prohibited,
1672—And finally stopped, 1764—Continued deficiency of
genuine coin under George III. leads to much forgery—
Birmingham's reputation for coinage—Some fine Birmingham
specimens—Issued by public-houses—And one by a brewery—
Modern metal checks—Used for "wet rents"—Some specimens
issued by Birmingham theatres, concert-halls, &c.

IN the library of the Guildhall is to be seen a collection
of old London tavern and coffee-house tokens. As the
practice of issuing such tokens prevailed throughout the
country, local collections of them would be of undoubted
interest in all provincial public museums. So common

were they in the seventeenth century that to say a man
had "swallowed a tavern token" became a cant phrase
for conveying the information that he had got drunk.

Throughout the seventeenth century, and indeed for
upwards of a century later, there was a most inconvenient
shortage in the copper coins and other small change
in circulation in this country; and to overcome this
deficiency authority was often given to traders and
others to coin their own pennies, halfpennies, and
farthings for the facilitating of business transactions.
These trade tokens, as they were called, became legal
currency as "promises to pay"; and the circulation
of them in all parts of the country grew to enormous
proportions. They were issued by business corporations
and traders of all sorts, and among them not a few innkeepers of the better class. Those of the last named
were generally brass farthings, and always bore the
sign of the inn from which they emanated and at
which they were redeemable in the current coin of
the realm.

A few words in explanation of this usurped privilege
of coinage may be necessary. In the sixteenth century
the want of authorised money for small change had
begun to make itself felt. The Government had coined
pence, halfpence, and farthings in silver, but the latter
were necessarily so small and thin as to be a loss rather
than a gain to the trader. German copper coins were
then imported and used, some known as abbey-pieces
and others as Nuremberg counters; for Queen Bess had
a magnificent contempt for any other than the precious
metal to bear her authorised effigy. James I. granted
a monopoly to Lord Harrington for the exclusive manufacture of copper tokens; but the issue thus authorised
was so disgraceful the public preferred to use those
issued by private traders. The circulation of traders'

tokens increased rapidly during the reign of Charles I. ; and throughout the Commonwealth there was scarcely an innkeeper of importance who did not issue his own coppers "for necessarie chainge."

The famous "Ship" at Greenwich issued a money token in the reign of Charles I., on which appeared a ship in full sail, and the inscription "Ship Tavern, 1640."

There is in existence a very rare small brass token of the "Boar's Head," High Street, Borough ; on one side it has a boar's head with a lemon in its mouth, surrounded by the words "At the Boar's Head"; and on the reverse side, "In Southwark, 1649." This house was part of Sir John Fastolf's benefactions to Magdalen College, Oxford ; and the benefactor was a brave general in the French Wars under Henry IV., who is not to be confused with Shakespeare's Falstaff.

A very curious sign is represented on a token issued by one Samuel Bovery, of George Lane, Southwark. The sign was "The Old Pick my Toe," which, it is suggested, was a vulgar representation of the Roman slave who, being sent on a message of importance, would not stop even to pick a thorn out of his foot by the way. If not this, what is the interpretation ?

Included among other preserved specimens of the tokens belonging to Southwark inns are those of the "Dogg and Ducke," St. George's Fields, 1651 ; the "Green Man"; the "Duke of Suffolk's Head," 1669 ; and the Bull's Head Tavern, 1667, which is mentioned by Edmund Alleyne, the founder of Dulwich College, as one of his resorts. Of the George Inn, Southwark, there are in the Beaufoy Collection at the Guildhall two seventeenth-century tokens, giving the names of different landlords.

The token issued by the Pageant Tavern at Charing Cross had upon the obverse a representation of the

triumphal arch erected near that house for the Coronation of Charles II.—a street decoration which was allowed
to remain standing for a twelvemonth after.

Another trade token was issued by the "Bear-at-the-
Bridge-Foot" in Southwark—a sign, no doubt, derived
from the famous Bear Gardens which stood close by
there in Elizabethan days, as the obverse of the specimen
preserved in the British Museum exhibits the figure of a
bear muzzled and chained. This hostelry, situated at the
south end of London Bridge, was one of some antiquity
and importance. It was used by travellers who wished
to go by water to Gravesend in the tilt-boat—a formidable
journey in those days; and its usefulness in this service
was recognised in 1633, for, while a number of licensed
houses were closed, this was specially exempted "for
the convenience of passengers to Greenwich." Pepys
mentions the house more than once in his Diary, while
its antiquity is referred to in an old poem of 1691, entitled
"The Last Search for Claret in Southwark":—

> "We came to the 'Bear,' which we soon understood
> Was the first house in Southwark built after the flood."

Considerable interest will always be attached to the
tavern token issued by the host of that house of Shakespearean renown, and doubtless the resort of the bard and
his dramatic brethren, the "Boar's Head" in Eastcheap.
This supposed scene of the Falstaffian revels was burnt
down in the Great Fire of London, 1666, but was rebuilt
two years afterwards. A stone-carved boar's head, with
the date 1668, was placed over the door; and when the
house was demolished, this sign was removed to the
Guildhall Library for preservation.

Trade tokens were issued by the "Three Cranes," the
Exchange Tavern, and a large number of other old
City houses of entertainment, not a few of which are

mentioned elsewhere in these pages, as the "Mermaid" in Cheapside, the resort of Ben Jonson and his literary friends, members of the club established by Sir Walter Raleigh in 1603.

Two doors from Temple Bar, on the south side of Fleet Street, stood the Devil's Tavern, as it was popularly called, though its proper name was the "Devil and Dunstan." As, however, the sign above the door, and the tokens issued by the proprietor of the house, contained a representation of the familiar legend of St. Dunstan gripping the Devil by the nose with his tongs, the name of the saint became neglected in favour of that of the greater personality depicted. The position of the house made it the favourite haunt of the lawyers and wits resident in the Temple; and hence, when they went forth to patronise this hostelry, they were wont to placard their chamber doors with the weird notice "Gone to the Devil." Aubrey informs us that "Ben Jonson, to be near the Devil's Tavern, lived without Temple Bar, at a comb-maker's shop." To this tavern he removed the wits from the "Mermaid" in Cheapside, and formed the renowed Apollo Club, writing his admirable "social rules" for its guidance in his favourite Latin, which piece of Jonsonian Latinity was rendered into English by Brome, one of his "poetic sons," as he termed the men he thus gathered round him. In Jonson's day the house was kept by Simon Wadloe, whose descendants seem to have been in possession at the later period, in the reign of Charles II., when the tokens were issued. Near the door stood a gilded bust of Apollo, and a "Welcome" in flowing, hearty rhyme, written by the great poet; this bust and the inscribed board found a resting-place in Child's Bank adjoining, when the tavern, in the course of time, came to be demolished for street improvements.

Also near Temple Bar was the Cock Tavern, mine host of which ancient hostelry, being obliged to close his house during the Great Plague (1665), advertised the fact like the honest man he was, announcing "to all persons who have any accompts with the master, or farthings belonging to the said house," that they might be paid their debts, and their tokens exchanged for the current coins of the realm. This is the house immortalised by Tennyson in "Will Waterproof's Lyrical Monologue," beginning—

> "O plump head-waiter at The Cock,
>   To which I most resort,
> How goes the time? 'Tis five o'clock.
>   Go fetch a pint of port."

The poem is too long to quote here *in extenso ;* but it is a happy illustration of the old custom of tavern frequenting, which was still indulged in quite freely, as Tennyson thus shows, till the middle of the nineteenth century.

Another famous old house called to mind by a token (dated 1657) in the Guildhall collection, was the Angel Inn, St. Clement Danes, once the resort of Cornish and West Country lawyers up in town on business. Concerning this "very old inn all gables and galleries," some interesting facts are recorded by Mr. Charles Gordon in his "Old Time Aldwych." We are there informed that in 1555, Bishop Hooper, after his condemnation to be burnt alive, was taken to this house previous to his martyrdom ; that in 1733 a notable duel took place here, in which one of the combatants was killed ; and that later it became a house much patronised by naval officers arriving from Portsmouth—for towards the end it was a very popular coaching inn.

Outside London a very interesting specimen belonging to Stratford-on-Avon may be noticed. This one was put in circulation by a man named Phillips, said to have been connected by marriage with the Shakespeare family, and who opened the Falcon Inn, opposite New Place. The "Falcon," it may be remembered, was Shakespeare's crest of cognisance; so on the obverse of the halfpenny appears the inscription, "Ioseph Phillips . . . At Ye," and a figure of that bird in the centre of the coin. On the reverse appears, "His Half Peny . . . 1668 . . . In Stratford-Vppon-Avon." Warwick, and many other old towns throughout the country, can produce similar examples of seventeenth-century tokens emanating from licensed houses.

Although the issue of private traders' tokens was prohibited in 1672, they continued to make their appearance, in defiance of the law, till 1764, when a final stop was put to the circulation of these base metal farthings and halfpennies and other insignificant pieces of brass, tin, or lead, all of which were so much below their nominal value.

The lack of genuine small money still continued to hinder trade till ten years after the accession of George III., although coiners at this period produced spurious copper pieces very extensively, and greatly to their own profit. As the forger's art thus flourished, the traffic continued, till the traders resolutely took the coinage into their own hands again, and, with tacit public approval, issued their own copper tokens of full intrinsic value.

Birmingham at that time having acquired a high reputation for the skill of its die-engravers and medallists, large quantities of these copper coins were produced there. Mr. W. J. Davis, in his "Token Coinage of Warwickshire," gives full descriptions of very many of them, some among them being issued from licensed houses.

An interesting and finely engraved specimen is a penny which was issued from the Coffee Tavern in Bell Street, which has been previously mentioned as the house of the "poet Freeth," and the headquarters of "The Twelve

Apostles"—a Jacobin Club. The obverse shows the bust of the host, wearing a cocked hat, and above it the inscription, "The Birmingham poet." The reverse contains, within an oaken wreath, the revolutionary sentiment, " Britons Behold The Bard Of Freedom Plain And Bold, Who Sings As Druids Sung Of Old."

A Birmingham halfpenny, also worthy of the artistic reputation of the town, was issued in 1792 by Henry Biggs, a licensed victualler, who kept the "General Elliott," in Moore Street.

Birmingham medallists at that time also turned out quantities of commemorative coins for all sorts of institutions. Among those which may be mentioned here were: one showing a front view of a building with four pillars and two weather-vanes, and inscribed, " New Brewery, Erected 1792 "; and a similar one to commemorate an hotel erected in the same year, and bearing a front view of the building with a sign inscribed " Hotel" over the door.

In recent times numbers of public-houses up and down the country have employed a system of metal checks, generally inscribed with the name of the house and figures to indicate some monetary value, their use being to facilitate, if not to promote, the house's interests in some form of "wet rent." For instance, the price of admission to a music-hall or pleasure-garden attached to a licensed house might be advertised at "sixpence, half returned in refreshments." The visitor paid his sixpence at the entrance, and received in return a metal check, which served not only as a ticket of admission, but was negotiable inside for the purchase of drinks to the value of threepence. Similarly, these checks have been used to hand to members of clubs and societies, holding their meetings rent free on licensed premises, as part of the receipt for their subscriptions, the agreement between the landlord of the house and the management of the club, in such cases, being that for the club's free use of his premises each member shall spend so much in drink every club-night. The collection of "wet rents" by this method of "public-house checks" was at one time very common in many of the more populous industrial regions of England.

Mr. Davis's comprehensive volume gives numerous examples of Birmingham checks and medalets made for concert-halls, theatres, societies, and public institutions. From pp. 111–115 may be selected a few connected with the subject here under consideration : "The Apollo Garden" (a place of resort now closed); "The Birmingham Musical Society, Colonade Hotel, New Street, Birmingham"; "Day's Crystal Palace Concert Hall, Smallbrook Street, Birmingham...3d. To be spent in the Concert Hall only The Same Evening As Received" (now the Empire Theatre); several similar brass checks for the Rodney Inn Concert Hall (now the Gaiety Theatre); and one for the "Spread Eagle" Concert Hall (now Criterion Inn); an oval specimen of the London Museum Music Hall, in Digbeth; and a hexagonal one for "Inshaw's Mechanical Lecture & Concert Hall. . . . For Lectures on Scripture Subjects," &c., available for 3d., to be spent at the Steam Clock Inn.

Almost in the same category are checks for "The Grand Sultan Divan, Needless Alley, New Street, Birmingham — American Bowling Saloon Refreshment Check 6d. W. H. H. Proprietor"; for the Town Hall; and for the Theatre Royal.

Perhaps the most interesting of this series is a milled brass token of the early nineteenth century, on the obverse of which is "Swan Hotel, Birmingham...George Hotel, Litchfield," while on the reverse appears "Litchfield and Birmingham 8 a.m. Tariff Omnibus 4 p.m."

XXVI

PUBLIC-HOUSE SIGNS

Signs not restricted to inns, anciently—As the Barber's Pole, &c.—
An unlettered age needed pictorial signs—The gaudier the
better—In London numerous enough to block the streets—And
the law had to intervene—Signs become compulsory in 1393—
A natural bush the most ancient of inn signs—Incongruous
combinations—Through the uniting of trade interests—The
hanging out of Family Arms—Hence the number of heraldic
signs—As Lattice, Chequers, Talbot, Crescent, &c., &c.—
Facetious corruptions and perversions—" Pig and Tinder Box"
" Bag o' Nails "—" Pig and Whistle "—" Cat and Fiddle "—
" Goose and Gridiron "—" Cock and Pye "—" Stewponey," &c.
—Jocular signs—" The Old Grinding Young "—" The Silent
Woman "—" World Upside Down "—" The Five Alls," &c., &c.
Puns and Rebuses—Historical and commemorative signs—
" Royal Oak "—" The Triumph "—" Royal " hotels—Signs of
Fishes and Insects—Animals and Monsters—Dignities and
Callings—Plants, &c., &c.—Modern signs—Railway Tavern—
Tramway Inn—Unique signs—" Soho "—" Now Thus ! "—" The
Widow's Son "—Signs wearisomely repeated—Commercial value
of a popular sign—Anecdotal illustrations—" The Parson and
Clerk "—The " Gray Ass "—The " Old Cock "—The " Baptist's
Head " — Religious signs — Enigmatic signs — " Who'd have
Thought it ? " — " The Same Yet," &c. — The ambiguous
wording of a sign—Highest sign—Largest sign—Swing sign
—Ornamental iron scroll-work on signs.

THE subject of trade signs and signboards is well-nigh
inexhaustible. So full of interest is it, however, and
more particularly so in connection with the licensed
trade, it cannot be summarily dismissed here.

In bygone times the use of signs was not restricted to publicans. As is well known we have vestiges of the custom in the "Three Golden Balls" of the pawnbrokers, the arms of Lombardy first used here by the money-lenders from that country, who, in 1299, replaced the banished Jewish merchants. The Barber's Pole reminds us that once upon a time a barber was also a leech, and practised phlebotomy, the red and white painted pole he hung at his door being supposed to represent the bleeding limb with the white surgical bandage twisted round it.

So in similar fashion the hosier hung out the form of a gigantic wooden stocking ; the glover displayed a huge golden glove ; the cutler the dummy of a mammoth knife ; while the bookseller generally exhibited the colophon, or distinctive device which he appended at the end of his books. In some few other individual cases the use of such signs has lingered on to the present day, no doubt being regarded as valuable advertisements to some established business reputation ; for in this respect a trade sign was once quite as valuable as a trade name.

When, in an unlettered age, reading was a rare accomplishment, a pictorial sign was a mark of identity which could be recognised by the most ignorant ; and a mark of identification was far more necessary when houses were unnumbered and streets were without name-plates.

To have in front of one's shop or place of business a showy sign, brightly gilt and gaudily coloured, for the direct purpose of attracting the attention of passers-by, was once the desire not only of innkeepers but of all traders who appealed to the general public for custom and support. However little may be the importance attached to signs nowadays, it will be readily seen that it was not so always.

So numerous and so ponderous were the tradesmen's signs of olden London, they invariably blocked the view and often impeded the free ventilation of the narrow, winding thoroughfares. When they rotted with age and neglect they were a constant source of danger to the passengers in the street ; and as they swung and creaked on the rusty hinges of their massive iron frames, they "made night hideous" with their shrieks and groans.

As Gay, in his "Trivia," notes of the inquiring rustic come to town—

> "He dwells on every sign with stupid gaze,
> Enters the narrow alley's doubtful maze."

The display of shop signs had grown to such extravagant dimensions in 1695 they attracted the notice of alert politicians, and a proposal was made to tax them ; in 1762 the active intervention of Parliament was more successfully invoked, and a measure was passed for their due regulation and restriction.

But while the use of signs by other tradesmen was purely optional, this was not the case with licensed innkeepers—a fact which no doubt accounts in a very large degree for the universal retention of signs by licensed houses to this day.

In 1393 the publicans of London were compelled by law to display signs ; and at Cambridge and some other old towns it was ordered by the authorities that whosoever brewed ale to sell must hang out a sign. It thus came about that the taking away of a publican's license was accompanied by the taking down of his sign. Massinger, in his "New Way to Pay Old Debts," says :—

> "For the gross fault I here do damn thy license
> Forbidding thee ever to tap or draw ;
> For instantly I will in mine own person
> Command the Constables to pull down thy sign."

A bush—the real natural object—was the sign used by the Romans to denote inn accommodation : a sign supposed to have been adopted from them by our fore-fathers, and (as noted in another part of this volume) very commonly used in mediæval England.

> " Ryghte as off a tavernere
> The greene busche that hangeth out
> Is a sygne, it is no dowte
> Outward ffolkys ffor to telle
> That within is wyne to selle."

When a natural bush was superseded, it may be accepted that among the earliest of English inn signs to be adopted, objects connected with brewing and agriculture were painted up ; as the " Plough," the " Wheatsheaf," the " Malt Shovel," and the " Barley-corn " ; and perhaps a little later came the " Woolpack," the " Fleece," and the " Packhorse." What could be more appropriate for an inn in the Eastern counties, where malting barley is so largely grown, than the sign of the " Malt Cross," which may yet be found in the market-place of one or two of its old towns ?

The most comprehensive work which has appeared on this subject is " A History of Signboards," by Larwood and Hotten, published in 1866. The authors have attempted to classify inn signs under fifteen head-ings, but not with any conspicuous success, owing to the extraordinary number of examples found to be in existence up and down the country everywhere, nearly every locality presenting some altogether new and un-heard-of sign. Then to add to their multiplicity are the numberless combinations it seems possible to meet with. No sense of absurdity or of incongruity has deterred the combination of two signs, which used individually may have been fit and appropriate enough, but which taken together side by side present ideas nothing less than ludicrous.

The following lines on the incongruity of the combinations then appearing on a number of street signs, was published in 1707 in the *British Apollo* :—

> "I'm amused at the signs
>   As I pass through the town,
> To see the odd mixture—
>   A Magpie and Crown
> The Whale and the Crow
> The Razor and Hen
> The Leg and Seven Stars
> The Scissors and Pen
> The Axe and the Bottle
> The Tun and the Lute
> The Eagle and Child
> The Shovel and Boot."

The way in which many of these strange combinations arose was simple enough. Two merchants (or two innkeepers, it may have been) had traded long and successfully under their respective signs; and then a time came when they wished to join in partnership or otherwise to unite their trade interests. If one had amassed money under the sign of the " Frog," and the other had built up a flourishing business under the sign of the " Flatiron," neither would care to abandon the outward and visible sign of his success, and so the joint venture would thenceforward be known as the " Frog and Flatiron," or some equally ridiculous combination.

As mentioned in Chapter IV., the term " hotel " has been correctly used to describe a family mansion utilised as a house of public entertainment. For in the Middle Ages the houses of nobility, both in town and country, whenever the family was absent, were used as hostelries for the accommodation of travellers. This practice, coupled with the fact that the family arms were hung

A "LIVING" SIGN.

THE "BEEHIVE," AT GRANTHAM.

[*Page* 313.

THE "MAN LOADED WITH MISCHIEF."

[*Page* 304.

GROUP OF FINELY-COLOURED TOBY JUGS.

(Date 1790-1810.)

[*Page* 345.

in front of the house, gave some shrewd innkeeper the idea of borrowing some conspicuous emblem from the heraldic device of a neighbouring noble, and adopting it for his own profit and advantage. For, as the best-known sign in the locality, it would be the most calculated to attract to his establishment the travellers accustomed to pass along that way.

Hence arose that large class of inn signs, the heraldic and emblematic, to which belong such as the "Crown," the "King's Arms," the "Lygon Arms," the "Red Lion," the "Talbot." For sometimes the innkeeper selected a nobleman's crest, as the Eagle and Child, that of the Earl of Derby; sometimes the supporters of the shield, as the Unicorn; and sometimes one of the charges, as the Crescent. He at times even adopted the field or background of the shield, as the heraldic *chequé*, commonly called the Checkers. This, if painted in red and white squares, is said to have obtained the slang name of the Red Lattice; which gives us the clue to the allusion in *Henry IV.* part 2, where Falstaff's page says to Bardolph—

"He called me, even now, my lord, through a red lattice."

A writer in the *Gentleman's Magazine* for September, 1794, makes the far-fetched suggestion that in olden times "the great earl Warren" was given the exclusive power of granting licences to sell beer; and that his agent might collect the tax more readily, he ordered that the door-posts of all licensed houses should be painted in Chequers—the arms of the Warren family. Where is the evidence in support of this?

A further corruption of Lattice, assisted by the substitution of green paint for red, is claimed to have been the origin of the "Green Lettuce," a sign once exhibited near Holborn. But it is more probable that these signs originated from the ancient custom of distinguishing houses at which malt liquor was to be sold by painting the lattices red ; and also it may be recalled that in the old times, when the different classes of public-houses in London were known as Osteries, Taverns, and Cookeries, those at which drink was to be obtained were usually known by their walls being painted in chequers, or lattice-pattern.

The "Talbot" readily became known among the vulgar as the "Spotted Dog." Similarly the "Crescent," a charge often found in the shield of a Crusader, was popularly converted into the "Half Moon." Butler, in his "Hudibras," queries—

> "Tell me but what's the natural cause
> Why on a sign no painter draws
> The *full* moon ever, but the *half !*"

As a matter of fact, the signs of the "Moon," and also of the "Full Moon" would not be difficult to find. Another heraldic charge is the "Blue Ball" (the heurte, or roundle of azure tincture), as it has been interpreted in the language of those unlearned in the science of armory.

But as the number and variety of heraldic charges were at the outset almost as infinite as the inn signs afterwards became, it will be as well to place a check upon our further investigations in this direction.

It may be pointed out that not only is heraldry responsible for a whole host of signs—and often in unsuspected instances, as when the Blue Pig usurps the place of the heraldic Boar azure—but it very frequently denotes the imminence of the seat and the local influence of the territorial family from whom any particular example has been borrowed. The sign of the "Eagle and Child," for instance, would almost always betray the vicinity of an estate of the Stanley family.

Perversions and corruptions, whether wilfully made or the result of pure ignorance, are responsible for the most interesting class of signs—those that excite curiosity and give rise to speculation as to their real origin. The consideration of a few will provide a fund of amusement.

The " Pig and Tinder Box " is a facetious rendering of the old armorial device more properly known as the " Elephant and Castle." The " Goat and Compass," a hostel sign of the Commonwealth period, is a verbal corruption of the Puritan motto, " God encompasses (us)."

The " Bag o' Nails " was originally the " Bacchanals " ; and, if accompanied by the Devil, it had been originally the " Satyr and Bacchanals " ; the " Bull and Mouth " was the Boulogne Mouth (or Harbour) where Henry VIII. met with a trifling success in 1544 ; the " Swan with Two Necks " (the sign of the Vintners) was really that bird with two " nicks," or marks cut in its bill, for identification at the annual swan-hopping time.

The " Pig and Whistle " is generally considered a corruption of the Peg and Wassail, a phrase associated with the ancient custom of drinking healths in tankards marked with pegs, somewhat as modern medicine phials are marked into measured doses.

A number of derivations have been put forward for this sign. Both words " Pig," and " Whistle," have had a diversity of origins given them. The favourite interpretation traces the phrase to some connection with the pegged tankard. At Pembroke College, Oxford, is a silver tankard, made after the model of similar wooden vessels, with a row of *pegs* running down the inside to apportion each man's amount of liquor as it was passed round. Hence the term to " Take a man down a peg "—*i.e.*, to cut off his turn at the bowl, for some offence against tavern etiquette maybe. This suggests it as a *very* probable sign for an inn—one of those bowls hung outside or painted.

In the same College, also, there are to be seen some curious silver mugs, or jugs, so made that you can turn the vessel up, when empty, and "whistle through the lower part of the handle" to call for more drink, when necessary. So this gives us choice of "Peg-o'-Wassail," "Piggin Wassail," and "Piggin Whistle"—*piggin* is an old English name for a wooden vessel with a handle for holding liquids.

Sometimes a religious aspect has been given to the signification of this odd combination ; as the "Pix and Housel" of the Sacrament of the Holy Eucharist ; and sometimes it was taken as a transformation of the virgin's greeting, "Pige Washael," which in Danish Saxon meant "Virgin hail !" or "Health to the maiden !"

Another sign very controversial as to its source and origin is the "Cat and Fiddle." The first and simplest explanation is that it refers to the nursery rhyme of "Hey diddle-diddle," and in some instances it is actually painted as a Cat playing a Fiddle, while the Dish runs after a Spoon, and all the rest of it. It is worthy of note that in Beverley Minster is to be found an old carving of a Cat playing a Fiddle. But this explanation seldom suffices for the controversialists. Says one, this sign is the English rendering of "Le chat fidèle" ; another that it is a corruption of Caton Fidèle, the faithful Governor of Calais ; and a third backs up what is practically the same theory by saying that the name "caton" (Cato) is often used by French authors to denote a man of strict probity—*e.g.*, Molière in "Tartuffe," has "Un caton dans le siècle où nous sommes," and Racine in "Les Plaideurs," "Ce Caton de basse Normandie."

The "Wig and Fidgett" is a less ancient sign, evidently going back merely to the days of our bewigged forefathers of the seventeenth or eighteenth century, when a fidgety man encumbered with a wig could scarcely but make a mark of some sort.

The "Goose and Gridiron" was a queer sign at the corner of St. Paul's Churchyard, which had supplanted the original one of the "Mitre." Previously to the destruction of this house in the Great Fire, the Society of Musicians had long been accustomed to hold their concerts in it. When the premises were rebuilt, after 1666, recognition of them as the headquarters of the society was made by displaying its badge, a lyre surmounted by a swan—a combination of emblems which the jokers were not slow to parody as the "Goose and Gridiron." As Ben Jonson justly exclaims—

> "It even puts Apollo
> To all his strength of art to follow
> The flights, and to divine
> What's meant by every sign."

Running through recent issues of the *Antiquary* have appeared a series of exceedingly informative articles on "London Signs and their Associations," by Mr. J. Holden MacMichael. We learn with regard to the origin of that not uncommon sign, the "Blackamoor," that in olden times travellers were acquainted with two kinds of Moors, the tawny natives of Morocco and the blacks, or "blackamoors" of the interior of Africa. But of more interest, being in the nature of a surprise, is Mr. MacMichael's explanation of the sign, the "Bleeding Heart," which lent its name to the tenements known as Bleeding Heart Yard, mentioned in "Little Dorrit." The sign "Bleeding Heart" was not allusive to any sanguinary crime, nor even to the sorrowful mysteries of the rosary; but, like so many more signs, it was simply of heraldic origin, the bleeding heart being the badge of the Douglases.

Thus Scott—

"The bloody heart blazed in the van,
Announcing Douglas' dreaded men."

Addison devotes one of his essays in the *Spectator* to London street signs, and says : " Our streets are filled with blue boars, black swans, and red lions, not to mention flying pigs and hogs in armour, with many other creatures more extraordinary than any in the deserts of Afric."

The perversion of heraldic charges and crests is responsible for a number of our curious old inn signs. Sometimes the perversion occurred through pure ignorance, but not infrequently was made quite wilfully through unrestrained pleasantry. For if the knight-errant was at liberty to choose as his device something as outlandish as the mythological Pan and his pipe, why not the humorist to change it into a pig and whistle ? And who was to deny the whimsical sign-painter rendering a dancing fawn as a goat in boots ?

The "Cock and Pye" in Old Drury Lane is said to have been a grotesque drawing suggested by the Tudor oath, " By Cock and Pye," which originated through the practice of knights-errant, in the decadent period of chivalry, when making their vows at a tournament banquet, of frequently swearing by the most gorgeous dish on the table, to wit, the peacock served up in all the glory of its magnificent plumage.

A sign that is unique and has excited much curiosity as to its origin is that of the "Stewponey," the name of a large inn near Stourbridge. The generally accepted explanation is that it was founded by an old soldier of Queen Anne's martial times, who had fought in Spain, and married his wife from Estepona in that country, and on settling down with her in Staffordshire had named his house in her honour the Estepona Tavern, of which the present name is a corruption.

Among the quaint and humorous the sign of the "Old Grinding Young" will deserve a prominent place. An example was to be seen in Dublin as late as forty years ago; and it was usually delineated as a grinding mill at work, old men and women being put into the hopper at the top, and coming out as sprightly young men and buxom young girls at the bottom. Next in order, perhaps, may be placed the "Labour in Vain," illustrated by a woman with a negro child in a tub, whom she is endeavouring to scour white. Then the "Silent Woman," who is represented without a head on her shoulders, but carrying that useful part of her anatomy under her arm, is by no means a bad example. At Pershore, in Worcestershire, some years ago, the "Silent Woman" was represented on a sign with her lips fastened tightly together by a padlock. The sign illustrated is to be found at Widford, in Essex; it improves on the idea that a woman deprived of her head is not only a "Quiet" woman, but one that is *fort bone*— "very good."

Akin to it is the "Honest Lawyer," also depicted in a like state of decapitation. The painter of the sign the "World Turned Upside Down," to be seen near Reading, confesses he derived his inspiration from old Gothic carving when he composed his subject; the resultant composition being a Donkey sitting in a cart, which a Man is pulling; a Pig killing a Butcher; a Bear conducting a Dancing Man; a Rat chasing a Cat; a Hare shooting a Man; and Dogs ridden by Foxes chasing a Man.

The "Five Alls" is one of the jocular signs which vastly amused our grandfathers, and was represented pictorially on five panels. In the first was painted the

King in his robes of State—in Rowlandson's time this was a caricature of his August Majesty, George IV.— labelled, "I rule all." In the next panel was seen the unctuous parson, in the clerical wig and gown of the period, labelled, "I pray for all." Then came the wily-looking lawyer, with the legend, "I plead for all." Fourthly, there was the fierce and swashbuckling soldier, against whom was written, "I fight for all." And lastly came the picture of the unhappy-looking taxpayer, over-burdened with the money-bags he was carrying to the "receipt of custom," as was sadly explained in the title, "I pay for all." In the one illustrated, which is to be seen at Marlborough, we have in the first section a Queen, in the second a Bishop, and in the fifth a Farmer. There is one of these characteristically English signs to be seen at Valetta, in Malta.

One Boniface, not satisfied with "Five Alls," made it into "Six Alls," adding a picture of the conventional devil, with orthodox tail and horns, wearing a smile of grim satisfaction, and armed with the formidable fork which gave significance to the words, "I take all." In some parts of the country this sign was modified into the "Five Awls," probably where the innkeeper added cobbling to his other calling. In fact, it is not to be assumed that variants of most signs are not to be found, individual fancy accounting for their vast multiplicity. On the other hand, dearth of ideas and lack of originality accounts for the constant repetition of "Red Lions," "Royal Oaks," and other commonplace examples which meet the eye with such wearisome frequency. A few more original-minded hosts like the modern cynic at Hull, who has named his house the "March of Intellect," would be welcomed.

A minor class is that consisting of Puns and Rebuses. The "Bolt-in-Tun," depicted as a bolt or arrow running through a wine tun, was nothing more than a copy of the punning rebus on the name of Prior Bolton, the last of the monastic rulers of St. Bartholomew's Priory. Another pictorial sign showing the "Hat [and] Tun," was the rebus of a witty host named Hatton. Even the "Bell Sauvage" in Ludgate Hill is said to have originated in nothing more romantic than a similar treatment of the Bell Inn, whose first hostess was named Arabella Savage, and the original sign of which was a bell hung within a hoop. Concerning which, Dr. Brewer in "Phrase and Fable," says : "It is remarkable that the sign of this Inn was a pun on the proprietress's Christian name, a bell on the Hope (hoop), as may be seen on the Close Roll of 1453. The hoop seems to have formed a garter or frame to most signs." Alluding to this house in Scott's "Kenilworth," chapter xiii., we may read—

"They now returned to their inn, the famous Bell Savage."

One class of sign may be designated the historical or commemorative. The "Royal Oak," for instance, helps to keep alive the memories of Boscobel ; but the majority in this class would be those which have reference to some great victory, like Waterloo, or to a popular victor, like the "Admiral Rodney."

There was a house at Charing Cross named the Pageant Tavern—sometimes miscalled the Triumph Tavern—to commemorate the triumphal procession which Charles II. made from Westminster to the Tower, as the preliminary to his coronation which took place the next day. It was to this house of resort that Pepys went with Captain Ferrars in May, 1662, to take a sly peep at the Portuguese maids of honour whom the new queen, Catherine of Braganza, had brought with her to England.

Another uncommon sign which appeared at the Restoration was the "Tumble-down-Dick," the Royalist nickname applied to Richard Cromwell, who failed so ignominiously to maintain the high estate to which his father had attained as Lord Protector of England.

There are inns and hotels which, having sheltered royalty only for a few short hours during a post-chaise journey, have proudly assumed the word " Royal" as part of their sign and title—examples of this could be found at Nottingham and Birmingham.

Larwood and Hotten have formed a class under the heading of Fishes and Insects. While such signs as the " Dolphin" and the "Three Fishes" are common enough, it is really difficult to find any house called after an insect. In the sign of the " Beetle and Pile" there is no allusion to a bug or any other coleopter ; in this connection a beetle would be a mallet or pile-driver. Similarly in Lincolnshire the " Three Gowts " (that is, sluices) has been perverted to the "Three Goats." The other classifications of these authorities must be dealt with briefly. Among Animals and Monsters come such examples as the " Reindeer" and the " Dragon " ; among the Birds and Fowls, the " Falcon," and the " Hen and Chickens" ; under the heading of the House and the Table must be ranged such examples as the " Lamp," the "Sugar-loaf," and the " Three Cups " ; under Dress, Plain and Ornamental, would appear the " Cap," the " Feathers," and the trade-mark of that famous hostelry the " Tabard," in Southwark, where Chaucer's Pilgrims lay ; among Dignities, Trades, and Professions, may be placed the " Mitre," the " Prince Regent," and the " Green Man " (the last named was merely a forester or ranger, so dubbed on account of his green livery) ; in the list of the Geographical and Topographical would appear the " Globe," and the " Dover Castle" ; and under Trees, Flowers, and Herbs we should have not only the " Rose," and the " Wheatsheaf," but that which claims, as an inn sign, the

highest antiquity of all—the " Bush." Even all these classifications do not exhaust the possibilities of the subject,
as Messrs. Larwood and Hotten found ; for they had to
fall back on that vague though convenient and comprehensive heading for the indefinable—Miscellaneous.
This chapter has but touched the fringe of the subject.

With the march of events, new signs naturally oust
some of the old ones ; and thus we get Railway
Taverns instead of the "Coach and Horses," or Tram-
way Inn, in place of the " Half-way House." Curiously
enough, though, present-day London boasts two
"World's Ends" and a " World Turned Upside Down."
There are also six " Elephant and Castles," and eighteen
"Angels," as well as Chaucer's "Tabard," and " St.
Thomas-a-Watering."

With all the vain repetitions and slavish imitations of
inn signs there are doubtless unique specimens to be
found in many parts of the country. At Oldbury, in
Worcestershire, the Chemical Inn reflects the nature
of one of the chief industries of the place. At Shone
Ridgway, in Kent, the village inn bears the sign Ye Olde
See Ho Tavern. It appears, however, that *See Ho* is
but another form of *So-ho*, the cry of the sportsman in
coursing, when a hare appears in sight.

A sign that is really unique is often equally quaint.
At Shinfield, near Reading, occurs the sign of the
" Merry Maidens," represented by four half-length stone
figures, each fitted into its own niche, and crowned with
a basket of flowers—figures of buxom, happy-looking
maidens, apparently well pleased with themselves and
the rest of the world. At Barton-on-Irwell, near Manchester, is to be found a curious sign, " Now Thus ! "
to the origin of which attaches a legend of the Civil
Wars, which is told in " Staffordshire Stories," a counter-
part of this sign being found on an old gravestone in

Leek churchyard. At that period William Trafford, a staunch Royalist, lived at Swythamley Hall, which fell into the hands of the Parliamentary troops. To save his property as much as possible, he sent away all his servants and his live-stock, and collecting his plate, cash, and jewels, buried them beneath the floor of a barn. When the Roundheads arrived, they found the owner of the property disguised as a farm labourer, busily engaged in threshing corn over the spot where his valuable portable property had been buried. He was apparently oblivious of everything but his work, swinging his flail, exclaiming at each lusty stroke the words " Now thus ! " The officers questioned him in every way, but he appeared a poor witless thing, who could say nothing but " Now thus ! " till at last they gave up their quest in despair, and went away as empty as they came. In commemoration of this successful ruse, we have to this day a carving on a Staffordshire tombstone, and an inn sign near the present Trafford property.

At Bow is a public-house known as the " Widow's Son," the story of which is rather curious, and which goes to explain the presence of strings of blackened buns hanging up in the house. The legend says that long ago the inn was kept by a widow, whose only son went to sea, making a promise that he would assuredly return on the following Good Friday. He failed to keep the promise. But the fond mother duly set aside for him his hot cross bun, that Good Friday ; and she continued to do so every Good Friday as long as she lived, for the son that never came back. A fresh bun is still added to the stock every year although widow and son have both long since passed away.

If a house had been successful under a certain sign, it was fondly hoped the hoisting of the same sign would attract a similar amount of custom to a new venture in the same neighbourhood ; and thus it comes about that in any one part of the country, the same sign, or group of signs, is to be met with over and over again. Popularity often ousts originality.

The commercial value of a sign after it has become well known far and wide all round the countryside is well illustrated by a case at Streetley, near Sutton Coldfield. An old house there was originally called the Royal Oak Inn ; but upwards of a century ago a bitter quarrel raged between the owner of the property and the rector of the parish. During the progress of the lawsuit involved, the landowner set up over the door of the inn, which was the property in dispute, a caricature of the rector and his clerk, the former bending his head in the attitude of prayer, and the clerk standing behind with uplifted axe as if about to chop off the bowed head of his superior. The inn, notwithstanding that the words "Royal Oak" continued to appear on the sign, became popularly known for miles round as the "Parson and Clerk"—in fact, when the property was recently rebuilt, it was deemed wiser to forego the older sign and to legitimatise the more popular name of the "Parson and Clerk."

Another amusing anecdote, illustrating the value of a sign which has become well known, is thus related :—

The worthy boniface of a small inn in the neighbourhood of Liverpool, not less known by its sign of the "Gray Ass" than by the virtues of its home-brewed ale, having taken it into his head that his symbol was scarcely commensurate with the dignity and importance of his establishment, resolved to change it the first fitting opportunity. The result of the battle of Waterloo, so exhilarating to all loyal Englishmen, afforded him an excellent excuse for carrying his intentions into effect. He accordingly employed an itinerant artist to paint him a portrait of the Duke of Wellington, which he substituted for the effigy of poor Neddy. In the meantime, a shrewd rival, who knew the value of a name, took a house immediately opposite mine host of the "Wellington," and adopted his discarded sign. The country people, who knew more of the character of the "Gray Ass" than of the qualifications of the great captain of the age, all flocked to the inn designated by their favourite appellative, until at length the elder publican had little or no custom left. Finding that his friends were ebbing from him like a spring tide with a breeze from the shore, he bethought him of an expedient to put a stop to the desertion. This *dernier ressort* was to attach to the portrait of his Grace of Wellington a supplemental panel, containing, in large and legible characters, the following pithy inscription : "*This is the Original Gray Ass !*" It is scarcely necessary to add that the intimation had the desired effect.

A good story, suggested by the alteration of signs, comes from Llandaff, where an inn once had for its sign the "Cock," but trade getting rather depressed, the landlord thought he would try the effect of a new sign. He accordingly put up a portrait of the Bishop of Llandaff, and called the house by that name. A rival in the immediate vicinity thought he saw his way to make fresh customers by this change, and straightway altered the sign of his inn to the "Cock," and reaped the anticipated benefits. Landlord number one, hearing of this, was greatly exasperated, and by way of check-mating his adversary he had painted up under the bishop's portrait, "This is the Old Cock."

The humour of this lies in the label, and recalls the fact that Hogarth in one of his pictures has copied a sign of St. John the Baptist's Head on a Charger and placed underneath the incongruous announcement, "Good Eating."

The last-named sign belongs to the class known as the Biblical and Religious, of which perhaps there were a greater number in pre-Reformation times. A few still remain to the present day, as the "Eden," and the "Adam and Eve." After the Reformation, however, a number of these "papistical" signs were changed to suit the altered opinions of the times. In this way the "Nuns" became the "Angels," and the "Catherine

Wheel" was disguised in the form of the "Cat and Wheel." Signs having inferential reference to the old religion are common still ; the "Salutation" has reference to the Annunciation, the "Cross Keys" were the arms of the Papal See, and the city of Nottingham boasted the curious sign "The Trip to Jerusalem," which dated from the days of pilgrimages, and was not inappropriately situated in Brewhouse Yard.

The enigmatic sign and the sign of the verbal quip make another distinct class. A well-known one is the "Who'd have Thought it ?"—the suppressed answer to which is generally supposed to be "that malt and hops would have bought it," and leading one to the inference that every innkeeper does not become prosperous enough to buy the freehold of his house. The adoption of "Hit or Miss" as a sign seems to be a direct challenge to fortune. The "First and Last" has many variants, and is a sign usually adopted for a house near to some boundary-line, because by its situation it offers the first opportunity for rest and refreshment on arrival and the last on departure. Another sign which is enigmatic and humorous as well is the "Three Loggerheads," a painting of two silly-looking faces labelled with the words, "We three Loggerheads be ! "—the unsuspicious reader, of course, making the third.

There is one of this category the origin of which is claimed to be clearly known, the "Same Yet," at Prestwich. The house originally bore the "Seven Stars," but many years ago it became necessary to have its faded sign repainted. When the painter asked the landlord what he was to put upon the board he received the answer, "The Same Yet." And the man took him at his word.

If the "Traveller's Rest" carries any advantage by virtue of its invitatory suggestiveness, what can be said

for "Pass By" as an inn sign? and is not the use of
"Come Along" of somewhat doubtful advantage?
Surely much more to the purpose are the signs Slip
Inn, and Dew Drop Inn; especially if the latter be slily
interpreted into the homonymous emphatic form, "Do
drop in." The shortest sign known, and at the same
time perhaps the most cryptic of all, is the "Q," to be
met with at Stalybridge.

The formal wording of public-house signs has given
rise to a misapprehension in past times which was not
a little amusing. It was generally written up on the
board that the landlord, John Jones, or William Smith,
or whatever his name might have been, was licensed to
sell ale and beer, cider and porter, wines and spirituous
liquors of all kinds, "to be drunk on the premises."
That blessed phrase, "to be drunk on the premises,"
which, of course, was intended to express that the house
had the benefit of an "on licence," was so frequently
understood to mean that it was the customer who was
"licensed to be drunk on the premises"; and indeed
such interpretation was so repeatedly pleaded by ignorant
licensees, summoned for "permitting" drunkenness, that
at last it was deemed advisable to alter the phrase into
"to be consumed on the premises." In which amended
form it is now most commonly met.

One of the highest signs was that of Keston Cross,
near Bromley, Kent. The inn was so-called because
it was situated at Keston, and its sign was a red
heraldic cross, painted on a board and erected high
above the finger-post of four cross-roads. An engraving
of this picturesque old house in 1827 is given in Hone's
"Table Book."

The inn reputed to have had the largest sign in old
London, "save and except the Castle in Fleet Street,"
was the "White Hart" in High Street, Borough.

STONEWARE JUG, BELLARMINE OR GREYBEARD, HAVING
ARMS WITH TUDOR ROSES.

(Late 16th Century.)

At British Museum.

[Page 345.

OLD PUZZLE JUG.

(Dated 1691.)

Victoria and Albert Museum.

[Page 347.

GROUP OF SUNDERLAND FROG MUGS.

Early Nineteenth Century.

(Photo kindly lent by Mr. Arthur Hayden.)

[Page 346.

The form taken by the public-house signboard of former days was nothing whatever in the nature of the modern sky-sign. One form for posting-houses and houses of call was the span-sign which, carried on two tall uprights, spanned the road, and with a sort of open-armed welcome struck the eye of the traveller from afar. Another was the swing-sign, that swung and creaked and flapped itself about in every high wind. We all remember the description of the one over the door of the "Blue Dragon," the village ale-house which figures in "Martin Chuzzlewit" :—

"A faded and ancient dragon he was, and many a wintry storm of rain, snow, sleet, and hail had changed his colour from a gaudy blue to a faint lack-lustre shade of gray. But there he hung, rearing in a state of monstrous imbecility, on his hind legs ; waxing with every month that passed so much more dim and shapeless, that as you gazed at him on one side it seemed as if he must be gradually melting through it and coming out upon the other."

This form of sign was one which offered scope for the skilled craftsman who could produce scrolled iron-work in ample lengths of artistic design. The ornamental iron-work which supported and often bordered a swing-sign could be fancifully wrought into flowers and flourishes, like the one over the door of the "Falstaff" at Canterbury, that quaint double-fronted inn of the sixteenth century, with its bulging bay-windows top and bottom, making up therewith an ensemble of picturesqueness such as we delight to associate with ancient hostelries.

The sign of the "Bell" at Stilton—an old Tudor inn where was first offered for sale the cheese bearing the name of this place, although it was produced at Dalby, in Leicestershire—is one of solid weather-beaten copper, supported by ornamental ironwork, wrought into the most complicated of flourishes. Real art ironwork is to be found on some of these old inn signs.

XXVII

SIGNBOARDS AND THEIR PAINTERS

The sign market—Signs by noted artists—Hogarth—and Kneller—
Pontack's Tavern—His head painted as his trade sign—Royal
Society's annual dinner at Pontack's—Isaac Fuller, artist—
Sign-painters or artists ?—The Birth Struggle of the English
School of Painting—Its first exhibition at Spring Gardens
(1761)—Hogarth's catalogue—The joke of the Nonsense Club—
A rival exhibition at Bow Street—Decay of sign-painting—And
the rise of English Art—Signs by Wale—David Cox—Old
Crome—Herring—and Millais.

WHEN looking at Hogarth's " Beer Street," and noting
the complacency of the professional sign-painter there
depicted at work, we are reminded that in those days
when signs were everywhere, there was a regular sign
market in Harp Alley, Shoe Lane. Hogarth himself, who
may be regarded as the true founder of the English
school of painting, has left us an example of his art
carefully expended on an inn signboard.

Hogarth's sign, the " Man Loaded with Mischief,"
depicting a man carrying on his shoulders, to which
she is fastened by the chain of wedlock, a drunken wife,
with a raven, and a monkey, all painted with a detail of
keen and caustic caricature, was once to be seen in Oxford
Street, London. There are still copies and imitations of
the " Mischief " to be found. One is at Wallingford,
another at Norwich ; the one illustrated is to be seen

a mile out of Cambridge on the Madingley Road. Underneath the original was the rhyme—

"A monkey, a magpie, and a wife
Is the true emblem of strife."

Sir Godfrey Kneller painted the portrait of a famous tavern-keeper of the eighteenth century. This was Le Beck, who won distinction in his line of business by providing only the best of viands, presenting them exquisitely cooked, and accompanied by the choicest of wines. He is represented by the painter as wearing a linen cap and holding a glass in his hand. The head of this high priest of Epicureanism served for the sign of another London tavern long after the man himself had passed away.

Another famous host whose head was painted on his sign was Pontack, who kept the French eating-house in Abchurch Lane; at which, till 1746, were held the annual dinners of the Royal Society. Allusions to this tavern are made by Swift; and Defoe, writing in 1722, says the best Bordeaux claret was named after him. Certainly he was always supposed not to practise the secret "stuming" or strengthening of his wines by introducing into them foreign infusions.

"What wretch would nibble on a hanging shelf
When at Pontack's he may regale himself?

Drawers must be trusted through whose hands conveyed
You take the liquor, or you spoil the trade;
For sure, those honest fellows have no knack
Of putting off stumed claret for Pontack."

Tavern signs were formerly the work of accomplished artists. In fact, at one time artists largely subsisted by sign-painting. Vertue, the Antiquary (died 1756), notes that Isaac Fuller, among others, was largely employed in this direction ; and when the first exhibition of pictures by living English artists was opened in 1760, the scoffers at native talent tried to belittle the show by pretended announcements of a rival exhibition of "curious signs by English sign-painters."

Next year came the great battle of the wits. London was startled by the announcement of a rival exhibition to be held "at the large room at the upper end of Bow Street," and which was to consist of "original Paintings, Busts, Carved figures, &c., by the Society of Sign-painters," together with "such original designs as might be transmitted to them," the whole being "specimens of the native genius of the nation."

In 1761 was held in the great room at Spring Gardens an exhibition which may be regarded as the progenitor of that which now opens at the Academy every May. The admission was by catalogues, which, besides serving as guides, were adorned by designs from the pencil of Hogarth and others, one symbolising the growth of the arts under the fostering care of Britannia, and the other ridiculing the miserable fate of the decayed "exoticks," which a connoisseur (typified by a monkey in Court suit and ruffles), magnifying glass in hand, is vainly watering. Thirteen thousand of these catalogues sold at a shilling each.

The "Society" was, of course, a myth. The burlesque originated with the famous Nonsense Club, its prime contriver being Bonnell Thornton, under whose super-intendence it was cleverly carried out in its every detail. The whim took. It was seen to be a harmless jest, and Hogarth himself, who had contributed some works to the Spring Gardens exhibition, readily lent assistance to the Bow Street parody, by giving a touch with his pencil where effect could be added by it ; thus in the companion portraits of the Empress, Maria Theresa, and the King of Prussia, we are told that he changed the cast of their eyes, so as to make them leer significantly at each other.

Indeed the fun was altogether of this order. The apothecaries' sign of the "Three Gallipots" had for its companion the "Three Coffins." No. 16 in the catalogue was entitled "A Man"; while the picture bearing this number was nine tailors at work. In No. 37 was "A Man Loaded with Mischief"—a satirical composition which has already been described.

Some of the jokes were rather broader than would be tolerated now, and some of the journals were disposed to treat the matter seriously; but the laughers carried the day. The jest was enjoyed, and it was not spoiled by repetition.

It cannot be denied that commissions for signs were often given at that period to painters of established reputation. The market for ready-made signs was still conducted in Harp Alley, although an Act had been passed for the removal of such signboards as obstructed the public ways; almost every shop still had its sign, and every tradesman strove to render his board more attractive than that of his neighbour, if not by beauty of design, by oddity of conception, or some sort of extravagance. The amusing incongruity of some of the pictorial compositions was treated in the last chapter. But from the date of this Act the decay of sign-painting set in steadily.

This branch of art outlived the famous Signboard Exhibition but a very few years; a more stringent Act was passed for the removal of signs (2 George III.), and that is really the reason why signboards have ceased to swing elsewhere than in front of taverns and inns.

The interesting point here is the evolution of the Academy and the English school of painting, from the more primitive craft of sign-painting. Wale, who was one of the first members of the Academy, its librarian and professor of perspective, was not above painting signs ; Penny and Catton, both among the first academicians, the former the first professor of painting, with others of equal standing, at least occasionally employed their pencils in a similar manner.

One of Wale's most famous signs was a portrait of Shakespeare, which hung across the road at the northeast corner of Little Russell Street, Drury Lane, and which, with its elaborate frame, is said to have cost £500.

The sign of the " Royal Oak," painted by David Cox, has also been carefully removed to the inside of that hotel at Bettws-y-Coed. Several signboards in and around London were painted by that drunken genius, George Morland. Old Crome, and Herring, left similar examples of their art ; and one public-house signboard can even be attributed to Millais—the " George and Dragon," at Hayes, in Kent.

In 1906 an interesting artistic freak of this kind fetched twelve guineas in an auction sale at Norwich. It was the signboard of the " Jolly Sailor," which formerly hung outside a Yarmouth public-house known by that name, the work of " Old Crome." As is well-known, John Crome began life in a very humble sphere, and in early manhood was content to paint signboards for a living. This one sold at Norwich depicts a jovial mariner wearing a red cap and a short blue jacket, standing on the shore and pointing seaward to his beloved ship lying close at hand.

If the facts could be ascertained, there are probably to be found up and down the country a number of village inn signs which have come from the brushes of artists during the rusticating period of their student days, and which they have not cared to father in after-years when overtaken by success and worldly prosperity.

XXVIII

SIGN RHYMES

Some hackneyed rhymes—Invitatory rhymes—Commendatory
rhymes—Rhymes allusive to the sign—A "living" sign—Sign
rhymes of combined callings—Rhymes allusive to the host—
Punning rhymes—Cautionary rhymes—Explanatory labels—
Competitive advertising rhymes.

A COGNATE subject to that of the preceding chapter
is the study of sign rhymes—those attempts at
versification which often take the form of an invitation
to sample the wares offered for sale inside the hospitable
doors of mine host, and not infrequently in a form
allusive to the sign which hangs in front of the house.
As thus, the sign of the "Traveller's Rest" may be
accompanied by these lines :—

> "If you go by and thirsty be,
> The fault's on you and not on me.
> Fixed here I am, and hinder none,
> So refresh, and pay, and travel on."

The invitatory verse distinguishes a large class of
sign rhymes. The one usually attached to the sign
of the "Dog" was noted in Dudley over fifty years
ago ; it ran :—

> "Step in, my friend, and rest awhile,
> And help the Lame Dog over the stile."

To some such sign as "The Gate," this rhyme is still very common :—

> "This Gate hangs well, and hinders none—
> Drink hearty, boys, and travel on."

Another variant of this couplet runs :—

> "This Gate hangs here for you to tell,
> Bill Spriggins has good ale to sell."

The sign of the "Red Cow" sometimes carries the curt couplet :—

> "The Old Red Cow
> Gives good milk now.'

The Malt Shovel Inn, at Chatham, once boasted its wares in this strain :—

> "Good malt makes good beer.
> Walk in, and you'll find it here."

The old "Fox Beerhouse" at Folkesworth, near Stilton, the place where George Borrow was first induced to try the nomadic life of gypsydom, as may be gathered from his "Lavengro," bore this weird legend :—

> "I HAM A CUNEN FOX
> YOU SEE THER HIS
> NO HARME ATCHED
> TO ME. IT IS MY MRS.
> WISH TO PLACE ME
> HERE TO LET YOU NO
> HE SELLS GOOD BEERE."

With the extension of "Mrs." into "Master's," and the proper spelling of the word "attached," the interpretation is easy; the rhymes also are easy of detection.

It will be observed how frequently the word "beer"

inspires the tavern rhymster. At Brighton many years ago this triplet appeared on an inn sign :—

> " Long have I traversed both far and near
> On purpose to find out real good beer—
> And at last I've found it here."

If the human traveller was not to be attracted by the beer, he was admonished by a whilom host of a wayside inn at Blean, in Kent, to consider the wants of his beasts :—

> "Stop, Brave Boys, and squench your thirst !
> If you won't drink, the horses must ! "

The invitation to the wayfarer is sometimes directly allusive to the sign borne by the house. At Castleton, near Whitby, the sign of the Robin Hood Inn was appropriately worded with :—

> "Ye gentlemen and yeomen good,
> Come in and drink with Robin Hood.
> If Robin Hood is not at home,
> Then stop and drink with Little John."

A variant of this, in another part of the country, ran :—

> "Robin Hood is dead and gone,
> So call and drink with Little John."

The sign of the "Round of Beef" illustrates an accompanying rhyme to this effect :—

> " If you are hungry or adry
> Or your stomach out of order,
> There's sure relief at The Round of Beef,
> For these or any such like disorder."

Occasionally the accompanying rhyme is more than allusive ; it may attempt to be explanatory, as did that attached to the pictorial representation of the "Cat and Shoulder of Mutton," at Hackney :—

> " Pray Puss, don't tear—
> For the Mutton is so dear !
> Pray Puss, don't claw—
> For the Mutton yet is raw !'

A good specimen of the rhyme allusive and invitatory was that of the Ship in Distress Tavern at Brighton :—

> " With sorrows I am compassed round,
> Pray lend a hand, my ship's aground."

At Plymouth the sign of the " Compasses " carried this appropriate admonition :—

> " Keep within the Compass
> And then you'll be sure
> To avoid many troubles
> Others have to endure."

Near Aintree racecourse, where a hill seems to give point to the warning, an inn sign runs in this benevolent strain :—

> " My ale is like my colour, bright roan,
> And for strength doth compare with my muscle and bone.
> So drink, and be thankful, but in drinking take heed,
> That howe'er good the liquor, you ne'er exceed."

It was surely the same benevolent disposition towards those inclined to imbibe to excess which induced a Reading innkeeper to dub his house the Moderation Inn.

Birmingham contained not many years ago an inn bearing the sign of the " Baker and the Brewer," on the sign of which appeared the verse :—

> " The Baker says, ' I've the staff of life,
> And you're a silly elf !'
> The Brewer replied, with artful pride,
> ' Why, this is life itself !' "

the landlord conducted a baking business next-door to his inn.

At Grantham, where the church steeple is 300 feet high, there has been set up as an inn sign a real bee-hive, with the following inscription :—

> "Stop ! Traveller, this wondrous sign explore,
> And say when thou hast viewed it o'er,
> Grantham, now, two rarities are thine,
> A lofty steeple, and a *living sign.*"

The sign of the " Beehive " in ordinary occurs in many places, and nearly always accompanied by some such rhyme as this, the original of which appeared at Birmingham :—

> " In this hive we all are alive,
> Good liquor makes us funny !
> If you be dry, step in and try
> The value of our honey."

How frequently the keepers of beer-houses and the publicans of the less-frequented class of inns had to eke out a livelihood by following other callings is well known. At Bradford there was once a publican chimney-sweeper who set forth on his sign :—

> " Who lives here ? Who do you think ?
> Major Lister. Give him a drink.
> Give him a drink ? For why ?
> Because when he's sweeping
> He's always dry."

The poetry of a barber innkeeper, painted on a sign-board below his barber's pole, was less interrogative and more witty :—

> " Roam not from Pole to Pole,
> But step in here,
> Where naught excels the Shaving
> But the Beer."

When John Pugh kept the Oak Inn at Kilpeck, Herefordshire, he rhymed his own name on his sign-board :—

> "I am an Oak and not a Yew,
> So drink a cup with good John Pugh."

In the use of the word "yew" there seems to be some cryptic reference to the churchyard and the sombreness of death. One Joseph Neale, who once kept a tavern in the High Street of Wednesbury, did not exactly put his name on his sign, but he is recorded to have left his own epitaph :—

> "Oh! poor Joe Neale
> Who loved good ale!
> For lack of good ale
> Here lies poor Joe Neale!"

In the dialect of the Black Country "Neale" was always pronounced to rhyme with "ale."

This kind of effort sometimes extended to punning as well as to rhyming on the landlord's name. Half-way up Richmond Hill at Douglas, Isle of Man, one Abraham Benjamin Lowe once announced his public-house entertainment in these lines :—

> "I'm Abraham B. Lowe, and half-way up the hill.
> If I were higher up, what's funnier still,
> I'm yet Abe below. So come, drink up your fill
> Of porter, ale, wine, spirits, what you will.
> Step in, my friend, I pray no further go,
> My prices, like myself, are always low."

This enumeration of alcoholic beverages recalls that "cider" as well as "beer" has given rise to a sign rhyme which has become very familiar through frequent repetition. Its original use, as given below, is said to have been on the sign of the Arrow Inn, Knockholt, Kent:—

> " Charles Collins liveth here,
> Sells Rum, Brandy, Gin, Beer.
> I've made this board a little wider
> To let you know he sells good Cider."

The habit of old-time sots and topers of running up ale scores at the taverns, which were sometimes chalked on the cellar door, or sometimes even on the flitches of bacon which hung from the kitchen ceiling, is well known. The identity of the trade benefactor who first attacked that vicious system of crediting the least creditable of all customers, will probably never be known; but that he was a genial reformer, and one who was not given to violent methods, may fairly be inferred from the traces he has left behind him in such jocular announcements as " Poor Trust is dead " and that " Bad Pay killed him "; and more particularly in the original draft of a familiar rhyme, of which the following is but one version of many :—

> " Gentlemen, walk in, and sit at your ease;
> Pay for what you call for, and call for what you please.
> As trusting of late has been to my sorrow,
> Pay to-day, and I'll trust you to-morrow."

Such notices may still be seen in the bars of old-fashioned village inns, but in the large towns where the hustle of a quick counter trade prevails—" perpendicular drinking " it has been called in the picturesque language of an up-to-date journalism—drink scores have become practically unknown.

At Trowbridge the " Lion and the Fiddle " sign is accompanied by the following couplet :—

> " Here is music without sorrow,
> Pay to-day, and trust to-morrow."

A tavern in the London Road, Manchester, many years ago had a flight of steps leading from the street down to its retail vaults, and a similar flight leading up to its public bar ; *apropos* of which the signboard was inscribed with :—

> " There are spirits above and spirits below,
> Spirits of bliss, and spirits of woe ;
> The spirits above are spirits divine,
> The spirits below are spirits-of-wine.'

Relative position, therefore, sometimes inspires the signboard rhymster. In a previous chapter reference was made to the sign " First and Last " occurring not unfrequently on the inns near to boundary-lines. On the edge of Dartmoor is an example of this sign, bearing on the side approaching the moor this rhyme :—

> " Before the wild moor you venture to pass,
> Pray step within and take a glass,"

while on the opposite side is painted—

> " Now that the bleak moor you've safely got over,
> Do stop a while your spirits to recover."

In the early part of the last reign a publican opened a house at Coopersall, Essex, bearing the sign of the " Queen Victoria," with this tag to a portrait of the young monarch :—

> " The Queen some day
> May pass this way,
> And see our Tom and Jerry :
> Perhaps she'll stop
> And stand a drop
> To make her subjects merry."

The original of this was said to have appeared on an Oxfordshire inn " dedicated " to Queen Mary.

Some old-time signs imperatively needed an explanatory label. There was, for instance, a curious eighteenth-century sign, "The Dog's Head in the Pot." Its purpose was manifestly that of a shaft directed against the shortcomings of sluttish housewives. The artist's composition showed the interior of a particularly disorderly kitchen, in which were two ancient beldames, one of whom was wiping a dish with the bushy tail of a large dog, while the animal itself was licking the inside of a capacious iron pot in which its head was entirely buried. Hence the appropriateness of these lines below the picture :—

> " All sluts behold, take view of me
> Your own good housewifry to see ;
> It is (methinks) a cleanly care,
> My dishclout in this sort to spare,
> Whilst dog, you see, doth lick the pot,
> His tail for dishclout I have got . . ."

and so on.

A history is sometimes attached to these sign rhymes, as to that, for instance, which once appeared on the sign of the " White Horse " on the old Bath Road. The story told of it is to the effect that a poor author once put up there, and incurred a bill which he was unable to discharge in the usual way with current coin of the realm. To appease the wrath of the angry host he promised to write him some lines which would help to secure him the custom of his nearest competitors. So underneath the figure of the gallant White Horse was painted :—

> " My White Horse shall beat the *Bear*,
> And make the *Angel* fly,
> Shall turn the *Ship* quite bottom up,
> And drink the *Three Cups* dry."

Needless to explain, the " Bear," the " Angel," and the

"Three Cups" were the three nearest inns and rival establishments.

Sign rhymes afford a subject of never-failing interest. No less personages than Lord High Treasurer Harley and his illustrious friend the Dean of St. Patrick once travelling together, as the latter informs us, by way of beguiling the tedium of the journey—

"Would gravely try to read the lines,
Writ underneath the country signs."

LIVERPOOL DELFT PUNCH BOWL.

(Decorated with military trophies in blue, and having three-masted man-of-war inside.) Diameter 20½ in.

(*At Victoria and Albert Museum.*)

[*Page* 352.

OLD ENGLISH DRINKING GLASSES.

(*Photo kindly lent by Mr. T. Rudd, 106, High Street, Southampton.*)

[*Page* 356.

OLD ENGLISH DRINKING GLASSES.

(Kindly lent by Mr. T. Rudd, 106, High Street, Southampton.)

[Page 356.

XXIX

COMPOUNDED BEVERAGES, WARM DRINKS, &c.

" Lamb's wool"—Twelfth Night wassail bowl—Gloucestershire
Christmas wassailing—A Midland wassail song—Herrick's
description of " Lamb's wool "—Piment—A fifteenth-century
recipe for same—Posset—A recipe for same—Cambridge
" Copus "—Oxford " night-caps "—Egg-flip—Beer-flip—Aleberry—Syllabubs—A recipe for same—Alegar—Ale used
medicinally—Barm used for poultices—Ale to mix mortar and
cement—Anecdote of Bess of Hardwick's building operations.

COMPOUNDED beverages and warm drinks were more
popular with our forbears than with us. Perhaps their
choice of good and palatable drinks was more restricted.

Although among the wealthier Anglo-Saxon house-
holds a favourite beverage was composed of some rich
wine, highly spiced and sweetened, with roasted apples
floating on the surface, it was more common to use ale,
mingled with nutmeg, ginger, sugar, toast, and roasted
crab-apples. It was essential that the roasted apples,
burst, white and fleecy, should form part of the mixture,
the whole forming a combination quaintly called " Lamb's
wool." When ready it was borne into the banquet-hall
in a huge bowl, decked with ribbons. Then each one at
the board drank, crying three times, " Wassail ! wassail !
wassail ! " after the head of the family had drunk to the
rest of the household.

In the royal household of Henry VIII. on Twelfth

Night the steward was enjoined, when he entered with
the spiced and smoking beverage, to cry "Wassail!"
three times, to which the royal chaplain had to answer
with a carol or song.

Numerous and diverse are the old customs of Christmas
wassailing; but that ale is the usual basis of the drink
may be gathered from the old ditties celebrating them.
Thus in Gloucestershire they sing—

> "Wassail! wassail! all over the town,
> Our toast it is white and our ale it is brown;
> Our bowl it is of the good maplin [maple] tree,
> So here's, good fellow, I'll drink to thee,"

—while in the North and the Midlands the Wassail Song
runs :—

> "Here we come a-wassailing,
>   Among the leaves so green ;
> Here we come a-wandering,
>   So fair to be seen.
>
> *Chorus.*
> Love and joy come to you
> And to your wassail, too,
> And God send you a happy New Year,
>   A New Year,
> And God send you a happy New Year,
> Our wassail cup is made of rosemary-tree,
> So is your beer of the best barley."

"Lamb's wool" was generally compounded with
good English "nut-brown ale," and finished off with
roasted crab-apples. Thus Herrick, in his "Twelfth
Night," sings :—

> "Next crown the bowl full
>   With gentle Lamb's Wool,
> Add sugar, nutmeg, and ginger,
>   With store of Ale, too,
>   And thus ye must doe
> To make the Wassail a swinger."

Another favourite drink of our ancestors was Piment. A fifteenth-century recipe for the making of Piment runs : "Take clowis, quibibus, maces, canel, galyngale, and make powdyr therof, temprying it with good wine and the third part hony, and clense hem thorow a clene klothe. Also thou mayest make it with good ale." In the writings of the times it is often mentioned; as thus :—

> "Mete and drynk they hadde afyn
> Pyement, claré, and Reynysch wyn."

A Posset was a warm drink of wine (or sometimes treacle) boiled with milk, taken before retiring to rest at night. Thus we may read how Sir John Falstaff, notwithstanding that he was known to be " given to taverns and sack, and wine and metheglins," and other copious drinkings, was graciously promised by Master Page (as we may read in the *Merry Wives of Windsor*, v. 5) that he should " eat a posset to-night " at his (Page's) house.

Says an old writer (1603) :—

"It is his morncing's draught when he riseth, his conserves or cates when he hath well dined, his afternoones nuncions, and when he goeth to bedde his posset smoakinge hote."

Copus is a drink made of beer, wine, and spice, heated together, and served in a Loving Cup, as at Cambridge University. The name is concocted from the Dog-Latin for *cupellon Hippocratis* (a cup of hippocras).

There were several Oxford " Night-caps " in vogue at that University a century or less ago—comfortable potations for the cold nights of the dreary winter season, supposed to be efficacious in strengthening the hearts of the healthy and cheering the spirits of the feeble. " Eggflip " was a famous concoction, of which a bottle of wine and the yolks of eggs were the principal ingredients ; but a modification of this, called Beer-flip, was a quart of strong home-brewed beer as a substitute for the wine. The eggs were beaten and put into the liquor after it had boiled, and the many flavourings included a glass of gin, sugar, cinnamon, juice of lemon—the quantities of each and the methods of mixing all being the subject of much careful instruction in the published recipes of the period.

A beverage made by boiling ale with sugar and spice, and having sops of bread in it, was known as Aleberry.

Ale has even been mixed with milk to make a once-popular beverage. Many people have heard of that old-fashioned drink called Syllabubs, but very few have tasted it. A century or two ago Syllabubs were sold in the London public parks and other similar places of public resort which boasted so much rurality as a green field and a cow. The usual composition of a Syllabub was milk, milked directly from the cow and made as frothy as possible in the process, into a bowl containing freshly mashed fruit, such as gooseberries, well sweetened with sugar, to which was then added wine or ale.

A recipe for making an Ale Syllabub says : " Place in a large bowl a quart of strong ale or beer, grate into it a little nutmeg, and sweeten with sugar. Milk the cow rapidly into the bowl, forcing the milk as strongly as possible into the ale, and against the sides of the vessel, to raise a good froth. Let it stand for an hour and it will then be fit for use. Cider may be used instead of ale, and the sugar should be proportioned to the taste of the drinker."

> " No Syllabubs made at the milking pail
> But are composed of a pot of good ale."

Punch belongs to a later century than most of these old English drinks, and the method of making this famous compound is given in the chapter on " Drinking Vessels," under the head of Punch-bowls. It may be recalled that the immortal Wilkins Micawber, in addition to his various accomplishments as a speechifier, letter-writer, and projector of bubble schemes, was no mean exponent of the art of punch-brewing.

As vinegar was the product of sour wine, so in olden times Alegar was prepared from sour beer.

The use of ale for any other purpose than that of a beverage is not common. Medicinally it has been re-garded as a stimulant, as an anodyne, as an enricher of the blood (in the case of boils and carbuncles), and as useful in several of the minor ailments treated at home. Barm, for instance, is believed to be very efficacious in drawing the pus from a wound or gathering. But out-side this range its uses have been very few, that of using it to mix mortar being almost the only one. In days of yore it was believed that mortar mixed with malt liquor possessed greater durability than that mixed with water ; and many old Church accounts contain entries relating to this, particularly to the joints in the steeples being re-pointed with this stronger kind of mortar or cement. Illustrative of the same point is the well-known tradition attaching to Bess of Hardwick, the historic " Lady of the Peak." The tale runs that a fortune-teller had promised her that death should not overtake her so long as she continued her building operations. These were some-what extensive, for she erected several noble structures in succession, including Hardwick and Chatsworth—two of the most stately homes of old England ; but, as the soothsayer had foretold, she succumbed at last during the severe frost of 1607, notwithstanding that her work-men tried to mix their mortar with hot ale—as they failed, she expired.

XXX

DRINKING SONGS

English songs chiefly in praise of ale—"Jolly good ale and old"—
"Gentle butler, fill the bowl"—A mediæval part-song—"Doll
thy ale"—In praise of "Cornie ale"—"Bring us in good ale"—
A Renaissance song in praise of wine—Also a tavern song—
Basse's song, "The Man in the Moon drinks Claret"—"Ale the
true liquor of life"—A dialogue between Wine and Bonny
Ale—In praise of ale—And of "Stout British beer"—"The
Leather Bottel"—A Wassail chanson—An equivocal song—A
song by Huffy White—Another by Crofton Croker—A song
from a Drury Lane drama (1826)—Derivation of the word
"grog."

"DRINKING," says Dryden, "is the soldier's pleasure";
and, according to some others, it is the poet's inspiration.

> "If with water you fill up your glasses,
> You'll never write anything wise;
> For wine is the horse of Parnassus,
> That hurries a bard to the skies."

But as England is not a wine country—

> "The poet divine that cannot reach wine
> Because that his money doth many times faile,
> Will hit on the vein to make a good strain
> If he be but inspired by a pot of good ale."

Germany is pre-eminently the country for drinking
songs inspired by the juice of the grape, as a fine col-

lection translated and published by J. A. Symonds amply testifies; here, however, it is proposed to restrict our notice as much as possible to those associated with the praise of malt liquor.

Mr. Symonds' collection is entitled " Wine, Women, and Song," and the bulk of his examples are translated from the mediæval Latin.

At the period when the whole Protestantism of Europe was arrayed in arms against the Catholic states, it was said of both Germans and English, that they loved a tavern better than a church, and a bowl of wine better than a sacramental chalice.

Bacchanalian ditties are about as old as civilisation, but the first drinking song that appeared in the English tongue is found in "Gammer Gurton's Needle," published in 1551, the earliest comedy but one written in English, and supposed to have been from the pen of Bishop Still, of Bath and Wells. This was the ballad " Jolly Good Ale and Old," of which the first verse runs in this wise—

> "But if that I may have truly
>   Good Ale my belly full,
> I shall look like one, by sweet Saint John,
>   Were shorn against the wool.
> Though I go bare, take ye no care
>   I am nothing cold,
> I stuff my skin so full within
>   Of jolly good ale and old."

There are seven more verses in the same strain, and the burden, so characteristically " Old English," will be recognised as that of the tippler's petition :—

> " Back and side go bare, go bare,
>   Both hand and foot go cold,
> But belly, God send thee ale enough
>   Whether it be new or old."

This song is quoted with evident gusto by Washington Irving, in his sketch entitled " Little Britain."

Let it not be thought there were no Old English lyrics of a date earlier than the one just named ; what is always to be remembered is that the old folk-songs were never written down, and such mediæval songs as have been preserved are generally the work of the minstrels. In the old song, "Gentle butler fill the bowl," the troubadour seems to betray his un-English origin in the line *Bevis a tout* (in which *bevis* is equivalent to "buvez") though not in the use of *bellamy* for "*bel ami*," meaning "fair friend." The first verse of it is :—

> " Jentill butler, bellamy,
> Fill the boll by the eye
> That we may drink by and by,
> With, How butler, how ?
> *Bevis a tout*
> Fill the boll, butler,
> And let the cup rout."

This seems to recall another old drinking song which begins—

> "Fill the cup, Philip,
> And let us drink a drain,
> Once or twice about the house
> And leave where we began."

Here is a mediæval three-part song also in the same strain :—

> " Tapster, fille another ale,
> Annone have I do.
> God sends us good ale,
> Avale the stake, avale
> Here is good ale ifounde,
> Drinke to me,
> And I to thee
> And let the cuppe go rounde."

In the foregoing the word *avale* signifies "lower" or "degrade"; the allusion to the ale-stake will be readily understood. In our next example, the famous old ballad "Dole thy ale," it is interesting to note the references made to the old manorial rights of stocks, blocks, and gallows :—

"Doll thy ale, doll, doll thy ale, doll
Ale make many a man to have a doty poll.

Ale make many a man to stik at a brere ;
Ale make many a man to lie in the miere ;
And ale make many a man to slepe by the fiere
        With doll !

Ale make many a man to stomble at a stone ;
Ale make many a man to go dronken home ;
And ale make man to breke his tone
        With doll !

Ale make many a man to draw his knife ;
Ale make many a man to make grete strife ;
And ale make many a man to bete his wife
        With doll !

Ale make many a man to wet his chekes ;
Ale make many a man to lie in the stretes,
And ale make many a man to wet his sheetes,
        With doll !

Ale make many a man to stombell at the blokkes ;
Ale make many a man to make his head have knokkes,
And ale make many a man to sit in the stokkes
        With doll !

Ale make many a man to rine over the falows ;
Ale make many a man to swere by God and Allhalows ;
And ale make many a man to hang upon the galows
        With doll !"

The next song to be quoted must be prefaced with glossarial explanations of at least three archaic terms :— *corney*, signifying " tasting of the malt " ; *nappy* or *noppy*, meaning " strong " ; and *stale* equivalent to " old " (*i.e.*, " strong old ale "). New ale was dubbed " ale-in-cornes."

> "A bone, God wot
> Sticks in my throat,
> Without I have a draught
> Of cornie ale
> Nappy and stale
> My life lies in great waste.
>
> Now give us drink
> And let cat wink,
> I tell you all at once,
> It sticks so sore,
> I may drink no more
> Till I have drunken once."

In similar strain is " We'll drink to the Barley Mow " ; but more famous is the old song which appears in a little volume of collections, " The Ipswich Minstrel" :—

"Bryng us in no browne bred, fore that is made of brane,
　Nor bryng us in no whyt bred, for therin is no game ;
　　But bryng us in good ale.

Bryng us in no befe, for ther is many bonys (bones),
　But bryng us in good ale, for that goth downe at onys (once)
　　And bryng us in good ale.

Bryng us in no bacon, for that is passing fate,
　But bryng us in good ale, and gyfe us i-nough of that ;
　　And bryng us in good ale.

Bryng us in no mutton, for that is often lene,
　Nor bryng us in no trypes, for thei be syldom clene ;
　　But bryng us in good ale.

Bryng us in no eggs, for ther ar many schelles,
　But bryng us in good ale, and gyfe us no(th)yng ellys ;
　　And bryng us in good ale.

Bryng us in no butter, for therin ar many herys (hairs),
Nor bryng us in no pygges flesch, for that wyl mak us borys ;
    But bryng us in good ale.

Bryng us in no podynges, for therein is al Godes good,
Nor bryng us in no venesen, for that is not for owr blod ;
    But bryng us in good ale.

Bryng us in no capons flesch, for that is ofte der,
Nor bryng us in no dokes (duck's) flesch, for thei slober in the
    mer (mire) ;
    But bryng us in good ale."

There is a type of English drinking song belonging to the Renaissance period, which is in praise of wine rather than of ale :—

    "Let's be jovial, fill our Glasses,
      Madness 'tis for us to think
    How the World is rul'd by Asses,
      And the Wise are sway'd by Chink.

    Let not such vain Thoughts oppress us,
      Riches are to us a Snare :
    We are all as rich as Crœsus,
      Drink away and drive off Care.

    Wine makes us as fresh as Roses,
      And our Sorrows quite forget ;
    Come, let's fuddle all our Noses,
      Drink ourselves quite out of Debt.

    When grim Death is looking for us,
      We're carousing o'er our Bowls,
    Bacchus joining in the Chorus,
      Cries, ' Death, begone, here's none but Souls.

    God-like Bacchus thus commanding,
      Trembling Death away shall fly,
    Ever after understanding,
      Drinking Souls can never die."

The next example, which is of the shameless tavern-haunting type, is also in praise of the rosy god :—

> " Farewel, my Mistress, I'll be gone,
> I have Friends to wait upon ;
> Think you I'll my self confine
> To your Humours, Lady mine ;
> No : your louring Looks do say,
> 'Twill be a rainy drinking Day,
> To the Tavern let's away.
>
> There have I Mistress got,
> Cloyster'd in a Pottle-pot ;
> Plump and bouncing, soft, and fair,
> Buxsome sweet, and debonair,
> And they call her, Sack my dear.
>
> Sack with no scornful Dread will blast me,
> Tho' upon the Bed she cast me,
> Yet ne'er blush her self to red,
> Nor fear the loss of Maiden-head :
> And tho' mute and still she be,
> Quicker Wits she brings to me,
> Than e'er I cou'd find in thee.
>
> Yet if thou wilt take the Pain,
> To be kind yet once again,
> And with thy Smiles but call me back,
> Thou shalt be the Lady Sack.
> Oh then try, and you shall see
> What a loving Soul I'll be,
> When I'm drunk with none but thee."

The ballad of " Old Mad Tom," printed in the " Percy Reliques," had as its second part " The Man in the Moon drinks Claret," which was sung at the Curtain Theatre, Shoreditch, in 1610, or even earlier. The reputed author of this was William Basse, a native of Thame, Oxford-shire, and a well-known poet of his time, among his works being lines on " The Death of Prince Henry,

1613"; some verses "On Mr. William Shakespeare, who died in April, 1616"; and a number of songs and ballads, among them the one here quoted :—

"THE MAN IN THE MOON DRINKS CLARET.

(As it was lately sung at " The Curtain," Holiwel.)

" Bacchus, the father of drunken nowles,
Full mazers, beakers, glasses, bowls,
Greasie flapdragons, flamish upsefriese,
With health's stab'd in arms upon naked knees.

Rich wine is good :
It heats the blood,
It makes an old man lusty,
The young to brawle,
And drawers up call
Before being too much musty.

Such gambles, such tricks, such figaries,
We fetch, though we touch no Canaryes ;
French wine till the welkin roares,
And cry out a plague of your scores.

There is no sound
The eare can wound
As lids of wine-pots clinking ;
There's no such sport when, all amort,
Men cry let's fall to drinking.

Our man in the moon drinks claret,
With powder beef, turnep, and carret ;
If he doth so, why should not you
Drink wine untill the sky looks blew ?

Hey for a turn thus above ground, hey !
O my noddle too heavy doth way !
Metheglin, perry, syder nor strong ale,
Are half so hevy, be they nere so stale.
Wine in our bodies can never rumble,
Down now and then though it makes us stumble ;
Yet scrambling up, a drunkard feels no pain,
But cryes,—sirra, boy, tother pottle again !

We can drink no more unless we have full
    pipes of Trinidado.
Give us the best, it keeps our brains
More warm than can friezado.
It makes us sing,
And cry, hey jing,
And laugh when pipes lie broken.
For which to pay,
At going away,
We scorn a mustard token.

If, then, you do love my oast claret,
Fat powder beef, turnep, and carret,
Come agen and agen,
And still welcome, gentlemen."

After the introduction of ardent spirits, there was a
note of regret in the Englishman's song in praise of the
old national beverage :—

" All history gathers
From ancient forefathers
    That Ale's the true liquor of life ;
Men lived long in health
And preserved their wealth
    Whilst barley-broth only was rife.

Ale is not so costly
Although that the most lie
    Too long in the oil of barley,
Yet may they part late
At a reasonable rate,
    Though they come in the morning early.

Chorus.
Sack is but single broth ;
Ale is meat, drink, and cloth."

A dialogue of the seventeenth century on this subject
is in this form :—

Wine.   I, jovial Wine, exhilarate the heart.
Beer.   March Beer is a drink for a King.

Ale.   But Ale, bonny Ale, with spice and a toast
           In the morning's a dainty thing.
Chorus.   Then let us be merry, wash sorrow away,
           Wine, Beer, and Ale shall be drunk to-day.

Wine.   I, generous Wine, am for the Court,
Beer.   The Citie calls for Beer,
Ale.   But Ale, bonny ale, like a lord of the soyl,
           In the country shall domineer.
Chorus.   Then let us be merry, &c., &c.

Here is a ballad of the same century :—

"IN PRAISE OF ALE.

" Come all you brave wights
   That are dubbed ale-knights,
      Now set yourself in fight ;
   And let them that crack
   In the praises of Sack
      Know Malt is of mickle might.

Though Sack they define
To be holy, divine,
   Yet is it but natural liquor ;
Ale hath for its part
An addition of art
   To make it drink thinner or quicker.

Sack's fiery fume
Doth waste and consume
   Men's *humidum radicale ;*
It scaldeth their livers,
It breeds burning fevers,
   Proves *vinum venenum reale.*

But history gathers
From aged forefathers
   That Ale's the true liquor of life ;
Men lived long in health,
And preserved their wealth,
   Whilst barley-broth only was rife.

Sack quickly ascends
And suddenly ends
    What company came for at first ;
And that which yet worse is
It empties men's purses
    Before it half quenches their thirst.

Sack makes men from words
Fall to drawing of swords,
    And quarrelling endeth their quaffing ;
Whilst dagger-ale barrels
Bear off many quarrels,
    And oft turn chiding to laughing.

Sack's drink for our masters ;
All may be ale-tasters.
    Good things the more common the better ;
Sack's but single broth,
Ale's meat, drink, and cloth,
    Say they that know never a letter.

But not to entangle
Old friends till they wrangle,
    And quarrell for other men's pleasure,
Let Ale keep his place,
And let Sack have his grace,
    So that neither exceed the true measure."

When the "Gin" question was exciting the public
mind, and "patriots" were declaring that the Government was attempting to oust "honest English ale" in
favour of foreign wines and spirits, the drinking songs
of the day (1757) assumed a political significance :—

"Ye true honest Britons who love your own land
    Whose sires were so brave, so victorious, so free,
Who always beat France when they took her in hand—
    Come join honest Britons in chorus with me.
        Let us sing our own treasures, Old England's good cheer,
        The profits and pleasures of stout British beer ;
        Your wine-tippling, dram-sipping fellows retreat,
        But your beer-drinking Britons can never be beat.

GARRAWAY'S COFFEE HOUSE.

[Page 366.

[Pictorial Agency.

Photo]

THE "BULL AND BUSH," HAMPSTEAD.

[Page 372.

The French with their vineyards are meagre and pale,
 They drink of the squeezings of half-ripened fruit ;
But we, who have hop-yards to mellow our ale,
 Are rosy and plump, and have freedom to boot.
    Chorus.

Should the French dare invade us, thus armed with our poles,
 We'll bang their bare ribs, make their lantern jaws ring ;
For your beef-eating, beer-drinking Britons are souls
 Who will shed their last blood for their country and King."
    Chorus.

A very famous old song, and one of the best known of
all, is that which praises the vessel for the sake of its
contents :—

" THE LEATHER BOTTEL.

" God bless the cow and the old cow's hide,
And ev'ry thing in the world beside,
For when we've said and done all we can,
'Tis all for the good and use of man ;
So I hope his soul in heaven may dwell
That first devised the leather bottel.

What say ye, to these glasses fine ?
Faith ! they shall have no praise of mine ;
For if you touch your glass on the brim,
The liquor falls out and leaves none therein,
And though your table-cloth be ever so fine,
There lies your beer, your ale, your wine ;
Whereas had it been the leather bottel,
And the stopper been in, it had been well.
So I hope in heaven his soul may dwell
That first devised the leather bottel.

What say ye, to these tankards fine ?
Faith ! they shall have no praise of mine,
For when the master doth send his man
To fill it with liquor as fast as he can,
The bearer thereof then runneth away
And is ne'er heard again of for many a day.
Whereas had it been the leather bottel,
And the stopper been in, why all had been well.
So I hope his soul in heaven will dwell
That first devised the leather bottel.

What say ye, to these black-jacks three?
Faith they shall have no praise from me;
For when a man and wife are at strife,
Which much too often is the case in life,
Why, then they seize on the black-jack both,
And in the scuffle they spoil the broth;
Not thinking that at a future day
They must account for throwing good liquor away;
Whereas had it been the leather bottel,
And the stopper been in, they could have banged away well.
So I hope his soul in heaven may dwell
That first devised the leather bottel.

And when this bottel is quite grown old,
And no more good liquor it will hold,
All off its sides you may cut a clout,
That will serve to mend your old shoes about;
T'other end, hang it on to a pin,
'Twill serve to put your odd trifles in;
Here's a save-all for your candles' ends,
For young beginners have need of such things;
So I hope his soul in heaven may dwell
That first devised the leather bottel."

An old wassail chanson, from " Poor Robin's Almanac," also trolls forth the praises of the containing vessel :—

" The brown bowle,
The merry brown bowle,
As it goes round-about-a,
Fill
Still,
Let the world say what it will,
And drink your fill all out-a.

The deep canne,
The merry deep canne,
As thou dost freely quaff-a,
Sing,
Fling,
Be as merry as a king
And sound a lusty laugh-a."

As a drinking song there is something equivocal about our next example :—

> "The wisest men are fools in wine,
> Experience makes us think ;
> Its magic spells are so divine
> We reason—yet we drink !
>
> Say, does not love and loving wine
> Inspire the weary soul ?
> The dullest fellows seem to shine,
> Reflected in the bowl !
>
> Oh, as the charmed glass we sip,
> We conquer care and pain.
> It woos, like woman's dewy lip,
> To kiss—and come again !"

A more typical song is that by Huffy White :—

> "Drink ! drink !
> Drink away !
> Never think
> On what's to pay !
> What is man ? A sigh, a vapour.
> What is woman ? Whitey-brown paper !
> Waiter ! Quick ! another lump
> Of sugar in my beaker plump !
> Pop it in my brimming cup !
> Bravo ! Now I'll drink it up.
> Drink ! drink !
> Drink away !" &c., &c.

A sprightly song of abandon is that by Crofton Croker, the Irish folklorist (1826) :—

> "Good liquor, good liquor,
> Makes the heart to beat quicker,
> And the blood to flow thicker,
> Good liquor, good liquor.

From black-jack of leather,
Cow-horn, cup, or mether,
Let good men drink together
  Their liquor, their liquor.

Though foot and tongue falter,
Pooh ! why should I palter ?
For all shrinking a halter !
  No liquor, no liquor.

They who leave it behind 'em,
A rope's end may find 'em,
So I'll drink, and not mind 'em,
  My liquor, my liquor."

A drama produced at Drury Lane Theatre, in 1826,
entitled " Benyowski," founded on the adventures of the
rascally Hungarian count of that name, had this drinking
song :—

"A toper's a thorough game-cock,
His head is as hard as a rock,
    He's frank and he's free
    For good liquor's the key
The hypocrite's heart to unlock.
Then drink, drink, hyprocrites drink
Tipple like fishes, and say what you think !

The poet whose fancy grows dim
For true inspiration and whim
    Finds Helicon's stream
    Has a bright rosy beam
In a goblet filled up to the brim.
Then drink, drink, merry bards drink
Tipple and wake up the Muse if she wink !

Your fighting man, Croat or Cossack,
If valour he happen to lack,
    His courage to jog
    Finds a rummer of grog
The best friend he has at his back.
Then drink, drink, Cavaliers drink
Tipple and hark how your weapons will clink ! "

For the complete understanding of the last verse it may be explained that the term " grog " signifies a mixture of spirit and water ; and that a " rummer " is a stout glass for containing the same when it happens to be made with hot water. Until the time of Admiral Vernon, British sailors had always had their allowance of rum served out to them "neat " ; but when the hero of Portobello was in command of the fleet he issued an order for the rations of rum to be served to the men mixed with water —an innovation which at first gave great offence to the sailors ; and as the admiral was in the habit of walking the deck in a grogram cloak whenever the weather was rough, they nicknamed him " Old Grog," and then called his watered liquor "Grog" as well. As to the term " Rummer," there is in Bristol an interesting old hostelry called by this name, which is evidently much older than the word itself.

XXXI

DRINKING VESSELS

Saxon ale-buckets—Norse skull cups—Lord Byron's ghoulish search
for a suitable family skull—Drinking horns—Mazers—Pewter
cups and mugs—The Pewterers' Company—Silver tankards—
The ballad of Syr Tankarde—Peg tankards—The Glastonbury
tankard—Dr. Pegge's specimen—His description of a peg-
tankard—Peg cups mentioned in 1102—Vintner's chained cups
—Ancient Staffordshire pitchers—Tygs—The Bellarmine, or
Greybeard jug—The Toby jug—Posset pots—Tricky jugs for
convivial joking—Toad cups—Puzzle cups—Fuddling cups—
The whistling jug—Anne of Denmark's jug—Margaret of
Voldemar's cup—English jugs of the thirteenth century—
Legendary cups—" The Luck of Edenhall"—Punch-bowls—
Derivation of the word " punch "—A fountain of punch—The
ingredients — A heady drink — Punch-bowls a recognised
household effect—Suitable for testimonials—Used as fonts—
Punch-bowls introduced into tavern signs—Anecdote of Spiller
—The " Old Slaughters' " Tavern, and its witty waiter, " Suck "
—Skin bottles—Leather bottles, black-jacks, and bombards—
Their shape and make—Literary allusions—" Jack " boots and
drinking " bouts"—The term " bumboat" derived from bom-
bard—Stoups and canakins—Drinking-glasses.

IN previous chapters allusion has been made to the
method of using the peg tankard, to the *raison d'être* of
the tumbler, and cognate matters. Here it is proposed to
go a little further into the history of these and other
specialised forms of drinking vessels.

Our Saxon forefathers, so " potent in potting," took

with them to their graves their ornamental ale-buckets and drinking cups—the latter made without foot or stand, purposely designed in this fashion so that they had to be filled and emptied by the drinker before they could be set down again on the festive board.

The Norsemen deemed the highest state of felicity to be a future state in which, seated in the Halls of Woden, they would for ever quaff strong liquors from the skulls of their enemies. This barbarous custom of converting skulls into drinking cups is mentioned frequently by the older dramatists.

In Middleton's *Witch* the Duke takes a bowl, and being told it is a skull, replies—

> "Call it a soldier's cup !"

Massinger has several allusions to the custom, and in Dekker's *Wonder of a Kingdom* a character says—

> "Would I had ten thousand soldiers' heads
> Their skulls set all in silver, to drink healths
> To his confusion first invented War."

Lord Byron was obsessed by this barbaric idea, and in his early youth he ransacked the graves of his ancestors at Newstead Abbey for a skull sufficiently capacious to be fashioned into a carousing cup.

The primitive drinking cup was a horn. In the Middle Ages a common form of drinking cup was the "mazer"— a vessel of maple wood—so called from the British word *masarm* (" maple "). Examples are extant in the Copus cups at Cambridge and the Loving Cup of the London Corporation ; and reference is made thereto in Scott's " Lord of the Isles " :—

> " ' Bring hither ' [he said] 'the mazers four
> My noble fathers loved of yore.' "

In olden times nearly all metals were much more valuable than they are now, and drinking vessels of metal were consequently rarer. The pewter trade was introduced into this country by the Dutch, and in 1482 the Pewterers were incorporated as the sixteenth Company of the City of London, which place has ever since remained the chief seat of the manufacture, although it was once carried on to a limited extent at Bewdley, in Worcestershire. Allusion has been made in Chapter VIII. to the "sealed quarts" made of pewter.

Old pewter drinking cups, bearing English marks, are prized almost as much as silver. The silversmiths of the sixteenth and seventeenth centuries whose drinking cups reached the highest pitch of art were those of Augsburg and Nuremberg, in Germany, the production of which took the form of men, animals, birds, &c.— all in the most grotesque designs. The air of antiquity in the following ballad arouses suspicion; it is in all likelihood a spurious composition :—

"SYR TANKARDE.

"Syr Tankarde, he is as bold a wight
  As ever Old England bred ;
His armoure it is of silver bright,
  And his colour is ruby red.
And whene'er on the bully ye call
  He is ready to give ye a fall ;
But if long in the battle with him you should be
The weaker are you, and the stronger is he,
  For Syr Tankarde is victor of all.

A barleycorn ear he mounts for a spear
  His helmet with hops is hung ;
He lights the eye with a laughing leer,
  With a carol he tips the tongue.
And he marshalls a valiant host
  Of spices, and crabs, and toast ;
And the stoutest of yeoman they well can overthrow
When he leads them in beakers and jugs to the foe ;
  And Syr Tankarde his prowess may boast."

Longfellow has given us as "an inscription for an antique pitcher," a drinking song beginning—

"Come, old friend! sit down and listen!
From the pitcher, placed between us,
How the waters laugh and glisten
In the head of old Silenus.

*   *   *   *   *

Bacchus was the type of vigour
And Silenus of excesses. &c., &c.

Peg tankards and peg or pin cups are largely treasured in the cabinets of antiquaries. Some notable specimens are extant. The Glastonbury Abbey peg tankard was one of the very few articles of value saved from Wardour Castle when it was surrendered by Blanche, Lady Arundel, after its siege in the Civil Wars of Charles I. This ancient drinking vessel is of oak, and has a handle and a cover to it. It holds exactly two quarts, and, being spaced with eight pegs, divides the contents into equal draughts of half a pint each. The exterior is elaborately carved, the Crucifixion appearing on the lid and the twelve apostles round the barrel, the design at the bottom being finished—in a style more conventional than ecclesiastical—with birds, animals, and serpents.

Another notable example of a wooden tankard, purchased at Yarmouth and presented to Dr. Pegge, the antiquary, was strictly ecclesiastical in design, and therefore not improbably it belonged originally to some religious house. The subjects carved on its sides included Solomon and the Queen of Sheba, Absalom suspended in the tree, David playing his harp, Jacob's Ladder, Abraham's Sacrifice, and the Creation of Eve; while on the lid appeared a representation of Abraham entertaining the three angels. Peg tankards have been reported, though not authenticated like these, of designs which would represent them as dating from the tenth or eleventh century.

Peg tankards, used like hooped pots for measured drinking, are, as we have seen, of great antiquity. They are thus minutely described by Pegge in his "Anonymiana" : "They have in the inside a row of eight pins one above another, from top to bottom ; the tankards hold two quarts, so that there is a gill of ale, *i.e.*, half-a-pint of Winchester measure, between each pin. The first person that drank was to empty the tankard to the first peg or pin ; the second was to empty to the next pin, &c., by which means the pins were so many measures to the compotators, making them all drink alike the same quantity ; and as the distance of the pins was such as to contain a large draught of liquor, the company would be very liable by this method to get drunk, especially when, if they drank short of the pin or beyond it, they were obliged to drink again." It is clear that this invention was as old as the Conquest, as in Archbishop Anselm's canons, made at the Council of London in 1102, priests were enjoined not to go to drinking bouts, or to drink to pegs.

The ingenuity exercised in days of old to compel the unfortunate Bacchanalian to drain the last drop of liquor or to expose his recreant sobriety was really marvellous.

An Elizabethan antiquary tells us (on what authority is unknown) that King Edgar, to prevent swilling and bibbing, caused iron cups to be chained at every vintner's door, with iron pins in them, to stint every man how much he should drink, and he who went beyond one of those pins forfeited a penny for every draught.

As early as the fourteenth century, when four quarts of ale could be bought for a penny, green-glazed pitchers of Staffordshire production were in use.

Of later date, perhaps, were the Tygs, a kind of many-handled earthenware mug, some having as many as ten handles, to be passed round from one guest to another, each person taking hold of a different handle, and putting his lips to a different part of the rim.

There was in vogue in the seventeenth century a corpulent sort of beer jug of stone pottery, having a man's face fashioned where the spout should be, and that face adorned with the large square-cut "cathedral" beard then peculiar to ecclesiastics. In England these jugs were usually called Greybeards, but sometimes they were known as Bellarmines, after the cardinal and Jesuit theologian of that name, whom they were intended (by the Dutch makers at Delft) to ridicule, because he had been sent into the Low Countries specially to hinder the progress of the Reformed Religion. The word "bellarmin," besides being applied to these large, handsome jugs, was sometimes used by drinkers to express a stout bottle of strong drink.

The eighteenth century produced the Toby jug, in which the potter somewhat overstrained his art to fashion a drinking vessel in the shape of a stout old toper, seated with jug and pipe, and wearing a three-cornered hat, the flaps of which conveniently offered themselves to form the rim of the jug. They were generally "coloured proper," and some of them are quite meritorious specimens of the potter's art. Less pretentious was the "little brown jug" used for ale, which is not to be confounded with the large earthern pitcher used for water, known as the "brown-george." There is a well-known song entitled "Little Brown Jug I do Love Thee"; and the Toby jug is mentioned more than once in Charles Dickens' novel, "Barnaby Rudge."

> "Toby Tosspot was as thirsty a soul
> As e'er drank to a health or emptied a bowl."

Special vessels came into use for the drinking of possets. Posset pots were manufactured in Staffordshire, the great seat of the pottery trade, at an early period ; after 1650 it became a somewhat common practice to date these bowls, some of which have become family heirlooms.

In the following century " Pretender glasses" were in use among certain of the stauncher Jacobite families —glasses bearing symbols and mottoes calculated to preserve the memory of the exiled Stuarts.

Drinking being regarded as an accomplishment worthy of the best among Englishmen, no little inventiveness has been exercised by them on the fashioning of the vessels for holding their liquors, particularly in the direction of enforcing the largest possible consumption.

While the peg tankard may or may not have been intended to regulate and restrain the practised toper, there can be no doubt the majority of whimsically fashioned drinking vessels were devised to entrap the unwary into drinking more than he bargained for.

When the more general use of china and earthenware began to prevail, the plastic art offered greater facilities for the production of whimsical drinking vessels. One form of mug in which convivial jokers once delighted was that designed for offering to a thirsty simpleton to be drained at a draught—and which, when the agreeable feat was accomplished, revealed a toad or other disgusting creature (in realistic earthenware, of course) at the bottom, to the dismay of the drinker and the amusement of the company.

Drinking vessels were made to display every device which the ingenuity of the potters could invent to raise a laugh among the topers in the taverns. There were puzzle jugs perforated with holes or fretted patterns, which made it impossible for the drinker to take a draught without spilling the liquor.

One puzzle jug in a famous collection bears the inscription :—

> "Gentlemen now try your skill,
> I'll hold you sixpence if you will,
> That you don't drink unless you spill."

There was one kind known as "fuddling cups," consisting of a group of cups or beakers cemented together, but with a hole drilled through each partition and connecting all the cups, so that the drinker could not empty one without emptying all.

A curious drinking vessel is the "Milkmaid Cup" of the Vintners' Company. It is a silver-gilt wine-cup, in the shape of a female, whose petticoat forms the cup ; she wears an apron with an enriched border, and an under-skirt which is pounced over to represent embroidery ; also an outer robe, open in front, thrown back and fastened behind with a clasp ; a tight-laced bodice, tight-fitting sleeves with deep ruffs, and her hair is dressed in the style of the seventeenth century. The "maid" holds above her head a milk-pail, on the underside of which is a Tudor rose ; this pail is hung on pivots let into scrolls in the hands of the figure. The whole forms a double cup, and is a "trick" arrangement ; for on the figure being inverted both the cups are filled with wine, and care must be taken when a person is drinking off the contents of the larger vessel not to spill any wine from the smaller one.

Another quaint form was the drinking cup which, unless held in one particular attitude, poured the liquor over the drinker. Then there was the whistle drinking cup. The drinker having swallowed the whole contents of this, blew up a pipe in the handle which gave a shrill whistle—probably as a peal of triumph at the accomplishment of so laudable a feat. The idea seems a borrowed one, as among the Bacchanalian verse of Burns is a song on a whistle used by a Dane in the retinue of Anne of Denmark ; which instrument was laid on the table at the commencement of an orgie and won by whoever was last able to blow it. The Dane conquered all comers until Sir Robert Lowrie, of Maxelton, after three days and three nights' hard combat, left the Scandinavian under the table.

A remarkable cup was that of Margaret of Voldemar, a Queen of Denmark, Sweden, and Norway in the thirteenth century. This convivial cup had ten lips, which were marked with the respective names of those whom she most honoured with her intimacy, who were the companions of her table, and permitted with special graciousness to taste the wine from the same vessel with her.

Not long ago there were exhibited to the local Field Club, by Mr. Edward Wooler, a Darlington antiquary, two ancient jugs said to date from Edwardian times. They had been found at the cleaning out of an old well at the Talbot Inn, Bishop Auckland, a very old tavern on the great Roman Watling Street. The rarer prize of the two was a fine example of potter's art, dating, according to expert opinion, from the thirteenth or fourteenth century. It is made of salmon-coloured clay, and is slightly glazed in parts, evidently through burning. In shape it is almost a small edition of a single-handed water jar, common in ancient Greece, and has been artistically moulded on the potter's wheel, of which it bears the mark ; and after six centuries the thumb-marks of the maker remain firmly printed above and below the handle.

Mr. Wooler's treasure is damaged by a hole in the side, evidently made by a sharp instrument used in excavating, and this discloses the interesting fact that though the exterior is salmon-coloured, the interior clay, which is burned quite black, is unlike any local clay. As the learned owner pointed out, the Romans introduced the potter's wheel, the Celts previously moulding their pots on wicker-work. It is not suggested, however, that this jug, though found by the Roman way, is earlier than the thirteenth century—it is English, and from it many a draught of good English ale has no doubt been quaffed by the proud owner of a vessel which was so superior to the common black-jack.

Of course there exists a drinking vessel with a legend attached to it. This is the cup called "The Luck of Edenhall." Edenhall is the seat of the Musgrave family, near Penrith, in Cumberland. The cup, which holds a pint, is of very thin glass, ornamented on the outside with a number of coloured devices; in shape it is tall, standing on a narrow base but spreading out to a wide rim at the top. It is carefully preserved in a leather case.

The legend is that the family butler having gone one night to the Well of St. Cuthbert, a copious spring in the grounds of the mansion, surprised a group of fairies disporting themselves around the well, on the headstone of which stood the mystic drinking-glass. The butler seized hold of it, and a struggle for its possession ensued between him and the fairies. The elves were worsted, and thereupon took to flight, exclaiming as they departed—

> " If this glass do break or fall
> Farewell the luck of Edenhall."

Such is one story, but the letters IHS on the glass betray an ecclesiastical origin—another version of the legend has been put into rhyme by Longfellow. The extreme thinness of the glass renders it very liable to

breakage, and it is said that on one occasion the wild
Duke of Wharton very nearly destroyed "The Luck of
Edenhall" by letting it fall from his hands. The butler,
however, luckily caught it in his napkin ; and as a poem
in celebration of this episode has it—

> "God prosper long from being broke
> The Luck of Edenhall."

The Punch-bowl is practically a modern institution,
because punch is a comparatively modern beverage.
The term "punch " is said to be derived from the Hindustani word *paunch,* signifying five, because this is the
number of the principal ingredients required to form
the mixture. The taste for this enervating drink was
brought to England, towards the close of the seventeenth century, by the naval officers engaged in the East
Indian trade.

In 1694 Admiral Edward Russell, commanding the
Mediterranean fleet, gave a grand entertainment at
Alicant. The tables were laid under the shade of
orange-trees in four garden walks meeting at a common
centre, where there stood a handsome marble fountain.
This fountain was converted for the occasion into a
gigantic punch-bowl. Four hogsheads of brandy, one
pipe of Malaga wine, twenty gallons of lime-juice, twenty-
five hundred lemons, thirteen hundredweight of fine white
sugar, five pounds' weight of grated nutmegs, three
hundred toasted biscuits, and eight hogsheads of water,
formed the ingredients of this monster potation. An
elegant canopy placed over the potent liquor prevented
waste by evaporation or dilution by rain. To crown
this titanic effort, a small boy was placed in a boat
expressly built for the purpose, to row round the fountain
and assist in lading the punch into the cups of the six
thousand persons who were invited to partake of it.

The five ingredients—spirit, water, sugar, lemon, and spice—were in time reduced to four.

> " Whene'er a bowl of punch we make
> Four striking opposites we take—
> The strong, the weak, the sour, the sweet,
> Together mixed, most kindly meet.
> And when they happily unite
> The bowl is pregnant with delight."

Toasted biscuits, once an ingredient of this Indian potation, were soon discarded. Throughout the eighteenth century, punch held a sovereign sway at all convivial meetings. At first a political significance was attached to it ; it being a favourite beverage with William III., the Tories were some time in coming to regard it with open favour. However, by the Augustan age of Queen Anne, the wits and essayists unreservedly acknowledged its supremacy ; soon it came to be praised as the choicest of liquors ; Johnson, Reynolds, Garrick, Sheridan, and Fox readily come to mind as among the men of note who were punch-drinkers. Songs innumerable were written to proclaim the virtues of punch, and even to extol it as a panacea for all diseases. A hard-drinking age might, and perhaps did, stand this strong and heady drink with impunity ; but its ultimate fall from favour was without doubt attributable to its unhealthiness, to the horrible headaches it inflicted on most of its votaries. Even the hard-drinking squire of Anne's reign who, when in London, frequented the tavern while his wife attended theatres, balls and routs, found the punch he was almost compelled to drink while in town far more potent than his strongest " October " at home.

However, while it was the vogue, punch-bowls were a recognised thing of household equipment. Young married couples always had one presented to them by some near relative ; a punch-bowl was considered quite a suitable present from a merchant or banker to his trusty clerk, or from a shipowner to a sea-captain.   Bowls were painted with special inscriptions and devices for testimonial purposes ; some of these are now among the valued contents of collectors' cabinets.

The punch-bowl was frequently one of the most cherished of household effects.   In dissenters' families even, they have acquired a kind of semi-sacred character from having been used as baptismal fonts.   And certainly clergymen of the Establishment always regarded punch as an orthodox liquor, if they have not perverted the use of its bowls.

As may be readily supposed, the punch-bowl found its way on to many old tavern signs, either alone or in combination.   Addison, in the *Spectator*, notices one sign which hung out near Charing Cross, representing a punch-bowl curiously garnished with a couple of angels hovering over and squeezing lemons into it.

But the most celebrated sign of this type was the " Spiller's Head," in Clare Market.   Its history is curious and cannot be omitted here.

Spiller was a fellow of infinite jest.   He started life as a landscape painter ; then took to the stage, became a popular actor, and was the original " Mat of the Mint " in *The Beggar's Opera*.   From one of his benefit tickets, engraved by Hogarth, he would seem to have been well acquainted with the inside of a debtors' prison.   During his last confinement he so charmed one of the turnkeys with his wit, that the man, on Spiller's liberation, resigned office and took a tavern, so that he might the oftener enjoy the comedian's laughter-provoking company.   As many notabilities and fashionables flocked to the house for the same reason, it presently became a

request, formally preferred by this " elegant company,"
that the sign—the " Bull and Butcher"—should be
changed to something less vulgar. The " concurrent
desire " was expressed one evening over a bowl of arrack-
punch ; and it was thereupon unanimously agreed to
rename the tavern the " Spiller's Head." The painting
of a sign representing the worthy, with a bowl of punch
before him, was undertaken by one of the gentlemen
present, Mr. Laguerre, who was an artist as well as a
musician of some ability. Underneath the portrait were
the lines :—

"View here the wag, who did his worth impart
With pleasing humour, and diverting art.
A cheerful bowl in which he took delight
To raise his mirth, and pass a winter's night.
Jovial and merry did he end his days
In comic scenes and entertaining plays."

As a matter of fact the popular Spiller was struck down
on the stage by apoplexy, a victim to the pernicious bowl
he loved so well. This tavern, it may be added (nicknamed the " Old Slaughters "), was a favourite haunt of
the wits and artists of the Hogarthian era ; at which
time there was a popular and witty waiter, whom the
painters dubbed " Suck," from his habit—tolerated as a
good joke in those days, but one which would now be
regarded with deep disgust—of slily drinking out of the
bowls of punch, as he carried them upstairs to the
company.

The Scriptural maxim, that " men do not put new wine
into old bottles," reminds us that there was a time when
the favourite vessel from which to imbibe the foaming
nut-brown ale was not of wood or of metal, neither
was it of glass or of earthenware. It was made, as the
bottles of the East still are, of the hide of an animal. The
Biblical bottle was generally the skin of a kid, stripped

off the carcase without opening the belly, the apertures made by cutting off the head, legs, and tail being sewn up ; and when filled it could be tied round the neck, as the water-carriers of Eastern lands use them to this day.

The Englishman has always declared there is "nothing like leather," and in former days, when his habits called for a really serviceable drinking vessel, he could find no material to suit his purpose better than the well-tanned hide. For his leather bottles, black-jacks, and bombards which he made of this material he could justly claim that they were unbreakable, unburstable, imporous, light, and of everlasting wear.

The Leathern bottle varied slightly in form, but it was usually barrel-shaped, made of one large piece doubled up, and stitched along the top, in the middle of which the aperture was left, and two flat ends sewn in each side. There were sometimes holes on each side of the neck or aperture for a sling or handle. The stopper was of wood, horn, or rolled leather.

The Black-jack was a large pitcher-shaped vessel, sometimes with, but often without, the pouring nozzle of a modern jug ; it was made of one large piece of leather curled round and stitched up the back, with a circular piece stitched in for the bottom ; the handle was of the same material, but of several thicknesses made hard and strong. Sometimes pitch was run over the inside to form a kind of glazed surface. Those of later make were ornamented or dated, but the earlier ones, used only for small beer, were not so highly finished. Mention is made of the black-jack in the well-known song, "Simon the Cellarer," and the references to it in older works are frequent.

A rhyme of 1630 has :—

> " Nor of blacke-jacks at gentle buttry bars,
> Whose liquor oftentimes breeds houshold wars."

In an old drinking song we have :—

> "John Black's a good fellow,
>   And he allows me
> To make myselfe mellow
> With good ipse-hee."

It was from the name of this jug that the tall riding boots of the cavaliers, which came well up over the knees, were called jack-boots ; and the phrase "drinking bout" is said to be a secondary derivative from this. An old satirist speaks of one drinking "boots-full" to his friends. And again, in Shirley's "Paralysed Soldier" (*circa* 1650) occurs :—

> "His boots as wide as black-jacks,
>   Or bombards toss'd by the King's guards."

A Bombard was a jack of gigantic size, and obtained this name from its resemblance to the clumsy kind of primitive cannon, so-called, which was short and thick and had a large mouth. A toper who could carry large quantities of ale was sometimes called a bombard-man.

The name "bumboat"—a boat carrying fresh food and not unfrequently spirits as well, to a vessel newly come to harbour—is a corruption of this term.

Just as there were canakins as well as tankards, so there were smaller-sized drinking vessels of leather ; the stoups, mugs, cups, and cans of leather being sometimes metal-mounted. The old and well-known ditty on "The Leather Bottel" is given in another part of this work.

In *Othello*, where, by the way, we have the phrase "Potations pottle deep"—a pottle being a two-quart measure—occurs the rollicking chorus :—

> "And let the canakin clink !
>   A soldier's a man,
>   A life's but a span—
> Why, then, let a soldier drink."

Old English drinking glasses afford an interesting study to some collectors. Many seventeenth-century glasses have large knops in the stem, also a folded foot ; that is, an extra piece is added to the rim of the foot to give it strength. Some examples of this period have *tears*, or bubbles of air in the stem, and sometimes, when the stem is made without knops, in the bottom of the bowl. Glasses of this period were rarely engraved. They were usually of very generous proportions, but as time went on grew gradually smaller in size and more ornate in design. About the middle of the eighteenth century the most artistic epoch was reached, and wine-glasses were often given *waisted* bowls ; that is to say, the bowl was made to curve gracefully inwards in the middle, and branch out again at the top. This type of glass has a dome-shaped foot. Venetian origin (or influence) is seen in those with spiral stems, of which there are two kinds ; in the opaque glass spiral, and the spiral formed of twists of air, the latter sometimes beautifully interlaced. In the bowls of this period there was no great diversity of shape ; they might be plain bowls, or waisted, or sometimes fluted. Old beer-glasses of the time of the eighteenth century are rather interesting ; they are of different sizes and shapes, and sometimes are appropriately decorated with designs of hops and barley. No collection would be complete without old grog-glasses, or rummers as they were sometimes called, though they would not add much to the beauty of the collection.

There is much spurious glass about, and the collector generally tests any specimen presented to his notice by giving it a sharp flick with his forefinger ; if it is spurious there will be little or no ring, whereas in genuine old glass there is always a sharp metallic ring. Again, the base is much smaller in the spurious than

in the genuine ; and the modern glass is always "buffed"
and brightened up by machinery—a feature which can be
readily detected. In old glass, too, there is always at the
bottom of the base a rough finish, as if the glass had
been broken off there.

XXXII

ADVENT OF THE COFFEE-HOUSE (1652)

The first coffee-house established in Cornhill by an Armenian—The
"Rainbow" in Fleet Street—Its proprietor, Farre, indicted for
a nuisance—Closed by Government during time of public
excitement (1675)—Homes of intrigue—Haunts of newswriters
—Macaulay's description of coffee-houses (1685-8)—Places for
social intercourse—And political discussion—The Londoner's
home—Centres of public opinion—Smoking taboo—Will's—
Sacred to literature—The resort of the quality—Dryden's chair
—Garraway's—Resort of the medical profession—Puritan,
Popish, and Jewish houses—Child's—St. James's—Jonathan's—
Each patronised by a separate clique—Tom's—George's—The
"Grecian"—The rendezvous of wit and learning—A lawyer's
house — Anecdote of an advertising quack doctor — The
"Rainbow" and Charles Lamb—Nando's—Where Thurlow
obtained his first brief — Groom's — Dick's — The scene of
Rousseau's play—Patronised by Cowper—The "Folly"—A
disreputable floating coffee-house—Coffee regarded as a dan-
gerous drug—Dubbed "Ninny-broth" and "Turkey-gruel"—
Yet coffee-drinking grew in favour—The drink of the wits—
Women's petition against coffee as dangerous to the race (1674)
—Coffee-drinking not popular with the lower classes—Tea first
sold at Garraway's—High price of the leaf—Chocolate-houses
—Mere aristocratic gaming houses—Coffee-houses not temperance houses—Became inns under another name—The
modern *café*—For business men's midday relaxation—Cocoa-
houses—Established by a Bristol Quaker.

A RIVAL to the tavern, in the shape of a public-house
vending a non-alcoholic beverage, came in appropriately
enough when England was under Republican govern-

ment. As a pamphleteer of the Restoration period put it, "Coffee and Commonwealth came in together."

The first coffee-house in London was started in 1652 at the instance of a City merchant, by his Armenian servant, Pasqua Rosee, who announced to the public that coffee "was made and sold in St. Michael's Alley, in Cornhill, by Pasqua Rosee, at the sign of his own head." The innovation, naturally enough, roused the active antagonism of the publicans and ale-house keepers, before which Pasqua Rosee was forced to retire, although afterwards an English partner he had taken, one Bowman, when left in sole possession of the concern, managed to make a success of it. Then other coffee-houses soon sprang into existence, one of the most notable of the time being that of James Farre, known by the sign of the "Rainbow," near the Inner Temple Gate. Any stick was good enough to beat a dog with, and this proprietor was accused by his rivals, the vintners, with "makinge and selling of a drink called coffee, where by in makinge the same he annoyeth his neighbours by evil smells, and for keepinge of ffire for the most part night and day, whereby his chimney and chamber hath been set on ffire, to the great danger and affrightment of his neighbours." Farre, however, who had been a barber, persisted ; he triumphed over his indictment as "a public nuisance," and his business grew and flourished mightily.

Even before the Restoration coffee had established itself in public favour as a drink, for we find some satirist paying unwilling tribute to its vogue :—

> "And now, alas ! the drench has credit got,
> And he's no gentleman that drinks it not.

Have I your leave, gentlemen, to repeat the last line :—

> And he's no gentleman that drinks it not" ?

In the troublous times which marked the end of
Charles II.'s reign it was not the taverns but the
coffee-houses which were closed by proclamation (1675)
as a means of coping with the popular discontents of the
times. The better-class coffee-houses were the meeting-
places of the most influential sections of the community,
and were recognised as the centres of intrigue from
which dangerous projects might be set afoot. The
Newsletters of the time, by which the inhabitants of
the larger provincial cities learned almost all they
knew of the history of their own times, were concoc-
tions of coffee-house gossip. The newswriter strolled
from coffee-house to coffee-house gathering gossip,
collecting reports, and getting together all those
materials for his weekly epistles destined to enlighten
some country town and find food for conversation on
some bench of rustic magistrates.

Macaulay, in his history of the events of 1685, shows
us how coffee-houses gained their popularity, and came
to be so well patronised :—

"The convenience of being able to make appointments in any
part of the town, and of being able to pass evenings socially at a
very small charge, was so great that the fashion spread fast.

"Every man of the upper or middle class went daily to his Coffee-
house to learn the news, and to discuss it. Every Coffee-house had
one or more orators to whose eloquence the crowd listened with
admiration, and who soon became, what the journalists of our time
have been called, a fourth estate of the realm.

"The court had long seen with uneasiness the growth of this new
power in the state. An attempt had been made, during Danby's
administration, to close the Coffee-houses, but men of all parties
missed their usual places of resort so much that there was a universal
outcry. The government did not venture, in opposition to a feeling
so strong and general, to enforce a regulation of which the legality
might well be questioned. Since that time ten years had elapsed,
and during those years the number and influence of the Coffee-
houses had been constantly increasing. Foreigners remarked that

the Coffee-house was that which especially distinguished London from all other cities ; that the Coffee-house was the Londoner's home, and that those who wished to find a gentleman commonly asked, not whether he lived in Fleet Street or Chancery Lane, but whether he frequented the 'Grecian' or the 'Rainbow.'

" Nobody was excluded from these places who laid down his penny at the bar. Yet every rank and profession, and every shade of religious and political opinion, had its own headquarters.

" There were houses near St. James' Park, where fops congregated, their heads and shoulders covered with black or flaxen wigs, not less ample than those which are now worn by the Chancellor, and by the Speaker of the House of Commons. The atmosphere was like that of a perfumer's shop. Tobacco in any form than that of richly scented snuff was held in abomination. If any clown, ignorant of the usages of the house, called for a pipe, the sneers of the whole assembly and the short answers of the waiters soon convinced him that he had better go somewhere else.

" Nor, indeed, would he have far to go. For, in general, the Coffee-houses reeked with tobacco like a guard-room. Nowhere was the smoking more constant than at Will's. That celebrated house, situated between Covent Garden and Bow Street, was sacred to polite letters. There the talk was about poetical justice and the unities of place and time. Under no roof was a greater variety of figures to be seen. There were earls in stars and garters, clergymen in cassocks and bands, pert Templars, sheepish lads from Universities, translators and index makers in ragged coats of frieze. The great press was to get near the chair where John Dryden sate. In winter that chair was always in the warmest nook by the fire ; in summer it stood in the balcony. To bow to the Laureate, and to hear his opinion of Racine's last tragedy, or of Bossu's treatise on epic poetry, was thought a privilege. A pinch from his snuff-box was an honour sufficient to turn the head of a young enthusiast.

" There were Coffee-houses where the first medical men might be consulted. Dr. John Radcliffe, who, in the year 1685, rose to the largest practice in London, came daily, at the hour when the Exchange was full, from his house in Bow Street, then a fashionable part of the capital, to Garroway's, and was to be found, surrounded by surgeons and apothecaries, at a particular table.

" There were Puritan Coffee-houses where no oath was heard, and where lank-haired men discussed election and reprobation through their noses ; Jew Coffee-houses where dark-eyed money-changers from Venice and Amsterdam greeted each other ; and Popish Coffee-houses, where, as good Protestants believed, Jesuits planned over their cups another great fire, and cast silver bullets to shoot the King."

Macaulay's graphic description of these popular places of resort cannot fail to enlighten us as to the anxiety of a responsible minister to close them during periods of public excitement, as the Earl of Danby had attempted to do. The better-class houses were invariably institutions of social, literary, and almost of political importance, conducted with never-failing dignity and decorum.

Every London coffee-house had its clique, and its regular frequenters gave it its distinctive characteristic. Thus Child's Coffee-house in St. Paul's Churchyard was much frequented by the clergy; in his first number the *Spectator* writes :—

"Sometimes I smoke a pipe at Child's; and whilst I seem attentive to nothing but the postman, overhear the conversation of every table in the room. I appear on Sunday nights at St. James's Coffee-house, and sometimes join the little committee of politics in the inner room, as one who comes there to hear and improve. My face is likewise very well known at the Grecian. . . . I have been taken for a merchant upon the Exchange for above these ten years, and sometimes pass for a Jew in the assembly of stock-jobbers at Jonathan's. In short, wherever I see a cluster of people I always mix with them."

Throughout the essays of Addison and Steele in the *Spectator,* and in the pages of the *Tatler,* constant reference is made to these resorts, particularly to Child's, "St. James's," the "Grecian," and Jonathan's, the four coffee-houses which represented respectively the Church, Politics, Literature, and Commerce. It was here, where men of affairs most did congregate, such keen observers of the age were able not only to glean news of passing events, but to feel the pulse of public sentiment, all of which they recorded deliberately in that delightful form of journalism which is not less than standard literature.

In Devereux Court, Strand, stood three well-known coffee-houses—Tom's, George's, and the more famous "Grecian," which last-named has been called the "Athenæum" of its day, patronised during its existence by a galaxy of talent, including Addison, Steele, Pope, Swift, Gray, Shenstone, Johnson, Goldsmith, Foote, and Sir Isaac Newton. To this rendezvous of wit, wisdom, and learning the young barristers of the Temple were naturally attracted, and those of them who aspired to be considered somebodies liked to be seen lounging at the doors of the "Grecian."

With Garraway's (mentioned by Swift in his ballad, "The South Sea Bubble"), which has been mentioned as the resort of doctors and apothecaries, a good story of an advertising quack is connected.

This quack, whose name was Hannes, impudently instructed his servants to stop the carriages of wealthy people going between Whitehall and the Royal Exchange and ask whether Dr. Hannes was inside, as he was wanted. One day one of Hannes' men rushed into Garraway's, crying, "Where is Dr. Hannes? Where is Dr. Hannes?"

The famous Dr. Radcliffe inquired who wanted Dr. Hannes, and the servant replied, "He is wanted by Lord D., Lord B., and Lord C."

"No, no, my friend! you are mistaken," said Dr. Radcliffe, deliberately setting down an empty cup of coffee, "it's Dr. Hannes who *wants* those lords!"

At a later period, about the year 1780, the grandfather of Moncrieff, the dramatist, who wrote *Tom and Jerry*, kept the "Rainbow." Charles Lamb was a frequenter of the "Rainbow."

Not far away from the "Rainbow" was Nando's Coffee-house, at No. 17, Fleet Street, once erroneously called "King Henry the Eighth and Cardinal Wolsey's

Palace"—it had once been the office of the Duchy of Cornwall. It was at Nando's that the famous Lord Chancellor Thurlow picked up his first brief in a remarkable manner. Nando's was a great house for barristers and lawyers, and Thurlow one evening argued vehemently with some friends the points of some *cause célèbre* of the time. Among his listeners, and quite unknown to him, were the leading counsel engaged on the very case. As they watched young Thurlow sipping his coffee, and heard him arguing with such amazing lucidity, they became so deeply impressed that on the following day Thurlow found himself appointed the junior counsel. The case won him a silk gown, and started him on the high-road to fame and fortune.

Groom's Coffee Tavern, the famous Fleet Street resort of barristers and solicitors, has receently been offered for sale. Facing Chancery Lane, it stood between two other notable houses—the Rainbow Tavern, which claims to be the second coffee-house started in London, and Nando's, of quaint architectural interest.

Groom's is noted for three things—a cup of coffee, a chop, and a game of chess. The business was originally established by a family of the name of Groom about the year 1700. The house, it is interesting to note, stands on the site of the shop of Bernard Lintot, the bookseller, who published Pope's " Homer." Included in the sale with the house was the original recipe for making coffee.

Dick's—also on the south side of Fleet Street, No. 8— was made the scene of Rousseau's comedietta, entitled *The Coffee House ;* and as there were a number of malicious allusions to its landlady in the play, the exasperated young barristers who patronised her attended the theatre in a body and hissed the piece from the stage. It was at Dick's Coffee-house that the poet Cowper first exhibited symptoms of mental derangement.

The history of the old coffee-houses is rich in biographical and anecdotal reminiscence.

Not the least remarkable coffee-house was the "Folly," a floating establishment on the Thames, where, in the reign of good Queen Anne, ladies of a certain degree of respectability were entertained by the beaux and gallants of the town. Its character as a place of genteel resort has been described by the popular literature of the time with expressive coarseness.

For a long time coffee was regarded as a dangerous drug, and those who indulged too freely in the new beverage were looked upon almost as drunkards. It was also ridiculed by having such nicknames as "ninny-broth" and "Turkey-gruel" bestowed upon it. Thus in 1705 one Edward Ward, a Tory publican, was twice put in the pillory for scurrilous pamphleteering ; but whether his spiteful muse was exercised more by hatred of Whiggery or by detestation of "ninny-broth shops," perhaps this description of one of the latter will show :—

> "Entering I saw, quite round a table,
> An ill-look'd, thin-jaw'd, calves-head rabble,
> All stigmatised with looks like Jews,
> Each armed with half a sheet of news,
> Some sucking smoke from Indian fuel,
> And others sipping Turkey-gruel."

This extract is from Ward's "Hudibras Redivivus," and the patrons of the coffee-house thus described are supposed to be Whigs and Low Churchmen.

The newer type of establishment, however, steadily grew in public favour, and in time the coffee-houses were not only recognised and regularly frequented as refreshment-houses—was there not, by the way, a waiter at Peele's, in Fleet Street, who was accustomed to insinuate to the hungry customer, with a smirk that overshadowed his grammar, "There are a leg of mutton and there is chops " ?—but became the rendezvous of wits and scholars, of fashionable beaux, and men about town—

> " I've heard much talk of the Wits' coffee-house.
> Thither, says Brindle, thou shalt go and see
> Priests sipping coffee, Sparks and Poets tea."

It has been said that the age of coffee-drinking was the age of wits, that by the use of coffee " the dull became witty, the wit's wit wittier."

The allusion to tea calls for note.   The satirists have reviled coffee—or kauhi, as the drink was first called—in no unmeasured terms, as—

> " Syrop of soot, or essence of old shoes
> Dasht with diurnals and the book of news."

Yet these critics had to admit the sway of fashion—that long ago " the drench had credit got."

But perhaps not the least curious objection was that raised in 1674 in " the women's petition against coffee," complaining that " it made men as unfruitful as the deserts whence that unhappy berry is said to be brought " ; and alleging that " the offspring of our mighty ancestors will dwindle into a succession of apes and pigmies ! "

On the other hand, a philosophical writer of 1659 observed that " this coffa-drink hath caused great sobriety—formerly apprentices and clerks used to take their morning draughts of ale, beer, or wine which often made them unfit for business.   Now they play the good fellows in this wakeful and civil drink."   The custom of drinking coffee among the labouring classes did not last, and popular prejudice ultimately ran in favour of tea.

It was at Garraway's Coffee-house, celebrated for two centuries, in Exchange Alley, that the public were first offered tea as a beverage.   In 1657 " the said Thomas

Garway . . . publicly sold the said tea in leaf or drink, made according to direction of the most knowing merchants of those Eastern countries."

The tea in leaf was retailed by this famous tobacconist and coffee-house proprietor " from 16s. to 50s. a pound " ; but the consumption of the tea at his tables was never so extensive as that of his coffee.

Later London had chocolate-houses as places of resort for frequenters of a somewhat more elegant and refined character. Against them, however, Roger North, a high Tory, and attorney-general to James II., thus inveighs : " The use of coffee-houses seems much improved by a new invention, called Chocolate-houses, for the benefit of rooks and cullies of quality, where gaming is added to all the rest." The chocolate-houses, in fact, were scarcely more nor less than the aristocratic gambling dens of the eighteenth century.

It must not be thought that the coffee-house of the seventeenth and eighteenth centuries was always a temperance institution, notwithstanding the definition of the Restoration rhymster :—

> " A Coffee House, the learned hold,
> It is a place where coffee 's sold ;
> This derivation cannot fail us,
> For where Ale 's vended that 's an Ale-house."

In those earlier days beer and wine were usually sold in the coffee-houses, one establishment making a speciality of its tiny ale-glasses " not as big as a tailor's thimble."

As time went on, coffee-houses became inns under another name. Daniel Defoe, in the description of his tour through the country between 1724 and 1727, says that on visiting Shrewsbury he found there " the most coffee-houses round the Town Hall that ever I saw in any town, but when you come into them they are but ale-houses, only they think that the name Coffee-house gives a better air."

The present-day successor to the coffee-house is presumably the up-to-date *café*, usually upholstered as a luxurious lounge, and boasting instead of the old-time sign some such new-fangled name as the "Mecca," or something perhaps more suggestive of Oriental self-indulgence. Here the business man in search of an hour's relaxation in the middle of the day, drops in to sip coffee and chat, or perhaps to glance through an illustrated paper as he smokes the calumet of peace, or maybe even to play a quiet game at dominoes or chess.

> "Waitress, my usual *café noir*,
>   My usual cigarette,
> Let business sleep, this hour I keep
>   To brood and to forget.
> I ask not that the day remit
>   Its tax on bone or brow ;
> I ask one thing—that each day bring
>   The calm I capture now."

The modern coffee-taverns, by whatever name known, no doubt meet a popular demand and fulfil a mission in the world of social intercourse.

It is little more than a decade or two since good Josiah Hunt placed his two cocoa-houses at either end of Almonsbury Tunnel, and the kindly Friends were led by his success to open their little shops at Bristol. Since then, and especially within the last few years, the movement has grown, till now there is scarcely a considerable town in England but has its own coffee-tavern or cocoa-house.

The coffee-houses of to-day differ from those of old London, in that they supply no wine, beer, or spirits to their frequenters. Still their popularity is said to be steadily growing—which is a sign of the times.

XXXIII

SUBURBAN TEA-GARDENS

Rural pleasures sought by the citizens—Morland's picture—"The Shepherd and Shepherdess," Islington—White Conduit House —"Jack Straw's Castle," Hampstead Heath—Dickens' and Forster's visit—The "Spaniards"—Visited by the Gordon Rioters—Who were circumvented by its wily landlord—The "Old Bull and Bush"—Its snuggery used by eminent men— Marylebone Gardens—Literary allusions—The "Yorkshire Stingo," Paddington—The "Dog and Duck," St. George's Fields—Sadler's Wells, Islington—Its music-house—Depicted by Hogarth—Bagnigge Wells—Its mineral springs—Described in "The Shrubs of Parnassus" (1760)—Closed 1841—Eighteenth-century craze for Spas.

FEW large towns a century or so ago, when a growing population first began to convert them into dreary congeries of bricks and mortar, but boasted a suburban tea garden, to which their citizens might resort for fresher air and pleasanter surroundings by taking an easy walk across field-paths or through green hedgerows, to arrive with sharpened appetites or pleasurable anticipations of the rural delights afforded by such establishments. The names of some of the old tea-gardens of London, though merely as names, linger very familiarly in the public memory, although too many of them became transformed into flaring gin palaces.

A fine picture of a tea-garden, as it was in the old time, has been left to us by George Morland.

The northern side of London preserved. its pastoral character to a comparatively recent time, and till the accession of Queen Victoria the marks used by the Finsbury archers in the days of Charles II. remained in the "Shepherd and Shepherdess Fields," between Islington and the Regent's Canal.   Herds of cows grazed where Euston Station now stands, all the country to Kentish Town being quite open, while the roads beyond it were then considered unsafe at night.   Traces of a Roman camp even were to be discovered in the vicinity of St. Pancras Church, and the view from "White Conduit House" over the fields to Highgate was unobstructed. Hampstead and Highgate could only be reached by "short stages" going twice a day, and the journey there two or three times during the summer would suffice the most active of Londoners.   Both these villages abounded in inns, all of them with large gardens in the rear ; and these latter were the objective and chief attraction of the Cockney holiday-makers who took their jaunts in that direction.

"White Conduit House" took its name from the contiguous conduit which originally supplied the Charterhouse.   Its gardens at the rear were surrounded by rustic arbours fitted for tea-drinking, and these were always crowded to excess on Sundays by patrons of its famous sixpenny teas, at which "White Conduit loaves" were as popular as buns were at Chelsea.

"Jack Straw's Castle" and the "Spaniards" were also fair samples of these bygone rural delights.   An old engraving of the latter, dated 1745, shows these resorts to have been laid out with that formal arrangement of the trees and turf introduced into England by Dutch William, and displayed on grander scales at his palaces of Kensington and Hampton Court.

"Jack Straw's Castle," on Hampstead Heath, occupies

the most elevated spot in the Metropolitan area. There is no evidence of the rebel of 1381 having had the least connection with the locality, but there may have been earthwork remains of an ancient castle from which the famous old tavern borrowed the latter part of its name. Its gardens were laid out in the usual imitation of the prim Dutch style, and in the fields behind them horse-races took place regularly till 1732.

Public and private dinner parties were long an "institution" at this snug inn, the catering at which inspired some minor poet to sing its praises :—

> " With best of food—of beer and wines,
>   There may you pass a merry day ;
> So shall mine host, while Phœbus shines,
>   Instead of straw make good his hay."

Charles Dickens loved the Heath, and often found his way to "Jack Straw's." In a note to John Forster he says : "You don't feel disposed, do you, to muffle yourself up and start off with me for a good brisk walk over Hampstead Heath ? I know a good house, where we can have a red-hot chop for dinner, and a glass of good wine." Forster adds, "This note led to our first experience of 'Jack Straw's Castle,' memorable for many happy meetings in coming years."

The "Spaniards" is situated on the northern boundary of the Heath, and the origin of this name is also difficult to trace. It is said to have been built on the site of a lodge at the entrance to the Bishop of London's domain, and that the lodge was once tenanted by a family connected with the Spanish Embassy ; another version attributes to a Spaniard the conversion of the lodge into a house of entertainment.

Near by stood Ken Wood, the mansion of that famous lawyer, Lord Mansfield. At the time of the Gordon

Riots, Lord Mansfield's house in Bloomsbury Square
was sacked and burned ; inflamed by success the word
was passed "To Ken Wood!" Mr. Prickett, in his
" History of Highgate " says :—

"The routes of the rabble were through Highgate and Hampstead to the 'Spaniards' Tavern, kept at the time by a person
named Giles Thomas. He quickly learnt their object, and with a
coolness and promptitude which did him great credit, persuaded
the rioters to refresh themselves thoroughly before commencing
the work of devastation. He threw open his house and even his
cellars for their entertainment, but secretly despatched a messenger
to the barracks for a detachment of the Horse Guards, which,
arriving through Millfield Farm Lane, intercepted the approach
northward, and opportunely presented a bold front to the rebels,
who by that time had congregated in the road, which then passed
within a few paces of the mansion. Whilst some of the rioters
were being regaled at the 'Spaniards,' others were liberally supplied
with strong ale from the cellars of Ken Wood House, out of tubs
placed on the roadside. . . . The liquors, the excitement, and the
infatuation soon overcame the exhausted condition of the rabble,
who in proportion to the time thus gained by the troops, had
become doubly disqualified for concerted mischief ; for, great as
were their numbers, their daring was not equal to the comparatively
small display of military, which the leading rioters felt would show
them no mercy ; they instantly abandoned their intentions, and
retired."

Distant a few minutes' walk from the " Spaniards " is
the picturesque and typical wayside inn (the fame of its
name was revived but a year or two ago in a very popular
music-hall song) known as the "Old Bull and Bush."
Originally a farmhouse, it became the country residence
of Hogarth, and later in the eighteenth century developed
into a house of refreshment frequented by the most
eminent men of the time.   Reynolds and Gainsborough,
Garrick, Cibber, and Foote, Sterne, Addison, and Steele,
Lamb, Coleridge, and Hone have all used " that delightful
little snuggery," the " Bull and Bush."

In other parts of London were to be found equally

popular places of resort, claiming patronage as tea-gardens, or as spas. Marylebone Gardens, in the north-west of the Metropolis, was an important place of amusement. It is mentioned by Pepys, two years after the Great Fire of London, as a " pretty place to walk in." In its famous bowling alleys Sheffield, Duke of Bucking-ham, " bowled time away" in the days of Pope and Gay. The latter alludes to the place in his *Beggar's Opera* as the rendezvous of the dissipated ; and in one of his Fables he speaks of the dog-fighting matches there—

> " Both Hockley-hole and Marylebone
> The combats of my dogs have known."

Toward Paddington was the " Yorkshire Stingo," near Lisson Grove, which also combined tea-gardens with bowling-greens, and to which admission was obtained on payment of sixpence. For this sum a ticket was given to be exchanged with the waiters for its value in refresh-ments—a plan designed " to keep out the low classes." This resort was always crowded on Sundays.

The " Dog and Duck" in St. George's Fields was originally known as "St. George's Spa," and obtained a wide celebrity through the disgraceful pursuit of " the royal diversion of duck hunting."

At Islington was the famous " Sadler's Wells." In early times the monks of Clerkenwell possessed a " holy well" here, and in the days of Charles II. the house and grounds were in the possession of a surveyor of the high-ways, named Sadler, whose men, digging for gravel, rediscovered the medicinal spring, which soon became immensely popular. He built a music-house, and succeeded so well in booming the place, that he often had as many as five or six hundred visitors in a morning to test the virtues of his healing waters. In Hogarth's picture, " Evening, " one of the " Four Times of the

Day" series, the entrance-gate to Sadler's Wells is introduced.

Then there was "Bagnigge Wells" nearer to town, and where a concert-room was added to the attractions of a spa and a pleasure garden.

> "The Cits to Bagnigge Wells repair
> To swallow dust, and call it air."

The house had once been the country residence of Nell Gwynne, and was first opened for public reception in 1757. There were two mineral springs in the grounds, one chalybeate and the other cathartic ; and in "The Shrubs of Parnassus" (1760) we obtain a curious description of the company usually to be seen there :—

> "Here ambulates th' Attorney, looking grave,
> And Rake, from Bacchanalian rout uprose,
> And mad festivity. Here, too, the Cit,
> With belly turtle-stuffed, and Man of Gout
> With leg of size enormous. Hobbling on,
> The pump-room he salutes, and in the chair
> He squats himself unwieldy. Much he drinks
> And much he laughs, to see the females quaff
> The friendly beverage."

As a place noted for tea-drinking, it is frequently mentioned by the authors of the eighteenth century. Colman, for example, has the reference :—

> "'Tis drinking tea on summer afternoons
> At Bagnigge Wells with china and gilt spoons."

An old print of the place is labelled "The Bread and Butter Manufactory, or the Humours of Bagnigge Wells." The gardens were much curtailed in 1813, and were finally closed in 1841.

These by no means exhaust the list of London's public tea-gardens and spas ; tea-gardens flourished in those

days in every outskirt of the city ; and as to spas, they
too were found practically all over England during the
eighteenth century, when nearly every spring that trickled
was exploited for its supposed medicinal qualities, if
only that the adjoining landowner possessed money and
enterprise, and an ambition to develop his property into
a rival, or at least an imitation, of the fashionable city of
Bath.   Spas were the craze of the period.

XXXIV

SMOKING

The tobacco habit—Conducive or a hindrance to drinking?—Incorporation of Tobacco-pipe Makers, 1619—Introduction of tobacco, 1586—Violent opposition to its use at first—Its high price in 1589—Duty imposed on it, 1614—Excessive smoking—" Moistening the clay"—The "Counterblaste" of James I.—A defence published in 1654—Pipe-smoking in seventeenth century—By women—And at the Universities—Smoking a tavern custom—The Smoke Room—And the pipe-rack—Gratuitous pipes sometimes refused—Public-house notices to that effect—Pipe-smoking a common habit with literary men—Invention of the cigar—Introduction of the cigarette—Snuff-taking.

THE influence of tobacco-smoking upon the circulation of the convivial cup must without doubt be distinctly appreciable either one way or the other. But in which direction does it lie? On the one hand, it has been urged that the convivial soul who divides his attention between his pipe and his glass is given to drink less than his glum-looking companion who is a non-smoker. The other side pooh-pooh this, and put it forward as an obvious fact that the smoking of tobacco must of necessity dry the mouth and parch the throat, and therefore lead to the imbibing of more liquid refreshment to allay the induced thirst—a thirst that has been purposely induced, insinuate the unscrupulous enemies of My Lady Nicotine. This latter view was manifestly the one taken by the first law-makers in this country to deal with the tobacco habit. " Item, you shall not utter," enjoins an ale-house licence of the time of James I., "nor willingly suffer to be utter'd, drunk or taken, any tobacco within your house, cellar, or other place thereunto belonging."

While James I. was fiercely fulminating against tobacco, a patent of monopoly, granted by Mr. Secretary Cecil, was enjoyed by certain tobacco-pipe makers ; and in 1619 the craft of Pipe-makers was incorporated, their privileges as a Company extending all over England and Wales. There were makers at Derby, Lichfield, and Wednesbury, and quite a dozen of them at Bath. The smoking-tube of a maker at Newcastle-under-Lyme was acknowledged as being a "gude cleane pipe and fayre," while the tobacco-pipes of Winchester won the praise of no less than "rare Ben Jonson." As yet Broseley had evidently not come to the front.

Let the controversialists settle it which way they will, the pipe has been so close and constant a companion to the glass from the first moment of its introduction into England that some brief account of the tobacco habit cannot be omitted here.

Tobacco was first brought into England from the West Indies by Sir John Hawkins in 1565, or by Sir Walter Raleigh and Sir Francis Drake in 1586; and the Pied Bull Inn at Islington is said to have been the first house in England in which the fragrant weed was smoked. How the novelty struck the imagination of the slow-witted stay-at-homes is well illustrated by the familiar anecdote of Raleigh's servant dashing a bucket of water over his master, who was quietly indulging in a pipe of tobacco, and whom he thought to be on fire.

Whether it was Sir Walter Raleigh or Sir Francis Drake who introduced tobacco into England as a substitute for drinking, it is certain that at first it met with violent opposition. It was a marvel to honest Cob, in " Every Man in his Humour," that men could find pleasure "in taking this roguish tobacco. It's good for nothing," said he, " but to choke a man, and fill him full of smoke and embers. There were four died in one house, last week, with taking of it."

In 1589 tobacco sold in this country at 3s. an ounce, and taking into consideration the relative values of money then and now, this price may safely be interpreted at about 20s. per ounce. And not only was it dear, but it seems as yet to have found but scant favour in the eyes of the " superior person" of the Elizabethan era—or, shall we say, with the untravelled Englishman hugging to himself his insular prejudices ? Stow, the chronicler of the times, calls it "that stinking weed so much abused to God's dishonour." In Elizabeth's reign a proclamation was issued against it, and the " Counterblaste to Tobacco," published by James I., is well known.

In 1614 the Court of Star Chamber imposed a duty of 6s. 1od. a pound on tobacco, and the cultivation of it was prohibited by an Act of Charles II. in 1684.

As by degrees the new habit of tobacco-smoking came gradually into favour with the phlegmatic Englishman, there were naturally some of them who pushed it to excess. Lilly, the famous astrologer, who lived between 1602 and 1680, tells us in his " Life and Times " of the Rev. William Breedon, Vicar of Thornton, Bucks, "a profound divine . . . and most polite person," who, " when he had no tobacco (and, I suppose, too much drink) would cut the bell-ropes and smoke them ! "

In this anecdote it will be observed that smoking to excess is associated with excessive drinking. And so, always, it has been assumed that the smoker cannot

possibly refrain from "moistening his clay"; that first he
dries his throat, and then proceeds to wet it, and that
dividing his attention systematically between his pipe
and his glass he can manage to devote too large a proportion of his time to the claims of sociality. Did not
the most convivial soul known to the nursery rhymster

"Call for his pipe
And call for his bowl
As well as his fiddlers three"?

Virtuous King James I., in his "Counterblaste to
Tobacco," published in 1604, condemns smoking as
"a branch of the sin of drunkenness, which is the root
of all sins."

It is, he says, "a custom loathsome to the eye, hateful
to the nose, harmful to the brain, dangerous to the lungs,
and in the black stinking fume thereof, nearest resembling
the horrible Stygian smoke of the pit that is bottomless."

"Herein," says this much over-righteous monarch, "is
not only a great vanity, but a great contempt of God's
good gifts, that the sweetness of man's breath, being
a good gift of God, should be wilfully corrupted by this
stinking smoke."

In a work published in 1654 we find one of the earliest
efforts in the defence of tobacco :—

"Much meat doth gluttony procure,
To feed men fat as swine ;
But he's a frugal man indeed
That with a leaf can dine.

He needs no napkin for his hands,
His finger-ends to wipe,
That hath his kitchen in a box,
His roast meat in a pipe."

A Frenchman travelling through England in the time
of Charles II. records—he instances the Stag Inn,
High Street, Worcester—that it was customary for the
landladies to sup with

"the strangers and passengers, and if they have daughters they
are also of the company, to entertain the guests with pleasant
conceits, where they drink as much as the men. . . . Moreover, the
supper being finished they set on the table half-a-dozen pipes and a
packet of tobacco for smoking, which is a general custom, as well
among women as men."

From a "Character of England," an old work printed
in 1659, it appears that "the ladies of greatest quality
suffered themselves to be treated in taverns, and they
drank their 'crowned cups' roundly, and exceeded the
bounds of propriety in their carousals."

Smoking had become a genteel accomplishment by the
beginning of the eighteenth century. Dean Swift heard
"more than one or two persons of high rank declare they
could learn nothing more at Oxford and Cambridge than
to drink ale and smoke tobacco." Yet a century earlier,
when the Puritanic spirit was abroad, smoking was
prohibited to schoolmasters, who were frequently also
divines. In the rules for conducting Chigwell School,
founded 1629, it was declared the master must be "a man
of sound religion, of grave behaviour, no tippler, and no
puffer of tobacco."

Certain it is that till a few decades ago it would have
been impossible to find any well-conducted tavern
without its supply of good clay pipes. The long Broseley
pipe, as "fine as a straw," or at the very least a solemn
"churchwarden" pipe, was to be had everywhere for the
asking ; and pipe-racks were always at hand, in which to
lay aside one's favourite "yard of clay" till the next
social gathering called it forth for the burning of more

incense. In fact, but for the association of this incense burning with the offering of libations to the festive gods, where would have been that never-failing institution in all licensed houses—the Smoke Room ? A licensed house without its Smoke Room is almost unthinkable.

The practice of exhibiting notices, cautions, and warnings in public-houses is an old and time-honoured one. The most common form is that directed against the use of bad language, which sometimes is tersely worded, "No Swearing Allowed," and sometimes is put with more poetic persuasiveness, as thus : " Friend ! Remember ! As a Bird is known by his note, so is a man by his conversation. Bad Language strictly forbidden here."

Another form of bar and tap-room notice is directed against customers expecting to obtain drink on credit, of which the following is a typical example, and is quoted here because exception is rather meanly taken in it to the common practice of supplying clay pipes to customers gratuitously.

"NOTICE.

"Those who bring their own tobacco must pay for pipes
as well as beer.

"My pipes I can't afford to give
If by my trade I am to live.
My beer is good, my measure just,
Excuse me, friends, I cannot trust.
Come then, be seated, call away
For what you please, and I'll obey.
There's one thing more I do desire,
You must not stand before the fire,
Nor on the table attempt to sit,
Unless you pay a quart for it.
Customers came who did not pay,
And afterwards they stayed away.

> By loss of beer and custom sore,
> I am resolved to trust no more.
> Chalk is useful, say what you will,
> But 'chalk' won't pay the maltster's bill.
> I'll strive to keep a decent tap
> For Ready Money, but not strap."

The literary man is generally a smoker, and so is the reading man. The habit is conducive to contemplation, to meditation, to the enjoyment of quietude. Charles Lamb sang :—

> " For thy sake, Tobacco, I
> Would do anything but die."

But with the exquisites of fashion there came a time when the recreation of smoking seemed to lack some of the elegance which was supposed to mark good breeding. When this idea had gradually attached itself to the smoking of a pipe, fortunately for the lovers of the tawny weed, the discovery was most opportunely made of a new mode of smoking it. This was by means of rolling up the fragrant weed itself, and making it perform the office of its own pipe. Thus was the cigar invented ; but as the new method was more expensive than the old, indulgence in it was consequently reserved for those of ampler means. The cigar gradually became fashionable, and early in the nineteenth century a Cigar Divan was established in King Street, Covent Garden, the frequenters of which were of course of the male sex solely—has not tobacco been described as " the tomb of love " ?—although coffee only was drunk there. For " coffee without tobacco," according to the Persian philosopher, " is like meat without salt." As James I. had written his indignant protests against tobacco-pipe smoking, so now George IV., another royal arbiter of fashion, did not think it beneath his princely dignity to lend his countenance to what he considered the more refined habit of cigar-smoking.

His present Majesty, King Edward VII., always enjoys a good cigar, and annually receives as a gift from a personal friend a quantity of fine Havanas, specially prepared for his smoking.

Cigarettes were first used in the streets of this country by the late Laurence Oliphant, and, curiously enough, the introduction of this method of smoking to the English people came as the result of the Crimean War. Our officers in Russia, among other hardships, could not procure tobacco or cigars, and learnt the use of the cigarette from their French, Italian, and Turkish allies, and also during their stay in Malta and Gibraltar. It took quite twenty years, however, to familiarise the English smoker with this form of using the weed.

As snuff-taking was never directly conducive to the drinking habit there is no need to treat of it at any length here. Till within a generation ago, a large snuff-box for the free use of customers was to be found in most well-appointed public-houses. It would sometimes be affixed to the counter of a bar, sometimes on a smoke-room table, or perhaps on a convenient chimney-piece. But nowadays it is seldom to be met with—it has been "routed by the cigarette," as one writer puts it.

Snuff-taking took its rise in England from the captures of vast quantities of snuff by Sir George Rooke's expedition to Vigo in 1702, and the practice soon became general. The literature of the habit of snuff-taking, of snuff-boxes, and of the whole etiquette of the practice when it was fashionable, is very interesting, but has no direct bearing on our main subject.

The habit of snuff-taking is a very modern one, and yet it is slowly but surely dying out. The habit of drinking alcoholic stimulants dates from the earliest dawn of civilisation, and has not died out. With the advance of human progress, drunkenness and excessive drinking will disappear along with other excesses and immoralities derived from our barbaric ancestors. But the moderate use of alcoholic beverages will never be entirely dispensed with, so long as human nature exists with its natural, its wisely ordained diversity of taste and inclination. And when the extremists of both sides of the great drink question have exhausted the controversy and drained the cup of disputation to the very dregs, this shall remain the last word. As witness the deliberate utterance of one whose trained intellect, matured judgment, and cultured taste have given him a right to be heard :—

"Wine is the drink of the gods, milk the drink of babies, tea the drink of women, beer the drink of Germans, and water the drink of beasts. Wine is the poetry of water, champagne the poetry of wine."

This was the dictum of the late Professor Blackie—the truth of it shall stand till such time as man alters his nature. For in an argument of this kind the immutability of human nature is a term that may never be left out.

INDEX

GENERAL

INDEX TO INN SIGNS